MINDING CLOSELY

MINDING CLOSELY

The Four Applications of Mindfulness

B. Alan Wallace

⊰⊱╫⊰⊱

SNOW LION PUBLICATIONS
ITHACA, NEW YORK

Snow Lion Publications
P.O. Box 6483
Ithaca, New York 14851 USA
(607) 273-8519 www.snowlionpub.com

Printed in USA on acid-free recycled paper.

ISBN-10: 1-55939-369-6
ISBN-13: 978-1-55939-369-0

Library of Congress Cataloging-in-Publication Data

Wallace, B. Alan.
Minding closely : the four applications of mindfulness /
by B. Alan Wallace.
p. cm.
Includes bibliographical references and index.
ISBN-13: 978-1-55939-369-0 (alk. paper)
ISBN-10: 1-55939-369-6 (alk. paper)
1. Meditation--Buddhism. I. Title. BQ5612.W355 2011
294.3'4435—dc22
2010039802

Designed and typeset by Gopa & Ted2, Inc.

❧ Contents ❧

⊰ Preface ⊱

Mindfulness, I declare, O monks, is helpful everywhere.
—BUDDHA SHAKYAMUNI, *MILINDAPAÑHA*

THE ABILITY to sustain close mindfulness is a learned skill that offers profound benefits in all situations. This book explains the theory and applications of the practice the Buddha called the direct path to enlightenment.
These simple but powerful techniques for cultivating mindfulness will
allow anyone, regardless of tradition, beliefs, or lack thereof, to achieve
genuine happiness and freedom from suffering. By closely minding the
body and breath, we relax, grounding ourselves in physical presence.
Coming face to face with our feelings, we stabilize our awareness against
habitual reactions. Examining mental phenomena nakedly, we sharpen
our perceptions without becoming attached. Ultimately, we see all phenomena just as they are, and we approach the ground of enlightenment.

The Buddha formulated the four close applications of mindfulness as
antidotes to four habitual misunderstandings that are the root of suffering in everyday life: We mistake the aggregation of mental and physical
phenomena called the body for the abode of a real self. We mistake feelings aroused toward apparent phenomena for genuine happiness. We
mistake the mind for a real self. And we mistake apparent phenomena
for real objects.[1] These mistakes lead to distorted perceptions, thoughts,
and views that generate mental afflictions like sensual craving and hostility, which produce endless unnecessary suffering.

As we engage in life based on these fundamental misunderstandings, we unwittingly fuel a vicious cycle of suffering. The conventional world we inhabit is known as the desire realm in Buddhism because the prime mover for all sentient beings is our desire for pleasurable feelings in body and mind and avoidance of suffering and pain. Without fathoming the true nature of our existence, we grasp at mundane pleasures in material things and experiences. Although we cling tenaciously to these things when we get them, they never last, and we only perpetuate more suffering by our efforts.

Instead, by applying close mindfulness to the body, feelings, mental events, and all phenomena, we observe with increasing clarity how these things actually are: illusory, unreal, and mere designations in conventional speech. Seeing the extent of suffering in the world, we cease clinging to the body as the true source of our existence. Seeing the misunderstandings that cause the world's suffering, we stop craving feelings as the true source of our happiness. Seeing that suffering can actually be extinguished, we release our grasping on to mental events as the true source of our identity. And seeing the actual nature of reality, we abandon all the entities habitually designated upon subjective and objective appearances as the true source of our experience.

The Buddha declared that mental afflictions, such as lust, anger, and delusion, are not inherent in our nature. He likened them to a pile of dirt in the middle of a crossroads, which represents our sensory and mental processes. Four chariots enter this intersection from four directions, representing mindfulness directed toward the body, feelings, mental states, and all phenomena, and they thoroughly disperse the pile of dirt.[2] When the mental afflictions are overcome, our true nature—which was merely obscured by these habitual misunderstandings—shines forth with unlimited benefit for ourselves and all beings.

This book was developed on the basis of a weeklong retreat I led in 2008 at the Old Mission in Santa Barbara, California. Cloistered within the walls of this "queen" of the series of Pacific Coast missions founded by Father Junipero Serra, we were blessed by contemplative seclusion and inspired by the tranquil gardens of a monastery in continuous use for over two hundred years.

The first meditation manual I ever read, back in 1970, was written by Nyanaponika Thera (1901–1994), a German-born ordained Theravadin monk, who lived in Sri Lanka. I met him many years after he wrote the classic text called *The Heart of Buddhist Meditation*.[3] This book made complete sense to me, and I took to it like a duck to water; for the first year or so, it was just about all that I practiced. The book focuses on the four close applications of mindfulness, once translated as the four foundations of mindfulness. These four avenues of meditation contain the heart essence of Buddha Shakyamuni's methods to liberate us from suffering and the inner causes of suffering.

After absorbing *The Heart of Buddhist Meditation*, I bought a one-way ticket to India and immersed myself in Tibetan culture, religion, language, and medicine. With a lot of studying, I became fluent in Tibetan. Eventually taking monastic ordination, I entered a monastery, the Institute of Buddhist Dialectics in Dharamsala. It was a very demanding academic curriculum, including debating for five hours daily, studying Buddhist philosophy, and memorizing hundreds of pages of material.

Then the famous Burmese meditation master S. N. Goenka came to Dharamsala, invited by a close friend of mine, who was like an older sister to me. She was determined that I should train with Goenka. His Holiness the Dalai Lama, who supervised our school, directed the entire monastery to attend the retreat. Goenka's ten-day insight (Skt. *vipashyana*)[4] meditation retreat has since become a classic that is still offered around the world, attended by thousands of participants annually.

We had ten very intensive days, meditating under Goenka's guidance for eleven hours daily, beginning at 4:30 a.m., watching the breath and scanning through the body. By this time I had already completed four years of fairly rigorous training, reading and studying philosophy, and engaging in analysis and debate. Suddenly, I found the experience of being alone with my mind for eleven hours nonstop to be absolutely unbearable.

Author Anne Lamott says, "My mind is like a bad neighborhood. I try not to go there alone." Being in the room with my mind all day, cold turkey, without anesthesia, was like being in a toxic waste dump crawling with snakes. I had been studying Buddhism's ethereal palaces while living in a filthy hovel. By the end of ten days, I couldn't stand it anymore. I ran directly from the retreat to His Holiness's residence and blurted out, "I just got a big glimpse of my mind—it's an awful place!"

I told him that I didn't want to pursue theoretical training for a while; I only wanted to purify my mind and ground my meditative practice in experience. The year before, wasted by my third case of hepatitis and down to 135 pounds, I had come within days of death. It would be unthinkable to die with this mind. I was determined to immerse myself in the experiential investigation of body, mind, and environment by practicing the four close applications of mindfulness.

Because of my tremendous reverence for His Holiness, I would have done anything he suggested. To my enormous relief, he said, "Good idea!" He asked his secondary tutor, Lati Rinpoche (1922–2010),[5] to guide me in the practice. From the collected teachings of the Buddha that are recorded in the Tibetan canon, Lati Rinpoche selected *The Sutra on the Close Applications of Mindfulness,* and I began to study this sutra.

Another of my primary teachers, Geshe Rabten (1920–1986),[6] gave me invaluable guidance in these practices as I trained with him. Around the same time we were joined in Dharamsala by a Theravadin monk, Ven. Kitti Subho, who introduced me to many of the core teachings of the Buddha recorded in the Pali Canon. He had just spent six years in Thailand, practicing mindfulness very intensively for up to eleven hours a day. He gave me very practical advice, and I immersed myself in mindfulness practice. My mental balance gradually improved, and later I returned to two monasteries in Switzerland for another five years of theoretical and meditative training in Tibetan Buddhism.

In the fall of 1979, I left my monastery in Switzerland; the following spring, at the invitation of His Holiness the Dalai Lama, I immersed myself in a five-month intensive shamatha retreat under his guidance in the mountains above Dharamsala. Eventually my visa expired, and I had to leave India. When I asked His Holiness, who was guiding my practice at the time, he said, "Why not go to Nepal? There are excellent lamas there to assist with your training." This seemed like a good idea. Then a fellow monk suggested that the fine teachers, hermitages, and locations conducive to meditation in Sri Lanka make it ideal for Buddhist monks.

I had already enjoyed such a delicious taste of mindfulness practice from the Theravadin tradition of vipashyana that this suggestion was enticing. I tried to contact His Holiness to ask whether Sri Lanka might be better than Nepal, but I couldn't get through to him—the Dalai Lama's schedule is incredible! Instead, I sought an interview with Kyabje Trijang Rinpoche (1900–1981),[7] a great lama who was one of His Holiness's tutors and my teacher as well. When I asked him about the possibility of practicing in Sri Lanka, he looked at me very carefully and said, "Good! Go to Sri Lanka."

I spent about six months in Sri Lanka, meditating primarily under Balangoda Ananda Maitreya (1896–1998),[8] one of that country's most beloved and revered teachers. Although he was retired, he welcomed me into his little temple. There were only about a dozen monks in attendance, so my training with him was very personal. He was an utterly marvelous embodiment of wisdom, kindness, and serenity. I consider him my primary teacher from the Theravadin tradition, and I would love to emulate his qualities. On several occasions I received teachings from Geshe Ngawang Dhargyey (1921–1995)[9] and His Holiness the Dalai Lama on the four close applications of mindfulness based on the "Wisdom Chapter" of the classic text *A Guide to the Bodhisattva Way of Life*.[10]

Most of my sources for this book are from the early Pali Canon and the Theravadin tradition, which has maintained a strong discipline in mindfulness practice. I've also included here the highly complementary views of my Tibetan teachers in the Great Vehicle (Skt. *Mahayana*) tradition.

I am very happy to be able to share these mindfulness practices and teachings with you. These teachings represent a noble lineage, and I have a deep reverence for all my teachers. My goal is to faithfully transmit to you the blessings of the lineages of teachings that I have received, with as little distortion as possible. I hope to give you some glimpse of the clarity and wisdom that my teachers generously shared with me.

⋙ 1 ⋘
Introduction

THE TEACHINGS on the theory and practice of mindfulness belong to the class of methods for cultivating insight (Skt. *vipashyana*). This book will give you an introduction to the vast theoretical framework and profound motivation of these contemplative inquiries, as well as an experiential taste of their rewards. My aspiration is that you will learn to engage effectively and confidently in a range of mindfulness practices. If you find them to be meaningful and beneficial, I hope you will be inspired to continue applying these transformative practices to all aspects of your life—the potential benefits are unlimited.

BALANCING THEORY AND PRACTICE

As we did in the retreat in 2008, we will begin here by developing the ability to be grounded and relaxed, a process of stabilizing and clarifying the mind. Mindfulness is a foundation for all other kinds of meditation. The practices we will explore do not require any religious beliefs; they can be used by atheists or by devout, fundamentalist followers of any religion—anyone who would like to improve attentional balance. Our supporting techniques will include the development of universally valued qualities of the heart: loving-kindness, compassion, and empathy. Developing an open heart is a worthy goal for any human being, regardless of creed or philosophy.

Practices to develop insight into the actual nature of phenomena incorporate more theory, but you need not swear your allegiance to the theory prior to utilizing the practices. These methods require empirical investigation: you must test the theory to see if the results are beneficial. By exploring the nature of the mind in deeper states of consciousness and dreams, you will finally arrive at the very nature of awareness itself.

These are fundamental teachings that make good sense, with rapidly evident pragmatic value. We need not practice for months or years to see the results. The techniques described here will deliver practical benefits in daily life, even without considering the possibility of transcending ordinary existence. My teachers, including His Holiness the Dalai Lama, Gen Lamrimpa,[11] Geshe Ngawang Dhargyey, Geshe Rabten, and Gyatrul Rinpoche,[12] have all strongly emphasized the importance of laying solid foundations as the prerequisite to more advanced practices.

I have attempted to find a middle way between the rich theoretical framework of scholarly analysis that illuminates the Buddhist understanding of mindfulness and actual engagement in meditative practice. Theoretical analysis has many merits, but there is no benefit unless the theory is put into practice. On the other hand, the practice of mindfulness is impoverished without being rooted in the vast, fertile field of contemplative wisdom that has developed and perfected these techniques.

The vitality of this middle way emerges spontaneously as the integration of theory and practice. One's experiences in actual practice resonate with reports from past adepts, bringing theoretical concepts to life. At the same time, theoretical analysis provides the context necessary for understanding one's own unique experiences. The synergies between theory and practice are powerful and dynamic.

MATRIX OF SKILLFUL MEANS

Mindfulness practices do not exist in isolation but are embedded within a matrix of diverse techniques with various purposes and prerequisites. These can be grouped into five primary categories: (1) refining the attention, (2) achieving insight through mindfulness, (3) cultivating a good heart, (4) exploring the ultimate nature of reality, and (5) realizing the Great Perfection—the culmination of the path to enlightenment.

Shamatha: Cultivating Meditative Quiescence and Samadhi

The first of these categories, historically as well as in practice, is meditative quiescence (Skt. *shamatha*), which is developed by training and refining the attention. The further goal of this contemplative technology is to achieve a state of highly focused and refined attention (Skt. *samadhi*). A refined mind becomes an accurate instrument for investigating the nature of reality, just as a properly cleaned and calibrated telescope provides the clearest possible observations of the cosmos.

The development of attention was mastered in ancient India, which led the world in formalizing such knowledge. Indian yogis were developing methods to refine their samadhi for hundreds of years before the Buddha's time. Contemplative practice had become a highly mature and sophisticated matrix of disciplines. These traditions were extensively adapted and developed as they spread throughout Asia, and they represent only one of India's extraordinary contributions to the world. Many generations of seekers found enormous benefits in extended samadhi practices that reached progressively subtler states. From the beginnings of shamatha, they strove to achieve increasingly refined absorptions in the form realm, where the object of meditation has a form, and in the subtler formless realm.

Mindfulness practice begins with the foundation of shamatha, which supports the development and cultivation of samadhi. Methods for developing meditative quiescence are not exclusive to Buddhist traditions, such as Theravada, Tibetan Vajrayana, Chinese Chan, and Japanese Zen; they also exist in the contemplative traditions of Vedanta, Christianity, Sufism, and Taoism. In fact, forms of shamatha are found to varying extents in all the world's great contemplative traditions. Practitioners have long recognized that if one wishes to devote oneself to meditation, the untrained mind presents an obstacle. The ordinary mind alternates between extremes of hyperactive mental activity and collapse into lethargy and sleep. During the daytime, one agitation follows another, and at night we are comatose; the next morning, we repeat the cycle. Ordinary people call this life. Contemplatives have identified it as the normal human condition.

The mind we bring to meditation needs refinement, and that is the purpose of shamatha. These extremely practical methods do not require us to retreat to a cave. They can be enormously helpful in our daily lives, personal relationships, and professional endeavors, as they transcend all barriers of religious traditions, affiliations, and beliefs. Scientific materialists, atheists, and religious fundamentalists alike will experience tangible benefits from a serviceable mind that is stable and clear. Such a mind can be applied more effectively to everything. Shamatha is also the indispensable foundation for more advanced practices, such as vipashyana.

Vipashyana: Achieving Insight through Mindfulness

Historically, the Buddha himself started with the development of samadhi, but then he moved on. Bear in mind that his world was well populated with contemplatives. Many were wandering ascetics, who were often countercultural figures, living on one meal a day and devoting themselves to the pursuit of truth. With so much competition, how did Buddha Shakyamuni distinguish himself over the others of his era? Of course there are many reasons, but from a contemplative's perspective, he stands out because he refused to take samadhi itself as the goal.

The Buddha's greatest innovation was to assert that the practice of samadhi—single-pointed concentration with highly refined attention, which enables very subtle states of consciousness that transcend the physical senses and lead to states of equanimity and bliss—only temporarily suspends the mental afflictions (Skt. *kleshas*). Instead, the Buddha sought lasting freedom. Standing upon the shoulders of the contemplative giants of his era, the young Siddhartha Gautama developed and refined his samadhi, but then he purposefully applied this stable, clear, and highly focused instrument to an experiential investigation. By closely inspecting his own mind, his body, and the relationships among mind, body, and environment, he founded the genre of meditation for cultivating insight, or vipashyana.

As the Buddha formulated it, insight practice begins with a solid foundation in ethics and a wholesome, noninjurious way of life. Upon this basis, the attention is refined into a reliable tool for investigation and employed to probe the ultimate nature of reality, with the mind at the very center of experiential reality. The Buddha's great innovation was the unification of shamatha and vipashyana. Prior to this discovery, contemplative inquiry into the nature of reality had not been linked with samadhi. The Buddha asserted that the fusion of shamatha with vipashyana is the key to liberation—an irreversible healing and purification of the mind. If the afflictive mental tendencies are irreversibly vanquished by severing the root of suffering, lasting freedom will be attained.

This search for insight and wisdom is not done for the sake of knowledge itself; it is a search to deepen our experiential understanding. Life is short, and we have many problems. The news media continuously remind us of the devastation of suffering. Profound outer and inner healing is needed. We are seeking the knowledge to live in harmony and flourish as human beings, in a balanced relationship with our environment. Mindfulness, the purpose of our expedition in this book, is central to both theory and practice in the traditions of Chan, Zen, and Vajrayana; the four close applications of mindfulness constitute the foundational vipashyana practices common to all schools of Buddhism.

A Good Heart: Cultivating the Four Immeasurables

The third category includes the practices of skillful means, which act as a counterbalance to insight and wisdom practices. This balance is symbolized by placing one's hands in the mudra of meditative equipoise, an element that appears in many Buddhist images. The Buddha and other great adepts are often shown with the left hand supporting the right and the tips of the two thumbs touching. The left hand symbolizes wisdom, and the right hand symbolizes skillful means, the essence of which is compassion. The union of wisdom and compassion is symbolized by the touching of the thumbs.

The cultivation of a good heart centers on what are known in Sanskrit as the four sublime abodes (Skt. *brahmaviharas*), often called the four immeasurables: loving-kindness, compassion, empathetic joy, and equanimity. The Mahayana tradition adds the vast intent of the spirit of awakening (Skt. *bodhichitta*), the altruistic motivation of a bodhisattva to bring all beings to the state of enlightenment. Also included here is the practice of mind training, or *lojong* (Tib. *blo sbyong*),[13] which consists of techniques to transmute all experiences of felicity and adversity into sustenance for one's spiritual growth.

Emptiness and Dependent Origination: Exploring the Ultimate Nature of Reality

The fourth category concerns a deeper dimension of insight, drawn from the Mahayana tradition's *Perfection of Wisdom* sutras (Skt. *Prajña-paramita*). Although it's generally translated as "wisdom," the Sanskrit term *prajña* denotes intelligent discernment resulting from study, contemplation, and meditation.[14] The perfection (Skt. *paramita*) of prajña culminates in the abolishment of delusion by direct realization of the nature of reality. The great Middle Way (Skt. *Madhyamaka*) teachings, promulgated by Nagarjuna (ca. 150–250 CE) and others, include quintessential meditations to develop insight into emptiness (Skt. *shunyata*) and dependent origination (Skt. *pratityasamutpada*).

One of the finest expositions of vipashyana practice is presented in a text by the extraordinary seventeenth-century Tibetan contemplative and scholar Karma Chagmé (1613–1678),[15] and it appears in *A Spacious Path to Freedom*,[16] which I translated under the guidance of Gyatrul Rinpoche. This teaching comes from the Tibetan Mahamudra[17] lineage, which accords philosophically with the Middle Way view. In the chapter on the cultivation of insight, the author probes deeply into the quintessential nature of the mind itself, striking at the very core of duality, in a mere twenty pages. This is an ontological probe: What is the relationship between the mind and what appears to the mind? What is the true nature of existence?

Complementing these daytime practices are the very potent nighttime practices of lucid dreaming. The Buddha said that all phenomena are like a dream. Becoming lucid within a dream entails realizing that you are dreaming rather than mistaking your experience for waking reality. The ancient Buddhist practices of dream yoga have been augmented by modern sleep researchers, such as Stephen LaBerge at Stanford University, who was the first scientist to empirically demonstrate the reality of lucid dreaming under laboratory conditions.

The Great Perfection: Accomplishing Buddha Nature

The fifth category concerns buddha nature, the deepest level of our own awareness, also called pristine awareness (Tib. *rig pa*). The practices of the Great Perfection, or *Dzogchen* (Tib. *rdzogs chen*), are said to represent the culmination of all lower practices, and their ultimate result is the realization of all buddhas—enlightenment.

PATH OF INSIGHT

Our expedition here belongs primarily to the second category of vipashyana, or insight meditation. In most cases, these five types of practice are best approached in sequence. However, they can each be explored profitably at any time. Every individual is different, with a unique psyche, various innate abilities, and diverse inclinations. Some people immediately gravitate to the practice of the four immeasurables in order to become more loving and compassionate. Others wish to transform their lives without abandoning their families, jobs, and responsibilities. Each person must follow his or her own heart in choosing the practices that are most meaningful and beneficial.

Many Methods

A single right way to develop insight in Buddhism does not exist. The Buddha's opening statement in his primary discourse on mindfulness begins, "This is the direct path," which some have mistranslated as "This is the only path."[18] The Buddha taught a multitude of different methods. Vipashyana is a direct path, but there are many levels of vipashyana practice and other approaches as well. These diverse techniques do not lead to the same result any more than diverse physical experiments lead to the same conclusion. Various degrees of sophistication and types of practice will produce differing results.

Our approach will be based on the metaphysical realism[19] of an early

Indian Buddhist school called the *Sautrantika*, a Sanskrit term that means "those who rely on the sutras." This philosophy asserts that real things are causally efficacious, while the imaginary, conceptual fluff we superimpose upon things has no causal efficacy of its own. This is a very pragmatic worldview in which to embed our practice, even though it ultimately suffers from some subtle, but important, contradictions.

The four close applications of mindfulness—to the body, feelings, mental events, and all phenomena—are foundational for the practice of vipashyana. Nowhere in these teachings on vipashyana practice does the Buddha say, "And now analyze the nature of the self." It never comes up. Instead, he encourages us to closely apply mindfulness to the body, inspecting it carefully in many ways. One strategy involves an analysis of the four elements, which are probed by direct observation as well as by the imagination. Each bodily part is examined closely, searching for anything that is suggestive of a person or a self. Am I the hand, heart, liver, kidney, lung, blood, bone, or marrow? If I were to donate an organ to you, would I be giving some of my self to you?

Pursuit of such questions requires direct observation of the phenomena that constitute the body. By carefully scrutinizing both our own and others' bodies in myriad ways, mustering intelligence and insight, we can see all there is to see of the body. Having so analyzed it, we are directed to see nakedly everything we call the body, its parts, its functions, and so forth: they are simply impermanent phenomena arising and not true sources of happiness. Nowhere among any of them—including the brain—can we find the self, I, or mine. Without directly addressing how we conceive of ourselves, we simply investigate the phenomena habitually grasped as "I and mine," to see what is actually there.

It is easy to be trapped in rationalizations, saying, "Of course, I know my brain is not me," while behaving as though it is. Or one might conceptualize: "I think, therefore I am," or "I have imagination and free will," or "I have a soul and will be reborn in heaven." But when we actually observe the entire array of impersonal phenomena nakedly, without the conceptually projected body, we find that none of it is the self, I, or mine.

Next, we will apply this same scrutiny to the origination, presence, and dissolution of feelings, by conducting a precise, penetrating investigation, both internally and externally, to see if there is anything in the nature of feelings that indicates the self, I, or mine. When we see feelings nakedly, we see that they too are simply phenomena.

Then we will direct the searchlight of mindfulness toward the gamut of mental phenomena, investigating every possible phenomenon from the first-person perspective. When we scrutinize objective and subjective phenomena to see whether they belong to a self, are generated by a self, or constitute a self, can we find any evidence? Once again, the conclusion is no—they are simply phenomena.

Finally, in the close application of mindfulness to all phenomena, we will examine the entanglement of our body with our feelings, which are enmeshed with thoughts, emotions, and mental processes, which are further intertwined with similar phenomena in other people. At this moment, your thought processes are arising in relationship to my words, which appear in dependence upon your visual perceptions, vocabulary, and experience—our phenomena are intimately entangled.

By recognizing the fact that internally and externally, all the relationships among various facets of reality are simply phenomena, one finally sees that there is no direct evidence for an autonomous self. Furthermore, one finds no indirect evidence or influence of an autonomous self. Everything operates quite naturally without one. This is not an intellectual conclusion but a direct perception.

Real or Not

The Sautrantika philosophy provides a simple, practical way to determine what is real. Those phenomena that can cause effects are categorized as real, a category coextensive with many others, including phenomena that are compound, impermanent, and those that can be directly perceived. Something that we simply imagine is not a real thing; however, when we directly perceive a dreamscape, it is as real—that is, as causally efficacious—as daytime reality.

Here's an example: This cup that I directly perceive visually and tactually, as I sip my tea, is effectively containing my tea—it's a real cup.

The fact that the cup is mine can't be seen, no matter how carefully we scrutinize the cup, so it's merely a designation—not real. Even if the cup were imprinted "ALAN'S CUP," it might not belong to me. Ownership is strictly a matter of conventions that are conceptually superimposed upon a real cup. The result of investigating the phenomena of immediate experience is to see that they are all empty of self, I, and mine.

At first, the goal of vipashyana is to realize the true nature of the experiential world. When we arrive at the Middle Way view, vipashyana becomes a deeper, ontological probe. We seek to realize experientially whether anything whatsoever has its own inherent nature. This is not simply an intellectual exercise and not something to be accepted or assumed. We directly investigate whether anything in the universe, including elementary particles, exists by its own inherent nature. Obviously, this involves a different type of vipashyana with a different strategy.

I have heard religious studies scholars who do not meditate express the view that meditation is brainwashing oneself with doctrine. It is true that meditation can be used in that way. This is why a central theme in Buddhism is the need to strike a balance between intelligence and faith. With intelligence but no faith, one would continue to question everything, never develop certainty, and fail to accomplish anything. Excessive skepticism sabotages one's pursuit of understanding.

On the other hand, there is a real danger of overzealous faith that suffocates intelligence. People who simply believe whatever they are told, without asking questions, will discover dogma rather than knowledge. The Buddha did not claim that his teachings were sacrosanct. Come and see for yourself, he said; hear my teachings, but test them, as if you were testing gold.[20] In classical India, a purchaser of gold would test its purity by melting it, cutting it, and rubbing it on a touchstone to avoid deception. Similarly, the stakes are high when we choose to follow this path. We are devoting precious days of our lives to this pursuit. It would be tragic if an ineffective teacher or corrupted teachings were to trap us in a dead end. After carefully verifying the teacher and teaching, we can proceed with confidence. We are not told to begin with the axiom: The Buddha was right—there's no self. We must actually investigate the issue. We must first understand exactly what type of self he refuted and invited us to challenge. Then we must see for ourselves.

As we gain clear insight, two different types of criteria can be used to evaluate our findings: epistemic and pragmatic. Epistemic criteria involve the application of intelligence to check for truth or falsity. But in the Buddhist view, life is too short to pursue knowledge for its own sake. Therefore, as we pursue knowledge, refined attention, and skills such as shamatha, we should never forget the second criterion, which is pragmatic value. How does it affect my life? Does it improve the quality of my mind, behavior, clarity of awareness, or openness of heart in some tangible way? Both epistemic and pragmatic evaluations are essential.

FOUR NOBLE TRUTHS

The foundation of all Buddhist teachings and practices is known as the Four Noble Truths. I was first exposed to these inaugural teachings of the Buddha in a one-year undergraduate course on India, taught by an anthropologist. When we got to Buddhism, I learned that the Buddha was quite a pessimist—India was such a horrible place that you couldn't blame him—and he asserted that everything was suffering. The Buddha's First Noble Truth was not very appealing to me!

Later, I was exposed to Buddhism as taught by those who understood it, which gave me a very different perspective. In Sanskrit, the Buddha's First Noble Truth simply means unsatisfactoriness (Skt. *duhkha*), but it is usually translated as suffering. This statement of truth is refreshingly honest and unambiguous. When hearing teachings about the nature of unsatisfactoriness, suffering, and discontent, if people simply cannot relate to this, then Buddhism is probably not for them. Most of us can easily recognize the nature of suffering in the form of feelings and experiences we do not want.

From the perspective of biology, pain is essential. If you didn't get hungry, you'd starve to death. If you walked into a fire and didn't feel pain, you'd probably die of your burns, and you wouldn't pass on your genes. For living organisms, pain is a powerful motivator that trumps the pursuit of happiness. We would all prefer not to suffer so much, often nursing the hope that we can search for happiness once our suffering ends. For many people living in poverty right now, it might be hard to imagine less suffering in life, not to mention the notion of leading a flourishing and fulfilling life. Life-threatening events are a perpetual source of human misery. Victims of natural disasters are primarily concerned with finding ways to survive. From an evolutionary perspective, suffering motivates us to take actions that prevent our species from vanishing.

Could mindfulness be useful from an evolutionary perspective? You are probably not interested in learning about mindfulness in order to acquire more money, fame, or opportunities to procreate. Even if you have plenty to eat, ample possessions, a comfortable home, good health, a supportive family, and a meaningful job, there remains an underlying dissatisfaction, which can be categorized as mental suffering. I felt it poignantly when I was twenty and in college. My life offered nothing to complain about—a loving family, good health, a new car, and fine career prospects—a life of comfort and satisfaction was virtually guaranteed. I looked ahead to marriage, kids, bigger cars, better jobs, retirement, sickness, and death—and it all seemed utterly pointless. I was tremendously dissatisfied.

Dissatisfaction presented quite a dilemma for Prince Gautama. He had been born with everything anyone could want, but he was not happy. Despite his father's efforts to ensure that the young prince never witnessed old age, sickness, or death, he eventually did see these things, and they made a strong impression. He abandoned his wealth, palaces, wife, and son for the life of a homeless beggar—with a mission: he wanted to find a way to overcome the world's suffering.

Why do we worry, even when everything is going well and we should be happy? There is always something to worry about because circumstances can change, and they inevitably do. The Second Noble Truth, of the causes of the arising (Skt. *samudaya*) of suffering, suggests that virtually everything in the world has the potential to create suffering due to craving and grasping. Can you imagine any occurrence in our society, in the lives of other species, or in the natural environment that could not possibly catalyze unhappiness somewhere? I've been pondering this for years now, and I haven't thought of anything yet. Even if world peace were to break out tomorrow, manufacturers of armaments would be devastated.

Such thoughts inevitably redirect the attention inward. Do we possess inner resources that can overcome the unsatisfactory conditions in the outside world? Many people have suffered adversities far beyond anything I could imagine. I had long conversations with Palden Gyatso,[21] a Tibetan monk who endured thirty-three years of brutal torture in Chinese prisons and labor camps. That he even survived is remarkable; even more so is his kind, calm, strong nature—utterly free of hatred. I have also met very wealthy and successful people who nevertheless suffer from long-term depression. Palden Gyatso is a poor monk, his health ravaged by torture, but he seems quite happy. What are the roots of dissatisfaction, unhappiness, and misery? If we can identify the underlying causes, is there any possibility of liberation? How have we come into existence? Who are we? What is our real nature? How much can we know about the world?

These existential questions must be faced by anyone dissatisfied with worldly pleasures, anyone striving to know himself or herself, and anyone who suspects that there is more to life than a struggle for survival. There are important truths in the history of evolution, but biology cannot explain every aspect of human existence. To me, the scientific materialists' creed is as dogmatic as the belief that every answer can be found in a particular scripture, even in the most sublime Buddhist text. I just don't buy it.

We are entering deep waters. What is our inherent nature? Have we been designed by God, nature, natural selection, or random genetic mutations? Are we condemned to an existence of suffering with no chance of freedom? Are the mental afflictions of delusion, hatred, and craving hardwired into us? Are the causes of suffering, asserted in the Second Noble Truth, determined by our biological nature? Is our survival dependent upon craving, aggression, passions, and a delusional separation of "I and mine" from everything else?

It seems likely that Homo sapiens knocked out the Neanderthals because they vanished and we are still here. Is our aggression genetically determined? These questions are too important to delegate to philosophers in academic enclaves. I have a lot of respect for philosophical studies, but theories must be verified in the laboratory of experience. Are we some noble experiment, destined to suffer from habitual delusion, grasping, craving, hostility, envy, and arrogance? Is there no possibility of escaping these causes of suffering?

One of the most extraordinary hypotheses ever formulated, but largely overlooked in the modern world, is the Buddha's Third Noble Truth, which asserts the possibility of the cessation (Pali *nirodha*) of craving and the freedom from suffering. He maintained that our nature is not afflicted to the core. A dimension of pure awareness can be unveiled, making freedom from suffering a real possibility. Not knowing with certainty whether or not you have the potential to be liberated, still you must bet your life on it every day—by taking action or not.

If it is truly possible to be radically free of suffering, there is an overriding justification to strive diligently for this result. If not, there is no harm in trying. This philosophical theme shares some similarities with French philosopher and mathematician Blaise Pascal's (1623–1662) wager in favor of the existence of an unknowable God.[22] It seems logical to bet your life that the infinite potential reward of liberation will outweigh the benefits of relying on circumstances and luck to find mundane happiness and avoid suffering. We cannot control our health, families, environment, or economy. As we grow older, we even lose control of our own bodies. Can the mind be controlled? If not the mind, can we find happiness beyond any need for control? What a relief that would be!

In the Fourth Noble Truth, the Buddha proclaimed that there is an ancient, eightfold path (Skt. *marga*) to liberation that has been traveled by the buddhas of the past.[23] This path is laid out in a magnificently sensible way. It begins with ethics: treating each other with kindness and doing our best not to cause harm. This is classically described as right speech, right action, and right livelihood. Wouldn't this make good sense on any planet in the universe? By treating others as we want to be treated ourselves, we will help each other, not only in pleasant times, but in adversity, aging, sickness, death, and in all of life's vicissitudes.

Upon the basis of an ethical lifestyle, the path continues with right effort, right mindfulness, and right concentration. With persevering effort to abandon harmful thoughts, words, and deeds while developing beneficial ones, along with cultivation of the four close applications of mindfulness and development of samadhi, the mind becomes balanced and healthy—a wellspring of happiness and fulfillment.

Finally, this balanced, healthy mind is applied to the investigation of reality on the paths of right view and right intention. The Buddha strongly encouraged the development of exceptional mental health and balance—far surpassing mere freedom from dysfunction. It is very good if a psychiatrist finds we don't need therapy, but the path of Dharma leads to Olympic-class mental balance, resilience, buoyancy, and suppleness. Upon this basis, as the Buddha states, "The mind established in equilibrium comes to know reality as it is."[24]

COMPLEMENTARY PERSPECTIVES

The result of following the Buddha's path is said to be attainment of knowledge of all knowable things, but the goal of knowing reality is not unique to Buddhism. The world's dominant paradigm for the acquisition of knowledge is science, for good reasons. This status was earned by adopting high standards of intellectual integrity, brilliant strategy, skeptical empiricism, and clear, rational thinking. In a mere four hundred years, a lineage of highly trained scientists has expanded knowledge and driven technological transformations in virtually all fields, as new disciplines proliferate exponentially. The frequency, speed, and impact of these radical transformations on the planet are unprecedented.

The Dalai Lama has a clear vision of science, and he is inspiring other Buddhists to engage in dialogue with scientists. He maintains that in order to continue to benefit all beings, Buddhists must be scientifically literate and must recognize the points of congruence and incongruence in various views. Although science is the dominant player in the knowledge game today, this unprecedented success is radically imbalanced. To a great extent, science does not acknowledge its most serious flaw—the crumbling foundations of metaphysical realism and scientific materialism that support its vast edifice.

Seeing Out

The explicit purpose of the pioneers of the scientific revolution—including Copernicus (1473–1543), Kepler (1571–1630), Descartes (1596–1650), Galileo (1564–1642), and Newton (1643–1727), as well as many of their followers well into the nineteenth century—was to see a God's-eye view of reality. The founding fathers of science were profoundly religious men, but they were not Taoists, Buddhists, Hindus, or Jews—they were all Christians. For them, the pursuit of a scientific understanding of the natural world—God's creation—was a way to know the mind of the Creator.

The universe was likened to a big clock, which was the cutting-edge technology of the time. Poets, philosophers, and scientists observed that such a beautiful mechanism, intricately assembled, reveals much about the nature of the God who designed and created it. Because they could not study the designer, they settled for studying his creation. In their mechanomorphic view, the clock would reveal the mind of its maker.

Although contemplatives throughout time have sought God, or ultimate truth, by following the mystical impulse to look inward, Galileo and his cohort looked outward instead. It was no coincidence that the Protestant Reformation and the scientific revolution occurred simultaneously within the mosaic of the European renaissance. Martin Luther (1483–1546) saw human beings as fallen sinners with unreliable intellects, wholly dependent on the grace of God for the gift of salvation—in the afterlife. In order to understand the universe from God's perspective, humanity's debased nature would have to be conquered.

To overcome their flawed condition, scientists employed the ideal of mathematics enshrined by Pythagoras (570–495 BCE) and the notion of reason championed by Aristotle (384–322 BCE) as springboards to leap beyond human perspective and think God's own thoughts, thereby achieving apotheosis—the ascent of the mind of man to the mind of

God. By the time of Galileo, mathematics was called the language of God. In order to understand God's thoughts, these researchers sought to quarantine their untrustworthy minds from the physical reality of creation. Technology, such as the telescope, was developed to yield objective knowledge, uncontaminated by subjective human thoughts, feelings, and motivations.

The tantalizing question of what exists beyond our anthropocentric perspective has inspired more than four hundred years of scientific investigation: What really occurs when no one is looking—other than God? Now that many scientists aren't religious, it's not called a God's-eye view anymore; one philosopher of science calls it a view from nowhere.[25] How does the world appear to nobody who is nowhere? The overriding need for an absolutely objective frame of reference remains central to the spirit of scientific inquiry.

Natural science based on metaphysical realism can be defined as the study of nature as it exists independently of the human mind. Its domain is the public sphere of intersubjective reality that is accessible to third-person inquiry. For example, most people who count the pages in this book will arrive at the same number. We all believe that there is a real number of pages, no matter who is counting, and even when nobody is looking. Most scientists are interested in phenomena that can be perceived externally, measured objectively, and verified by others. But this approach should not be considered sacrosanct.

Seeing In

The Buddhist view, like the ancient Indian contemplative perspective in which it is rooted, considers the external approach to understanding reality to be of distinctly secondary importance. As with the great Christian contemplatives, the Buddha's primary approach was an inward search for experiential insight. Consequently, he started with a very different question: Why is there so much suffering in the world? The notion of suffering with nobody to experience it would never have occurred to him.

The world of interest to a hundred generations of Buddhist contemplatives and philosophers is our lived world, and this world of experience (Skt. *loka*; Ger. *Lebenswelt*) is central to the movement of phenomenology that originated with German philosophers Edmund Husserl (1859–1938) and Martin Heidegger (1889–1976). The world of experience is quite different from the world independent of experience—the God's-eye perspective. Rather than imagining what exists when nobody is looking, the challenge is to understand the world as we actually perceive it.

Buddhist physics describes an ancient atomic theory, with atoms that are quite different from those depicted in modern theories. These are not atoms existing independently of experience; they denote a wholly different domain: the structure of experience itself. Each experiential atom is more like a molecule with eight components, including the four primary elements and the attributes of visual form, smell, taste, and tactile qualities—the things we call subjective qualities, or qualia. From this perspective, visual forms are what we actually see, not what travels through space, and a physicist or neuroscientist would agree. The visual cortex doesn't act like a catcher's mitt in catching colors that travel through space.

Color vision is particularly interesting. According to the perspective of modern physics, no color exists objectively. A blue object is not composed of blue molecules. Photons of various energies are emitted from this object, but photons have no color. The photons entering the eye strike the retina and catalyze a complex sequence of electrochemical events leading to the visual cortex, but there is no blue area of the visual cortex. Finally, in some mysterious way that nobody understands, the color blue appears to visual perception. Blueness is not in the object, in the brain, or in between. Blueness is a basic phenomenological constituent of the human visual field.

For the first three hundred years in the history of science, the mind was largely overlooked. There was little interest in the mind or consciousness because the goal was to understand an absolutely objective reality as it exists from God's own perspective. Seeking to describe reality independent of human experience, scientists shunned the human mind as a subjective source of error. Consciousness itself did not become a legitimate topic of scientific study until the late twentieth century, and it is still widely regarded as a mere emergent feature of complex neural networks.

In contrast, the starting point in Buddhism is the world of subjective experience. This is dictated by a highly pragmatic motive: the eradication of suffering and the causes of suffering on the path to liberation. If one is trying to understand the world of experience, then the mind is central to the inquiry. The mind makes experience possible; without awareness, there is no experience.

Seeing Beyond

After having trained and experimented extensively in samadhi and other practices, Prince Gautama sat down beneath what became known in Sanskrit as the *bodhi* (awakening) tree. He vowed not to rise from his seat until he had achieved the liberation he was seeking. On the night of his enlightenment, he investigated the essential nature of the mind. Probing beyond his own mind—a particular psyche influenced by biology, social environment, and personal history—he delved into a deeper dimension of consciousness underlying the psyche.

Then he traced this continuum of consciousness back across thousands of lifetimes that manifested in the particular psyche of Prince Gautama. Probing the nature of consciousness, he reported that he directly observed a vast sequence of past lives, each with its specific circumstances. This was his first act of vipashyana: probing beyond the ordinary mind into the underlying continuum of a subtle dimension of consciousness that carries on from lifetime to lifetime.

The elegance of the Buddha's path continues to hold me in awe. It begins quite pragmatically with our feet firmly planted on the road of an ethical life. It is easy to become enthusiastically involved in abstract meditations, esoteric books, or exotic rituals, without spending sufficient time attending closely to our conduct in the world. We may develop lofty views and opinions of ourselves, while scarcely considering our impact on others and the environment.

From an ethical perspective, how are we treating the other people, nations, and species on the planet? How can we not only avoid injuring them, but also bring them benefit? How can we be of the best possible service? We enter into meditation from this point of departure and return to it continuously. The contemplative search for insight is always grounded in our way of life.

Settling the Body, Speech, and Mind *in Their Natural States*

The practice of meditation begins with settling the body, speech, and mind in their natural states of equilibrium. The body rests in comfort and ease—still as a mountain. The speech rests in effortless silence—still as a lute with cut strings. The mind rests in nonconceptual awareness— still as space. Please find a comfortable position, seated or supine, in which to explore the following practice, whose primary purpose is the relaxation of body and mind. You should follow these steps to begin each session; the later descriptions will include progressively briefer recaps of the points mentioned here.

GUIDED MEDITATION: Settling the Body in Its Natural State I

Attend to the tactile field— balancing relaxation, stillness, and vigilance

Reality is what is occurring right here and now, for you. At the start of each practice, I invite you to bring forth your highest aspiration for the greatest possible benefit to yourself and others.

Now bring your awareness into the field of the body. Be mindfully present within the field of tactile sensations in the feet, legs, torso, arms, neck, and head. Stop being compulsively caught up in thoughts—rest your awareness. Release all thoughts and let awareness settle into the field of the body.

Adopt a witnessing mode of bare attention without analysis or commentary. Simply remain present with tactile sensations of solidity, heat, cold, and motion as they arise. Maintain continuous awareness of these sensations as they change from moment to moment.

Settling the body in its natural state requires a balance of three qualities: relaxation, stillness, and vigilance. Relaxation is paramount. Relax deliberately as you exhale, and set your body completely at ease. Loosen further with each out-breath. Feel a delicious melting sensation as you surrender all excess muscular tension to gravity. Release tightness in the shoulders. Soften the muscles of the face, jaw, and mouth. Open the forehead, particularly between the eyebrows. Relax all the muscles around the eyes.

Let your body be still as it settles into progressively deeper comfort and ease. Apart from the natural movement of the breath, remain as motionless as possible. Keeping your sessions short makes it easier to remain still without being distracted by various sensations and urges to move.

Adopt a posture of vigilant attention, whether you are sitting upright or prone. If you are sitting, let your spine be straight, with the sternum slightly raised and the abdominal muscles soft and loose. Feel the belly expand with each inhalation and contract with each exhalation.

Continue relaxing more deeply with each exhalation. Maintain a motionless balance between relaxation and vigilance. Involuntary thoughts are bound to arise out of habit. Rather than becoming caught up in them or trying to stop them forcefully, simply release them with each out-breath. Let them go, as if with a sigh of relief.

Settle the speech—including the "inner speech" of mental chitchat—in its natural state of effortless silence, with no need to speak and no thought of verbalizing. Immerse your awareness in the silent, motionless, nonconceptuality of the body. Attend closely to whatever tactile events arise within this field. Observe them nakedly from moment to moment, without thinking, cogitating, or ruminating. Each moment of experience is fresh, unprecedented, and unique.

In the process of settling the speech in its natural state, settle the breath in its natural rhythm, releasing all control. This is a subtle challenge, not easily mastered, because the breath is so easy to influence and control. Let the breath be unimpeded and spontaneous, flowing as effortlessly as possible. Be mindfully aware of the sensations of the breath rippling throughout the body. Let the body breathe itself without any influence of desires, expectations, or preferences.

Whether the breath is deep or shallow, fast or slow, smooth or irregular, just let it be. Quietly and nonintrusively observe the sensations of the breath. With each out-breath, release all thoughts, images, memories, and fantasies, returning your awareness to the field of tactile sensations. Relax increasingly deeply, while sustaining the innate clarity and luminosity of awareness of the field of tactile sensations. Be embodied mindfully.

Finally, completely release all aspirations, imagery, desires, and mental objects. For a short while, let your awareness rest in its own nonconceptual nature.

To conclude each practice, I invite you to bring forth your most meaningful aspirations for your own flourishing and fulfillment, embedded in your wishes for the world around you. Arouse the yearning that the time and effort you have devoted to study and practice will lead to the realization of your own and others' most meaningful aspirations. This is known as dedicating the merit. ☙

On Familiarization

Mindfulness includes not only present-centered mindfulness, but also retrospective memory of your experiences. Following each practice, note how well you maintained your object of attention. Were you able to follow the practice instructions? How did your experience compare with expectations? What will you do differently next time? Exercise prospective mindfulness by remembering this when that time comes. The essence of practice is familiarization by repetition. Repeat each practice until you can perform it confidently from memory and you experience a taste of the results.

A book is an excellent way to learn about the theory and practice of meditation, but it is not a substitute for spiritual friends who support your progress on the path or for the blessings that come from your personal connection with a spiritual teacher. Take responsibility for your own welfare by evaluating your progress with a critical but nonjudgmental eye. Overcome the doubts that will inevitably surface in your practice by studying the vast and profound Dharma literature, seeking clarification from more experienced practitioners, and establishing a relationship with a qualified teacher.

CONTEMPLATIVE SCIENCE

The theory and practice of mindfulness is fundamental to the discipline I refer to as contemplative science.[26] This is a true science, whose primary mode of observation and experimentation is not the technological examination of external phenomena but the examination of experiential reality as a whole, starting with understanding the mind itself. A simple fact might be surprising: if we are fundamentally interested in mental phenomena, we can observe them only by mental perception.

Direct Observation

If we were studying the planets and galaxies in an external pursuit of reality, we would augment our vision with the best telescopes available. In four hundred years, Galileo's thirty-power visible-light telescope has led to the Hubble Space Telescope and observations across the entire electromagnetic spectrum. Exquisitely sensitive detectors for trace elements far exceed the sensitivity of our tongues and noses. Computer-enhanced vision and hearing detect images and sounds far beyond the limits of our physical organs. Spectroscopy details the chemical composition and motion of astronomical bodies across the universe. These technologies illuminate our world with amazingly precise observations.

But if we are interested in the nature of the mind and consciousness, our only instrument is the mind itself. The scope of psychology, as defined by American psychologist William James (1842–1910), is the phenomena of the mind in firsthand experience, such as thoughts, dreams, mental imagery, desire, suffering, and joy. Behaviorists observe only the physical expressions of a living being. Neurobiologists observe only the neural correlates of mental processes. No instrument devised by a psychologist or neuroscientist allows direct observation of a mental event in the way that a telescope permits the direct observation of a celestial event.

Only one mode of observation can actually illuminate the nature of mental events themselves, and that is mental awareness—not one of the five physical senses. We may draw inferences about other people's mental states and processes, for example, by looking at someone and judging that they look angry, sad, joyful, bored, or excited. But mental phenomena themselves are directly observable only by the individual mental perception that accompanies them.

Mental perception is a term that does not appear in the psychology textbooks I've read. This sixth mode of perception, extending beyond the five physical senses, is the one that enables us to observe mental phenomena, states, and processes. Mental events, such as thoughts, images, and dreams, are invisible to all instruments of technology. They cannot be detected with microscopy, blood analysis, electroencephalography (EEG), or functional magnetic resonance imaging (fMRI). It is only mental awareness that directly illuminates the nature of mental phenomena.

Instrument of Refinement

Mental phenomena can certainly be observed. But when we try to observe the mind, our attention typically vacillates between hyperactive excitation and lethargic stupor. Can mental perception be refined and stabilized into a rigorous instrument of inquiry that produces reliable observations? Among the six modes of perception, only one—mental perception—can be significantly refined and rapidly enhanced, with no upper limit.

For example, someone who conducted five thousand hours of rigorous investigation in the context of a meditation retreat might discover truths about the nature of the mind, consciousness, the origin of mental events, and the relationship between the mind and body. Someone else might replicate these discoveries, which would encourage others to follow suit, and this might continue for hundreds of generations. By developing rigorous methods of inquiry and a common language, these discoveries could be reported, replicated, analyzed, refined, and deepened. Theoretical explanations could be offered, tested, and challenged. This is precisely what has occurred in Buddhism over the past twenty-five centuries.

The introspective mode of inquiry is the dominant theme of mindfulness practice because it is the only way to observe mental phenomena. Sometimes it seems that the world has developed a kind of imagination-deficit disorder concerning the study of the mind. Science has been tremendously successful in developing knowledge, power, and technology, but the field of philosophy has been far less successful. Is there any consensus among twentieth-century philosophers except concerning their lack of consensus? There often seem to be as many views as there are philosophers, each arguing for the supremacy of his or her own beliefs. There is no contest between science and philosophy in terms of their respective bodies of consensual knowledge and the practical applications that have been developed.

Theology is running in distant third place. Atheists believe that theologians study something that does not exist. Even within a single religion such as Christianity, there are myriad denominations and sects, each with differing interpretations. What sort of theological consensus would there be if we included the other Abrahamic religions of Islam and Judaism, not to mention Taoism, Hinduism, and Buddhism? How many theologians believe that theirs is the only true religion—despite fundamental tenets unambiguously repudiated by scientific explanations?

Scientists appear to have won a four-hundred-year Olympic race to describe and explain reality. Theologians and philosophers have made no comparable progress in that time. To many people, science is where the knowledge is—the only show in town. To the skeptic, religion seems to be loaded with superstitious dogmas, many of which are implausible or contradictory. Meanwhile, philosophers never tire of arguing among themselves, without ever achieving any fresh discoveries of their own. If you want the truth, rely on science; everything else is a waste of time.

But there is a downside to the tremendous success of the natural sciences—they only look outward. Even the mind itself is studied only by looking outward: interviewing subjects, collecting survey data, measuring behavior, and studying neurophysiological correlates. These attempts to scientifically understand the nature of the mind by measuring physical processes are profoundly limited by their methodology, which guarantees that the mind will be found to be a mere byproduct of physical phenomena. This conclusion is preordained.

Complementary Understanding

Rather than competing with externally focused methodologies, contemplative science offers a profoundly complementary approach to understanding reality. Scientific acuity, rigor, and skepticism are practiced while looking inward to directly observe the subjects of interest themselves—mental phenomena. With proper refinement, the mind becomes a reliable, accurate instrument for introspective probes into the very nature of the mind and body in relationship with the environment and other people. Contemplative science provides a real means of discovering, validating, and propagating knowledge.

Science has been remarkably successful in illuminating the physical universe, making breathtaking and revolutionary discoveries, but it carries some heavy metaphysical baggage. Fundamentalists in every field insist that theirs is the only way. If we limit ourselves to studying physical phenomena, we are sure to find that only physical phenomena exist. The complementary mode of contemplative inquiry into the nature of reality studies mental events by observing these phenomena directly. By making careful observations with well-balanced instruments, a rigorous science of mind can develop accurate data and verifiable theories.

Contemplative science is revolutionary, and it is not religion. I am a religious person, and I love philosophy too, but this is science! It begins with the direct observation of the phenomena in question, followed by the formation of hypotheses, which are then put to the test of experience. We are following in the footsteps of giants of the past, who probed these issues deeply and presented their conclusions as hypotheses to be verified. Could there be any greater or more meaningful adventure than to discover the truth of our own existence in relationship to our fellow beings and the universe at large?

This expedition begins by looking inward. Is there any other way we could possibly understand the world as we actually experience it? Dogmatic assumptions are inherently unscientific. We need all the integrity, open-mindedness, and healthy skepticism we can muster, especially James's sense of radical empiricism: the mind of the observer can never be separated from the observation to yield a completely objective result. Let us probe into the nature of experience and fathom it thoroughly because life is short. My hero Henry David Thoreau (1817–1862) put it well:

> I went to the woods because I wished to live deliberately, to front only the essential facts of life, and see if I could not learn what it had to teach, and not, when I came to die, discover that I had not lived.[27]

GUIDED MEDITATION:
Mindfulness I

Attend to all mental and sensory appearances—
observing without distraction, grasping, or aversion

Begin each session by settling the body, speech, and mind in their natural states of equilibrium. Bring awareness to the field of the body, becoming mindfully present from the soles of the feet to the crown of the head. Rest in a witnessing mode: nonreactive, nondiscursive, and nonconceptual, with awareness approximating bare attention. Attending to the sensations arising throughout the body, you may notice areas of constriction. Breathe into them and release the tension as you breathe out. With each out-breath, release any tension in the shoulders, softening and relaxing the face, especially around the eyes.

As you settle the body in a posture of ease, remain in stillness except for the movement of the breath. Stillness of the body supports coherence of awareness and mindfulness. While maintaining the sense of relaxation and stillness, assume a posture of vigilance. Keep the sternum slightly raised if you are sitting upright, while letting the abdominal muscles relax.

Settle the speech in effortless silence, with no need for words or discursive thoughts. Settle the respiration in its natural rhythm, unforced and uninfluenced by will or expectation. Let the abdomen remain loose and relaxed, expanding and contracting naturally, without forcing the breath down into the belly. In progressively deeper breathing, first the belly expands, then the diaphragm, and finally the chest expands. Let the breath flow naturally and effortlessly.

Now settle your mind in awareness, hovering ever so simply in the present moment, without directing or isolating your attention to any particular object. The object of mindfulness is whatever arises in the immediacy of the present moment. Let your awareness remain motionless—not scurrying after the various sights and sounds appearing to the five physical senses. With your eyes at least partially open, allow all appearances to arise to awareness, without inhibiting or avoiding any thought, image, memory, desire, emotion, or sensation.

No matter what arises in the present moment, hover there, simply taking note of all that appears. Notice all the comings and goings of sensory and mental phenomena, while awareness remains still, unattached, and nonreactive. Thoughts are bound to arise; don't block them or identify with them. Don't allow the mind to be carried away by distractions, obsessive thinking, or compulsive grasping and aversion toward the objects of thoughts. Simply let thoughts arise from moment to moment, attend to them, and note them for what they are.

As thoughts arise in the space of experience, together with visual imagery, sounds, and tactile sensations, let your awareness remain motionless in its own place, without grasping or aversion toward anything. Be present with every appearance, engaged from moment to moment, and not spaced-out. Remain in stillness, amidst a whirlwind of appearances to the mind and senses, like a gracious host surrounded by unruly guests.

Let this meditation flow in a spirit of ease, remaining present while releasing everything and relaxing more deeply with each out-breath.

Note whatever appears to the mind without distraction, conceptual projection, grasping, or aversion. Be discerningly present with appearances to awareness from moment to moment.

Finally, release everything and rest in nonconceptual awareness. Conclude by bringing forth your most meaningful aspirations for yourself and others, and dedicate your merit, benefit, and virtue to their actualization. ☙

On Seated Postures

Many people are uncomfortable sitting on the floor. Our backs ache, our knees hurt, and we can't sit still without fidgeting or cutting off the circulation in our legs. Without being comfortable, the essential goal of relaxation cannot be approached. This is a practical issue that calls for experimentation instead of dogmatism. Hatha yoga offers a matrix of techniques specifically designed to develop the physiological capacity for extended sessions and samadhi. The *Yoga Sutras of Patañjali* begins with ethics and goes immediately to physical postures (Skt. *asanas*), the breath, and so forth.[28] Regularly performing slow stretches to loosen the hamstrings and strengthening exercises for the back and abdominal muscles will improve sitting comfort.

The *zabuton*, a Japanese-style sitting cushion, is comfortably firm, without cutting off the circulation in one's legs. I use it with a fairly thin, firm wedge under the coccyx, at the base of the spine. Resting on this solid support, the spine can be held erect with very little effort. I like my legs flat, and although I've tried many different postures, such as full lotus and half lotus, as I'm getting older, I prefer what's called the comfortable posture. You should experiment to see what works for you.

I've lived with yogis who have spent twenty or thirty years in retreat, real professionals who make me look like a rank amateur. Yogis I've known who meditate twelve to sixteen hours a day do not generally sit in the middle of a rug for serious, long-term meditation; they will usually have a solid support behind them, whether sitting on a cushion or a firm bed. Some yogis don't even lie down to sleep. One seventy-nine-year-old lama I know about meditates sitting on his bed and sleeps barely two hours per night. We're not quite sure when he sleeps because we haven't had the audacity to interrupt him.

In 1978, I was translating for a very senior lama, probably seventy-five at the time, who was quite well known for his extraordinary abilities. Two friends and I sought instruction from him, and he said, "Come over at the end of the evening." We arrived at ten o'clock, and he was joking around, enjoying the company of some other lamas. This went on until about one o'clock in the morning. Then he said, "Okay you three, come on in." At one-thirty in the morning, he started giving the teachings at great length. Then, right in the middle of the teachings, he paused and just went out! He had a support, so he didn't keel over. After about ten minutes, he continued the teaching. That was his night's sleep!

When the lamas fled Tibet in 1959, many joined a great encampment of lamas and monks in East Bengal. The British government had created a fort, called Buxa Duar, to incarcerate political prisoners such as Gandhi. After Indian independence, thousands of Tibetan lamas and monks were housed in this big prison for months, while the Indian government tried to decide what to do with them. The monks thought, "We've got a great big monastery here," so the senior ones started teaching. Quite a number of my lamas, including Gyatrul Rinpoche, Geshe Rabten, and Geshe Ngawang Dhargyey, were in that great encampment. One of the senior monks, Song Rinpoche (1905–1984), was well known for teaching around the clock. When he saw that nobody needed him, for example, at two o'clock in the afternoon, he would take a little siesta. Then he would resume teaching.

Such extraordinary abilities take time to develop, so experiment to find a comfortable but solid support for your lower spine. Try various positions for your legs. Experiment with chairs. One participant, who was not very limber and had back problems, attended a three-month retreat with me in 2007 while sitting in a portable, zero-gravity chair. The chair reduced the stress on his body and kept his spine quite straight. He was very relaxed and comfortable in extended sessions. It's fine to make use of technology!

❧ 2 ❧

Engaging in Practice

CONTEMPLATIVE EXPEDITION

ALTHOUGH YOU might not have access to an ideal setting, such as the Old Mission in Santa Barbara, I encourage you to find the most suitable environment available to you. Take the time to explore and engage in the meditative practices described here, until you become familiar with the taste of their results. Only through your own experience will you come to understand the subtle truths pointed to by these simple but profound techniques. New depths will emerge each time you revisit these practices.

A totally secluded environment might be difficult to obtain; see if you can carve out of your daily obligations a space of virtual retreat in which to explore these teachings. Dedicate time to read and practice away from diversions and interruptions, and maintain your silence as much as possible. When you must interact with others, try to keep your talk and activity meaningful.

The ability to rest in silence is a rare opportunity in our hyperactive, multitasking world. In a formal retreat setting, it can be quite beneficial to maintain one's silence. The absence of speech naturally promotes a quieter mind and body, and this leads to a deepening of meditation practice. In a very strict retreat, even eye contact might be avoided.

There are times when it's best to retreat, resting and recouping one's energies; then one may be ready to set out on a contemplative expedition. The etymology of the word "expedition" suggests extricating one's feet from the ruts in which they have become stuck. This is an opportunity to break old habits and explore the freedom of new realms of experiential insights and discoveries.

Practical Matters

If you have already established a regular practice of meditation, you can easily augment your practice with these techniques. Here are a few considerations, based on my own experience, which may assist you in realizing the most benefit from mindfulness practice:

- ► Give yourself a daily allowance of one or more dedicated times for meditation. Early morning hours are classically favored; you are refreshed and least likely to be interrupted.
- ► Retreat to a solitary, quiet, softly lit place with fresh air and no distractions. Create good habits by using this space exclusively for meditation—not for work, sleep, or entertainment.
- ► Establish a comfortable seat, in a sitting or supine posture. Arrange firm support from cushions to minimize discomfort. The best position depends on the practice and your needs.
- ► Maintain short sessions. Finish while you're still fresh and wouldn't mind continuing. Slowly increase the length and frequency of sessions, but never past the point of freshness.
- ► Relish your meditation! Seeing the results of improved mindfulness and focused attention, you will look forward to meditation and not succumb to procrastination and excuses.

The Buddha taught meditation in four postures: sitting, lying down, standing, and walking. Between formal sessions, you are bound to be standing and walking, so you will have plenty of opportunity to apply these teachings and practices in those modes. In formal meditative practice, I encourage you to explore two primary postures. The first is seated on a chair or in a cross-legged position on the floor, whichever is most comfortable for you. Second, explore the very useful option of meditating while lying down: the supine position. Alternating between seated and supine positions is also beneficial.

A session of twenty-four minutes is a good starting interval; for most people, it is neither too short nor too long. This ancient Indian measure of time (Skt. *ghatika*) is one-sixtieth of a twenty-four-hour day, and this is the session duration that the eighth-century Indian Buddhist contemplative Kamalashila recommended for beginning meditators. Having multiple, short meditation sessions—with quick breaks in between—is better than struggling through long, tiring sessions.

Unlike receiving verbal guidance in a group, you can use this book to practice at your own pace. An essential aspect of mindfulness training is remembering the instructions; the result is that you will not need to continually refer to the book. Repeat each practice until you can perform it confidently from memory. Brief instructions above each practice summarize the primary instruction and corollary points. Each practice builds on the progression of earlier ones, so follow the sequence. In some cases, two practices fit well together. If you are still fresh after the first one, take a short break to stretch and have a drink, and then continue with the second session.

MATTERS OF FORM

The Buddha's teaching of the Dharma was called "Good in the beginning, good in the middle, and good in the end,"[29] and these can also be explained as three aspects of successful practice. One of several ways of interpreting this statement in the context of practice is that good in the beginning refers to personal motivation: start each session by generating your highest aspiration for the practice. Good in the middle refers to maintaining a continuity of focused attention, which is at the heart of all practices. Good in the end refers to dedicating the merit of your practice to the achievement of the most meaningful aspirations of yourself and others.

At the start of each session, I invite you to bring to mind your highest aspirations for the benefits you would like to derive from this practice. How would you love to enrich and transform your life, your mind, and your engagement with the world? What would you love to offer to the world? After engaging in a variety of practices involving observation, inquiry, and analysis, always conclude by dissolving all such questions and simply resting your awareness in its own nonconceptual nature—sheer luminosity and cognizance. Finally, at the close of each session, bring to mind your most meaningful aspirations and envision their actualization with the yearning, "May these wishes be fulfilled by the merit of this practice, with great benefit for all."

GUIDED MEDITATION:
Mindfulness II

Sustain unwavering mindfulness of all appearances—
observing without distraction, grasping, or aversion

Begin each session with a sense of ease. Release your awareness into the field of tactile sensations throughout the body, remaining mindfully present. Settle your body in its natural state, imbued with relaxation, stillness, and a posture of vigilance. The supine position is profoundly relaxing, and if you are resting in comfort, it will not be difficult to remain still, without moving or fidgeting. If you adopt a psychological stance of vigilance, the supine posture can be very suitable for meditation.

Embrace the subtle challenge of settling your respiration in its natural rhythm, allowing the breath to flow of its own accord; with no intervention and no notion of correct breathing—long or short, deep or shallow, regular or irregular—just let it be. Breathe effortlessly, as if you were deep asleep, but remain mindfully attentive to the sensations of the breath arising throughout the body.

With your eyes at least partially open, so that visual appearances arise, let your awareness hover motionlessly in the present moment. Having no preference, desire, or aversion, engage mindfully and attend to whatever thoughts and sensory images appear. With your awareness like space, simply be present, without reacting to any appearances. Release any grasping tendencies, allowing your awareness to remain in its own place. Attend to whatever arises in the present moment, without distraction, grasping, or aversion, and sustain an unwavering flow of mindfulness. 🙏

On Supine Postures

I'm a strong advocate of the supine posture in addition to seated postures. Recommendations for using the supine position are found in two of the greatest commentaries in the Theravadin tradition. One is Upatissa's first-century-CE classic, the *Vimuttimagga,* translated as *The Path of Freedom,*[30] in which he recommends postures for vipashyana practice based on personality. The typologies in Buddhism include two major groups: those dominated by anger and those dominated by craving. This text recommends sitting and reclining postures as particularly suitable for angry personalities, while standing and walking are best for lustful personalities. If you're craving, walk it off; if you're angry, back off by sitting or lying down!

Vipashyana can and should be practiced in all four postures, as the Buddha clearly states in his primary discourse on mindfulness. The modern Vipassana movement strongly emphasizes walking meditation between seated sessions, which can be very helpful. Deep stabilization of the mind in shamatha practice is best done in the more grounded postures: seated and supine.

The fifth-century Indian Theravadin scholar Buddhaghosa, in the *Vishuddhimagga,* or *The Path of Purification,*[31] simply states that there are the four postures of standing, sitting, walking, and lying down; whichever posture is effective for developing concentration is the one to be adopted. The Buddha taught these four postures, and each one can be useful. The Tibetan tradition strongly emphasizes the lotus posture with the seven points of Vairochana,[32] which has important benefits. Some practices require specific aspects of posture, such as precise placement of the hands and the contact point of the thumbs. A detailed technology of posture is integral to the highest stages of practice. Nevertheless, the lotus posture is not the only acceptable one, and we must take great care not to injure ourselves in trying to accomplish it forcefully.

Relaxation is more difficult for us in the modern world than it was for people living in traditional rural or nomadic societies. In the lifestyle that we accept as normal, the importance of relaxation cannot be overstated. Among my own teachers, Gyatrul Rinpoche encouraged me to practice in the supine position. Having taught in the United States since 1972, he knows that our stressful lives call for the supine position's ability to promote deep relaxation. Simply by relaxing our body and mind, we will find that continuity, coherence, and stability of attention emerge and increase quite naturally and effortlessly. This is a valuable discovery, even without considering the benefits of using such stability to investigate phenomena in the practice of vipashyana.

◁ 3 ▷
Wheel of Dharma

THE BUDDHA'S TEACHINGS begin not with a leap of faith to affirm some metaphysical truth or hypothesis but by drawing our attention to something we already care a great deal about: we don't want to suffer. We don't need a religious persuasion to want to avoid suffering. But rather than avoid it or sugarcoat it, the Buddha encourages us to face the reality of suffering. This is the First Noble Truth of four truths outlined in the Buddha's first discourse, known as his first turning of the wheel of Dharma.

Short aphorisms capture each of the Four Noble Truths. Here is the reality of suffering: understand it. Here is the reality of the origin of suffering: abandon it. Here is the reality of the cessation of suffering: realize it. Here is the reality of the path to the cessation of suffering: follow it. These four constitute the whole of the Buddha's teachings— everything else is a commentary upon them.

TRUTH OF SUFFERING

Directing our attention to the reality of suffering, the Buddha counsels us: Attend to it. Investigate it. Understand it. You already care a great deal about it. The Buddhist analysis of suffering (Skt. *duhkha*) covers the entire range from mild malaise to physical and mental anguish. We sentient beings are all too familiar with the coarse level of suffering— experiences of suffering and pleasure define our condition.

Blatant Suffering

The coarsest dimension of suffering is called blatant suffering: unwanted feelings that are inescapable; pain and discomfort in the body; sadness, anxiety, and fear in the mind. Blatant suffering often arises in conjunction with an appearance to one of the sense fields, such as something heard, seen, or felt. When such an appearance arises, suffering occurs, and we feel averse to it. Pointing to the appearance, we think, "I want that person, place, object, or situation to stop because it causes my suffering."

In thinking this way, we have forged a connection between the appearance and our suffering, which we wish to stop, so we will do everything possible to avoid a recurrence. "Don't say that to me! Stop acting this way! I want nicer weather!" We try to manipulate the world to conform with our wishes, so that the world will not make us suffer anymore. We react to appearances and associated effects, typically looking only at external causes, without probing into the underlying causes at all. "This happened and I am suffering because of it. If you behave properly, I won't suffer anymore." We find the origins of suffering to be always outside of us. "I'm okay—you're not okay!"

Such blatant suffering is literally called the suffering of suffering, and it is obvious to every sentient being. Cockroaches are sentient beings, and they will run away if you light a match or throw water at them. Humans are no different from cockroaches, earthworms, and all other sentient beings in recognizing the pain of blatant suffering and striving to avoid it.

Suffering of Change

Next, the Buddha advises us to look a bit more deeply. As human beings, we have exceptional abilities to probe a deeper, less obvious dimension of suffering, called the suffering of change. In addition to appearances that give us physical and mental discomfort, some appearances are conjoined with pleasure. For example, we may eat a tasty meal and think, "Oh, this is good! This is so delicious that I'll have seconds, especially the dessert!" For those of us with a sweet tooth, if one dessert is good, two are better, and three, even more so. Pleasurable appearances can be as simple as dessert, as complex as loving relationships with family, and as meaningful as satisfaction with work. There is nothing wrong with these, but there's a catch. When appearances arise in conjunction with a sense of pleasure, satisfaction, security, or fulfillment, we think: "I've got it!" Then the mind grasps like an octopus's tentacles: "You're making me happy. Stick around and give me more—I like it!"

When we grasp on to our pleasures, a suffocating clinging develops in our relationships with objects, families, friends, jobs, and situations. "I've finally beaten the system—the cycle of existence (Skt. *samsara*). This makes me happy, so I'll hold on to it and hope it never changes." Hoping things won't change is like hoping the sun won't rise tomorrow. Things will change—it's assured. Mastering samsara—landing the right relationship, job, home, and so forth, and then freezing things while they're good, grasping on to appearances as though they were the very source of our well-being, security, and fulfillment—is a fool's game!

Undeterred, we grasp at objects as though they were the actual sources of our well-being. Then we hold on tenaciously, thinking: "I'm in control, the object that I'm holding is solid, and my grip is durable. This is my ticket to happiness." The Buddha, watching our little chess game, sees checkmate in a finite number of moves; it is a game we will lose, as certain as death itself. Wake up! It doesn't work that way. We are clinging to appearances that are not true sources of happiness. They may catalyze happiness, but appearances, people, jobs, situations, possessions, homes, and money are not true sources of happiness. We need to look more deeply.

As soon as attachment and clinging appear, we are guaranteed to lose the game in disappointment. The minute we imagine, "That would give me happiness, if only I had it," we have already lost. Checkmate! Grasping is the problem, both in yearning for what we don't have and in holding on to what we do. This deeper dimension of suffering may not be obvious to insects, birds, and other mammals; it takes a bit more insight. But human beings can probe deeply to see whether appearances themselves are actual sources of discontent, suffering, pain, security, happiness, and fulfillment.

Suffering of the Aggregates

As we probe even more deeply, we come to the third and deepest dimension of suffering. This is not explicit suffering, but it exists simply due to grasping on to "I" and "mine." No one word really captures this suffering that is said to be ubiquitous—saturating every experience of happiness, lethargy, euphoria, misery, and even the deepest states of samadhi, when all attachment to appearances is released—all experiences in samsara are contaminated by grasping.

This was the Buddha's brilliant insight, which might have been historically unprecedented. He saw that—even when slipping into very deep samadhi, releasing attachment and aversion to all appearances, resting very deeply in the nature of awareness itself, with the senses utterly withdrawn from the world in a luminous, blissful, silent space of awareness—all is unsatisfying. This is not blatant suffering; samadhi feels quite nice, with no grasping on to appearances because there aren't any. You are resting in a state that can easily be mistaken for buddha nature, pristine awareness, Atman, Brahman, ultimate reality, or God consciousness. Nevertheless, this is merely a quiescent mind resting in its own luminous, blissful, silent, relative ground state. The Buddha recognized a deeper dimension of suffering that is due to our habitual grasping on to appearances.

This most subtle suffering is called the suffering of the aggregates (Skt. *skandhas*), which are the elements that constitute our existence, including our body and mind. If someone asks where you are, you'll answer, "Here I am." I'm where my body is. I'm not where you are. We identify very closely with the aggregates that constitute our existence— body, feelings, recognitions, compositional mental factors, and states of consciousness—calling them "I, me, and mine," as opposed to "you and yours." We hold these collections of elements very closely. They are often referred to as "the aggregates subject to clinging."

There is something that seems to be inherently mine in my body, along with my mind, my tactile sensations, my flesh, my bones, my perceptions, and the sound of my voice. My thoughts and memories seem to be distinctly mine. I'm sure they're not your memories because you didn't live in Scotland when you were four. These are *my* desires, fantasies, and emotions, and *I'm* in touch with them. Each of us cherishes these elements and identifies with them, feeling that they constitute the very essence of our unique, separate, independent existence. I'm over here, and I'm absolutely sure I'm not you or anyone else because you and everyone else are over there. We all think like this instinctively.

Our closely held identification with the aggregates is the result of the mind's tentacles grasping for "I, me, and mine" and latching on. "I'm okay. I'm here and not over there." This tight hold on the aggregates—grasping on to my body, my feelings, and my mind—is the root of our deeply ingrained vulnerability to suffering on all its levels. The aggregates themselves are not the problem; they are just the body and mind. But holding them closely, identifying with them, clinging to them, and thereby isolating ourselves creates a tear in the very fabric of our existence.

From the whole matrix of dependently related events—appearances arising in mutual interdependence throughout the universe—I rip out one part and cling to it, declaring: "Here I am with my thoughts, feelings, perceptions, body, and mind. My territory is separate from everyone and everything else. My body, sensations, mind, memories, and fantasies are all mine!"

The Buddha declared that as long as we hold these aggregates closely, we will suffer. It's only a matter of time. You might go into samadhi for a thousand years, but it will come to an end. Samadhi is like inflating a balloon—no matter how good the rubber, it will deflate. You can pump it up again, but eventually you'll be back where you started. The Buddha's brilliance was to recognize samadhi as being a necessary step on the path to enlightenment but insufficient by itself. One should develop an extraordinary balance of mind and focus of attention, with increasing finesse, but without mistaking this as the goal. Use this instrument to explore the nature of reality.

Recall that, in the first mindfulness practice, we remained present with whatever appeared rather than trying to withdraw into some deeper dimension of awareness. Our goal was to remain wide-open, spacious, and utterly present from moment to moment. This practice of mindfulness entails holding on to nothing whatsoever, while being closely present with everything that arises. With proficiency, events of the body and mind emerge continuously—but with no owner—and awareness is as open and invulnerable as space.

Benign Grasping

Grasping occurs in a broad spectrum. It may be extremely coarse and afflictive or subtle and innocuous. At a coarse level, possessiveness can be very destructive: "Don't touch—it's mine!" Aversion, hatred, and aggression are simply the negative pole of the grasping mind. At a subtle level, even recognizing a person you know can be a form of grasping. Simply recognizing someone, as one would do if asked whether that person were in the room, is a practical form of communication. But isolating someone from everybody else, labeling him or her with a name, and acting as if he or she were an independently existing entity constitutes grasping.

When we pose questions about reality, following the Buddha's guidance in the four close applications of mindfulness, the very act of inquiry is an expression of grasping. This is not necessarily delusional, even if it does isolate us from everything else. As a temporary strategy to achieve a higher goal, vipashyana can be very useful for overcoming active delusion. If we were not so strongly habituated to delusional ways of apprehending and distorting reality, then it would not be necessary to engage in inquiry. But such habits are quite firmly entrenched.

Consider the psychosis of thinking, "I am Napoleon." If I really believed that I was Napoleon, I would suffer because nobody would treat me with the respect I think I deserve. My therapist might ask me some pointed questions: "*Parlez-vous français?*" And if I answer, "No, but I can speak English with a quasi-French accent," that might be a clue! Or she might ask, "Look in the mirror—are you a short, balding man?" A skillful therapist, posing questions concerning the reality that I was experiencing, could precipitate a breakthrough for me: "I'm not Napoleon after all!" I would be relieved of my suffering as soon as I saw through the veil of my habitual, delusional belief that I was Napoleon. I would recognize that this isn't Napoleon's body, and I don't speak French or know anything about battle strategies.

Pointed questions that shatter delusion constitute a benign type of grasping, which can be used to destroy more malignant forms of grasping. When the delusion is demolished, the questions are no longer needed, and we can dispense with grasping altogether. In such cases, we are using grasping as a tool to transcend grasping, like a finger that points at the moon.[33] The finger is grasping, but the moon is not.

FOUR CLOSE APPLICATIONS OF MINDFULNESS

The four close applications of mindfulness (Skt. *smrityupasthana*; Pali *satipatthana*) constitute the bedrock of the Buddha's teachings on insight, or vipashyana, optimally fused with meditative quiescence, or shamatha, in a mind finely honed in attention and samadhi. Classically speaking, one is cultivating the mental faculty known as mindfulness (Skt. *smriti*; Pali *sati*) along with its corollary, introspection (Skt. *samprajaña*; Pali *sampajañña*).

Observing the breath might sound boring, but the development of attentional skills is not done for entertainment. These practices stabilize and enhance the quality of attention. The principal method to shape, refine, and polish mindfulness is the practice of shamatha. Both mindfulness and introspection are developed in shamatha and utilized, or applied closely, in the four close applications of mindfulness.

Mindfulness of the Body

The first close application of mindfulness is directed to the body and our immediate experience of the physical environment in our lived world, or Lebenswelt. When the Buddha speaks of the close application of mindfulness of the body, this means corporeal embodiment. At this moment, what tactile sensations of embodiment are arising? How does it feel to move the body? Of course the body does not exist in isolation but is inextricably embedded in a broader physical environment. To attend to the body while ignoring the environment makes no sense. The body is embedded in the world, breathing it, being breathed by it, taking it in, and giving it out.

The close application of mindfulness to the body implicitly entails mindfulness to all five physical sense fields: visual, auditory, olfactory, gustatory, and tactile. I'm attending to my body when I hear the sound of my own voice, observing that this sound is embedded in the domain of experience of hearing. When I look at my own body, the visual appearances of my body are simply part of a larger constellation of appearances. My visual field includes the form of my body as well as that of someone who is nearby. I don't have one field for attending to my body and another one for everyone else. It is simply a visual field in which bodies appear.

When I attend to tactile appearances, a plastic bottle of water in hand feels cool, firm, and slightly squishy. At the same time, I have a proprioceptive awareness of my hand itself. Our awareness of our own body is embedded in our sensory awareness of the environment. This is the first application: close mindfulness of the body embedded in the fields of the five physical senses.

Mindfulness of Feelings

The second close application is mindfulness of feelings (Skt. *vedana*), in a very fundamental sense. The usages of the English word "feel" are very broad, including expressions such as "I feel like chocolate ice cream" and "You hurt my feelings." But the term *vedana* is not as multifaceted as the English term. It simply refers to our basic experiences of pleasure, pain, and indifference—we like, don't like, or don't care. When a feeling arises, it's the sheer sensation rather than the appearances that happen to occur simultaneously. Feelings occur in two domains: physical and mental.

When you eat something tasty, hear pleasant music, or smell a nice fragrance, there is a physical arousal of feelings of pleasure associated with the body's five senses. It seems quite possible to purchase such feelings. If you order a good meal, it is bound to give pleasant tactile, gustatory, and olfactory sensations. I was recently treated to a marvelous dinner—fourteen courses at the top restaurant in all Australia. It was quite an affair, starting at seven-thirty in the evening and lasting almost to midnight. Waiters introduced each of the fourteen courses as if they were describing their loved ones. Each tiny, elegant morsel was dramatically presented and distinctively lovely. "The chef's an artist—dare I touch it?" I wondered. A waiter announcing the cheese course detailed its creation and provenance in France, prompting me to think, "Wow, I'd like to visit just hearing about it. This dish sounds great!" My nose caught a whiff: "Mmm, that smells good!" It looked good, sounded good, and smelled good. And then I popped it into my mouth to discover a delicious flavor with a range of textures, chewy and creamy. Pleasure arose from all sense fields.

Fourteen courses were presented in a carefully orchestrated sequence. There were preliminaries of a half dozen hors d'oeuvres, followed by four main courses and four desserts. It became clear that our chef was number one in Australia because each dish was a pleasure to all the senses. Furthermore, a lot of money was paid for that dinner, so we all thought, "This is bound to taste good—it cost enough!" The experience appealed to all six senses. The final dessert, following thirteen courses in four hours, consisted of tiny chocolate bonbons, only three, but each one a delight. Our chef achieved his goal of triggering an avalanche of pleasant feelings across all the senses.

We have all known something similar when our experiences have hit the bull's-eye. Of course, feelings of pleasure may arise in the body at the same time as mental experience is dominated by pain. Even while the body tastes a delicious meal, the mind might be bitterly resentful of someone's insulting comment. "What a horrible thing to say. Oh, that tastes good! I really hate that guy." Pleasure and pain can occur simultaneously or alternately, like the sound of bongo drums: physical pleasure, mental pain, physical pleasure, mental pain. Then the meal's over, the bill must be paid, and the bathroom scale inflicts more pain!

Why are feelings selected as the second object or domain for this practice? We closely apply mindfulness to feelings because we care about them intensely. We will endure extreme hardships to indulge in certain feelings and avoid others. Because we care so much, closely applying mindfulness to feelings—understanding how they arise, how they are present, how they dissolve, and how they interrelate with appearances—is worth a good deal of careful examination. Feelings manifest as soon as we become aware of our bodies in space and time. Here I am physically, and then . . . "Ouch! That hurts!" Pleasure and pain catch our attention immediately, making it natural to focus upon, probe, and understand feelings as the second object of mindfulness.

Mindfulness of Mental Events

The third object of close mindfulness includes all mental events not already discussed. We have already attended to mental feelings of pain and dissatisfaction, pleasure and euphoria, boredom and indifference—the whole array of such feelings. Now, like directing a great telescope, we direct our attention toward the other phenomena of the mind and attend with closely applied mindfulness. What's happening in the space of the mind?

We are being selective in choosing not to attend to the five physical sense fields but to the often-dominant—even domineering—field of appearances experienced exclusively by the mind. Attend closely and inquisitively to phenomena in this domain of reality that is invisible to all instruments of technology: ideas, thoughts, mental images, dreams, emotions, desires, and fears of all kinds. What is the nature of the phenomenon we call mind, and what populates its domain? Probing closely into this mental space, so central to our very existence, is the close application of mindfulness to the mind.

Mindfulness of Phenomena

Finally, the fourth object of close mindfulness is called *dharmas* in Sanskrit, which in this context simply means "all phenomena" rather than the Buddha's teachings. Having carefully taken the preliminary steps of closely applying mindfulness to the body embedded in the fields of the five physical senses, followed by feelings, and then to the whole domain of the mind, what remains? The final frontier is the matrix of interrelationships among these domains, called dependent origination. We investigate phenomena with wide-open attention and discerning intelligence. Closely applying mindfulness to all phenomena is comparable to a bright bulb illuminating everything in all directions, instead of a telescope focusing on one region of the sky. We attend to all phenomena as we did in the first sessions, but now we are far better informed.

Are the appearances arising in the six fields of awareness simply manifesting randomly? Science is based on the observation of regularities. When we drop a ball on Tuesday, it falls; on Wednesday, it falls in the same way. These orderly relationships are often called laws, but Buddhism speaks of patterns of regularity and causal sequences. There is meaning to the madness of appearances that sometimes seem to arise randomly. Careful inspection reveals patterns of interrelationship. Because this arose, that arose; because this didn't arise, that didn't arise.

To look at these patterns of causality in the fourth close application of mindfulness literally means to make sense of the world. This is what the Buddha did in the third watch on the night of his enlightenment. In the first watch, he fathomed the nature of his own mind, penetrating to countless experiences in his own past lives. In the second watch, he fathomed the nature of the minds of all sentient beings and the interrelationships among their many lifetimes. In the third watch that night, he examined these profound interrelationships of dependent origination and natural causality and fathomed the way the whole world works, how samsara arises, and how it comes to an end.

What is the nature of the phenomena that arise from moment to moment? In a crucial point for Buddhism, can they be seen to arise interdependently, without the necessity of positing a supernatural ego? This is the crux of the story. The Buddha's great discovery—attending to the body embedded in the physical environment, intertwined feelings in body and mind, and mental phenomena, all arising interdependently with the appearances of the environment, other people, and so forth— is the natural arising of the phenomenal world. Because this arose, that arose; this didn't arise, so that didn't arise. Nowhere did he find the finger of an independent ego poking through the causal fabric of dependently originating phenomena in the natural world saying, "I'll fix this." There was no evidence of intervention by a supernatural being.

There is a famous story of Pierre-Simon Laplace (1749–1827), the French mathematician and astronomer, in a conversation with Napoleon, about two hundred years ago. Laplace laid out his understanding of the nature of the universe according to physics and astronomy, showing how the behavior of the stars, planets, and terrestrial phenomena accorded with the known laws of classical physics—it all made sense. At this, Napoleon asked why there was no mention of the Creator in this exposition, and Laplace responded, "I have no need for that hypothesis."

Newton believed that God created a machine that was unable to operate without supervision, but Laplace found the universe to be perfectly sensible without God tinkering to maintain the planets in their orbits. As scientists understood more, they found the universe to work quite well without control by supernatural forces. At the human level, there was no evidence for a metaphysical self, supernatural ego, soul, or the "real me" operating the body or mind. Humans get along just fine without any such controller. Likewise, at the cosmic level, there was no evidence for a supernatural being that stands outside the world and interacts with creation. Interdependent relationships provide natural explanations for everything within the world of nature.

Still, there is a huge difference between what Laplace and the Buddha had in mind. Science was exclusively extrospective for three hundred years since its beginnings with Copernicus, Kepler, Galileo, and their followers, while paying virtually no attention to the mind. Science's domain was the natural world, which was equated with what can be observed from the third-person perspective, shared by multiple observers. The mind was left out of the natural world due to the inherent limitation of scientific methodology: mind is not observable from outside. Therefore, the mind came to be seen as having no role in the physical universe.

A great irony is that by the time modern psychology originated, around 1875, physicists believed that almost all the questions about the physical universe had been answered. Scottish mathematical physicist and engineer William Thomson, Lord Kelvin (1824–1907), reportedly stated that physicists' knowledge of the natural world was virtually complete. They were finished before psychology got started; the mind was left out and it didn't seem to matter! Not being in the public domain, the mind was deemed unfit for study. Moreover, until then, the mind was very closely associated with the soul, which was the domain of theologians and philosophers—scientists kept out of this turf.

The fourth close application of mindfulness is quite extraordinary because we are making sense of the world by observing from inside out, rather than outside in, from some imaginary God's-eye perspective. Mental phenomena are as real as anything else. They have causal efficacy. Who could doubt that our desires, intentions, hopes, and fears have real effects? Nevertheless, there are intelligent people so indoctrinated in the tenets of scientific materialism that they ignore or dismiss introspection as a valuable method for exploring the mind. For such people, anything that cannot be seen and demonstrated outwardly does not exist, so they say, "That doesn't exist—it's only in your mind." How ridiculously dogmatic!

Causal Efficacy

Bear in mind that reality does not define itself. The word "real" has been defined by human beings, not by nature, God, or anybody else. My spirit is very much with the radical empiricism and pragmatism of William James. One possible definition of the real (as proposed in the Sautrantika philosophy) is that it actually does something: it's causally efficacious. A real phenomenon arises in dependence upon causes and conditions, and it acts as a cause or condition for other phenomena.

Focusing on things that matter to us makes this a very pragmatic definition. It has a therapeutic orientation that goes to the root of our existence: Why do we suffer? How can we suffer less? How can we find greater fulfillment and meaning, spiritual awakening, and liberation? In such a context, anything that is real must be relevant to the health of the planet, the ecosphere, and other species as well as our own. We take seriously anything that affects our well-being, for better or worse, whether it is global communications or viral mutations. Real mental processes lie at the root of mental distress and societal conflict. There is much practical value in attending to that which is real and not getting caught up in imaginary things. Anything that affects our lives, our environment, our interpersonal relationships, and so forth is real.

The Sautrantika school's distinction between real and imaginary phenomena based on their causal efficacy constitutes a philosophical view of metaphysical realism, which asserts that things really exist out there and in here, independent of conceptual designations. There are real physical and mental events, real feelings, and real emotions, which have causal efficacy. This notion of reality hinges on the criterion: Does the entity in question have causal efficacy? By its own nature, does it affect anything else?

This is a very robust, practical philosophy. You can call a bottle of water whatever you like; it really doesn't matter—it is what it is. Your verbal designation is merely an overlay. When it smacks into my hand, it makes an impression on my hand. My hand is real, and it makes an impression on the bottle. Feeling it, I experience a cool, mildly pleasant sensation, and that sensation is real. The bottle is real, regardless of humankind's designations. My thoughts are real too, such as my belief that this is my bottle of water. But the fact that it is mine is purely a conceptual designation based on human conventions. There is nothing whatsoever in the nature of the bottle itself to indicate that it belongs to me or anyone else. The designation "mine" is an imaginary phenomenon.

If this is my bottle, and I didn't steal it, the notion that it's mine is a fact. But the fact that it's mine is not to be found anywhere in the bottle; this fact of being mine has no causal efficacy in and of itself, although the *belief* that it is mine certainly does have results. Given that people continue to wage wars over imagined borders, how can we claim that the fact of ownership has no causal efficacy? The Sautrantika view asserts that the fact that something is mine has no causal efficacy at all, but the belief that it is mine, and my grasping on to it, certainly do. These mental processes are as real as cannonballs. Mental processes have causal efficacy, and the bottle has causal efficacy, but the fact that the bottle is mine has no causal efficacy of its own.

The notion of ownership is quite ephemeral. If someone were thirsty, I might give my bottle to him. At that moment, it would become his and no longer mine. This would happen just because of a shift in our conceptual framework—we agreed on a change in ownership. There are many other examples of superimposed conceptual designations that have some existence due to conventional agreements but have no causal efficacy inherent in their own nature. Border wars occur only because we grasp on to such concepts.

The view of robust metaphysical realism is quite compatible with classical physics, which is based on such a worldview. The realist believes that our concepts correspond to real space, real time, real mass, real energy, and real phenomena that result from various interactions. Furthermore, most physicists until the nineteenth century believed in the mind, God, and souls, and so of course they believed in the causal efficacy of a mind that prays. About 40 percent of American scientists today believe that prayers directed to a transcendent God can have causal efficacy and that God intervenes in nature to answer them.[34]

Unlike scientific materialism, the Sautrantika view does not attribute causal efficacy exclusively to configurations of mass and energy. It does admit to the causal efficacy of mental processes, but it disqualifies the whole realm of conceptual designations that exist only by agreement. We might declare that a bottle of water is a performance-enhancing elixir, a paperweight, or a superb example of product design, but our designations do not change its sheer causal efficacy. If I throw it through a window, it will break the window no matter what you call it. Conceptually designated agreements have existence but no independent causal efficacy.

My experience of something as pleasant is real, regardless of whether anybody agrees with me. For example, I bake a pretty good pizza, and from my perspective, my pizzas are the tastiest in Santa Barbara. No other pizza in this town measures up. This is a truth—for one person. Nobody can deny that I find my pizzas the tastiest in Santa Barbara, regardless of my limited data and possible bias. My evaluation of my pizza is real, with causal efficacy, because I will stay at home for pizza instead of buying one at a pizza parlor. My wife agrees that in fact, my pizzas are the best in town, which means that we have a consensus, but she could change her mind any day. The supremacy of my pizzas has no causal efficacy because it is merely an agreement subject to change.

I began my formal monastic education in 1973, at the Institute of Buddhist Dialectics in Dharamsala. Our class was immediately introduced to basic logic and the Sautrantika view. We cut our teeth on this philosophy, tested ourselves in debate, and explored the following categories:

- Real things: anything that is a cause, an effect, compounded, and impermanent
- Causes: phenomena with causal efficacy
- Effects: anything real, causally efficacious, impermanent, and compounded
- Impermanent: anything arising and passing from moment to moment
- Compounded: anything coming together in dependence on causes and conditions

Anything that arises and passes from moment to moment is impermanent by nature, compounded, a cause, an effect, and real—these categories are coextensive. Using them, we immersed ourselves in debate, grappling with metaphysical realism to see how sensible it is. This system of metaphysical realism is not materialism because it includes the causal efficacy of mental states as well as physical states. The crucial point is that the relationships between mind and body are nonmechanistic.

Does it make sense to say that physical phenomena, mental phenomena, and the interrelationships between the mind and body are all real if they have causal efficacy? This view of reality makes sense to many people, but I will not try to persuade you of it. Frankly, the distinction is not ultimately convincing—it's a can of worms. Nevertheless, like classical physics, this is a very reasonable and pragmatic view that can be useful in many ways.

Classical mechanics makes good sense. Atoms are like billiard balls bumping into each other in absolute space and time, each one having a certain velocity and mass. In a similar way, the Tibetan Buddhist introduction to classical mind science says that there is real matter externally, along with real mental processes internally. Grasping has causal efficacy, even if that which one is grasping on to is completely nonexistent. I may think that I'm Napoleon and become outraged if you disagree with me, even though I'm grasping on to a nonexistent identity.

The Sautrantika view is not the final word, but it can stimulate your investigations. You may find that it makes sense and is useful to a certain extent. Grasping has causal efficacy even when the object of grasping —such as the conventional border between Palestine and Israel—has no causal efficacy. Such conventions are commonplace. How black does your skin have to be to make you black? If your grandmother on one side was black, does that make you black? If one out of eight of your great grandparents is Hopi, are you? These are merely conventions, and yet we can become very upset due to grasping on to such notions.

Having engaged with this view, my class in Dharamsala entered the more advanced stages of monastic training, which employ the sword of the Madhyamaka view to see whether metaphysical realism stands up to rigorous analysis. First we see whether something is sensible or not, and then we probe for inconsistencies. This becomes quite interesting. The consensus among Tibetan Buddhist scholars is that metaphysical realism collapses like a house of cards. Classical physics was sensible enough to have withstood three hundred years of scrutiny by the brilliant minds of Newton, James Clerk Maxwell (1831–1879), and many others. Only when confronted with questions like "How would the universe look if you were riding a photon at the speed of light?" did the edifice of metaphysical realism in classical physics begin to crumble. Quantum mechanics delivered the final blow.

The first indication of anomaly came in 1887. It had been assumed that there was a mechanical explanation for everything, and this was why everything fit together so well. The principle of the conservation of energy was ironclad. There was near-universal belief in a luminiferous ether, whose ripples explained the propagation of light waves. But thirteen years before quantum mechanics, and eighteen years before special relativity, the Michelson-Morley experiment demonstrated that there is no mechanical explanation for the propagation of light— no luminiferous ether fills space.[35] This discovery signaled the end of strictly mechanical explanations of the physical universe, and it opened the door for Albert Einstein's (1879–1955) brilliant assertion of the relative nature of space and time. If light could have been explained as mechanical ripples in the ether, then there would have been no impetus for special relativity.

GUIDED MEDITATION:
Mindfulness III

Sustain unwavering mindfulness of all appearances—
observing whatever arises in the present moment

Begin each session by settling the body in its natural state, imbued with the three attributes of relaxation, stillness, and vigilance. You may round off the initial settling of the body with three slow, deep breaths, breathing into the abdomen, then the diaphragm, and finally into the chest. Breathe in, almost to full capacity, and then release the breath effortlessly. Be mindfully attentive to the sensations related to the breath arising throughout the body as you repeat this three times.

Now release all preferences and give up control of the breath. Let it flow in and out as effortlessly as the tide, at its own pace. Mindfully attend to the sensations of the breath throughout the body, while releasing any sense of control or influence.

With all senses open and the eyes at least partially open, cultivate a deepening ease in body and mind. Let your awareness rest in its own place of innate stillness, without grasping or aversion. Remain open and attentive to all appearances arising in the six fields of experience. If you find yourself distracted, having lost mindfulness, you might naturally bear down and try harder; counterintuitively, relax more deeply and release the grasping that distracted you.

Awareness, by nature, illuminates appearances and knows, or cognizes. Sustain awareness with an ongoing flow of unwavering mindfulness. Whatever arises in the present moment to the six modes of perception is the object of mindfulness. Attend to these appearances without distraction or grasping. ☞

MENTAL FACULTIES

Mindfulness and introspection are classically described as mental faculties, and you can get a clear sense of the meaning of these terms from some of the wisest voices in the Buddhist tradition. There are no disagreements or sectarian issues here; in fact, there is a strong congruence in the usage of these two key terms throughout the Indian, Theravadin, Zen, and Tibetan Buddhist traditions.

Mindfulness

The term "mindfulness" (Skt. *smriti*; Pali *sati*) is enormously important in Buddhism and has been defined by the Buddha and many of the greatest Buddhist commentators. The four close applications of mindfulness have been splendidly presented and extensively practiced for over two thousand years in the Theravadin tradition, from which we will examine two classic definitions. The first was given by the Indian Buddhist monk Nagasena, a liberated being who realized the culmination of nirvana (Skt. *arhat*), as taught by the Buddha in his early discourses recorded in the Pali Canon.

Nagasena conducted the first East-West dialogue on record, in the second century BCE, with a Greek king who governed one of the principalities created during Alexander the Great's (356–323 BCE) brief and unfortunate occupation of India. King Menander I, known in Pali as Milinda, was a well-educated Greek citizen who eventually converted to Buddhism. In the *Milindapañha*, the text recording their dialogue, the king asked Nagasena what is meant by the term "mindfulness." Nagasena was very generous in his answers to the king's many questions, and he responded that mindfulness has both the characteristic of "calling to mind" and the characteristic of "cultivating":

> Mindfulness, when it arises, calls to mind wholesome and unwholesome tendencies, with faults and faultless, inferior and refined, dark and pure, together with their counterparts . . .

> Mindfulness, when it arises, follows the courses of beneficial and unbeneficial tendencies: these tendencies are beneficial, these unbeneficial; these tendencies are helpful, these unhelpful. Thus one who practices yoga rejects unbeneficial tendencies and cultivates beneficial tendencies.[36]

In this quote, "counterparts" means the other concomitant mental factors operating simultaneously with mindfulness. "One who practices yoga" refers to a follower of the spiritual path. Mindfulness requires discerning, ethical concern. Which processes and activities arising in the body and mind give rise to beneficial results? Which give rise to detrimental results? We must differentiate, applying mindfulness strategically and discerningly because we care about ourselves. Are we flourishing, or are we sowing the seeds of our own misery and discontent? According to Nagasena, mindfulness means attending closely to what is occurring in the mind and body.

For the second definition, we look to the most authoritative commentator in the Theravadin tradition, Buddhaghosa. In his extraordinary compendium, *The Path of Purification,* which draws on over nine hundred years of Buddhist contemplative study and practice, he says first of mindfulness: "By means of it they [that is, the concomitant, or simultaneous mental processes] remember, or it itself remembers, or it is simply just remembering, thus it is mindfulness."

Buddhaghosa conveys the sense that mindfulness itself recollects or remembers. The very experience of recalling something is his first emphasis in defining mindfulness, and it was also the Buddha's emphasis when he defined this term. We would call it memory because it means retaining something in the mind. What did you have for breakfast? Where did you live when you were six years old? What's your mother's name? How many fingers do you have? The faculty that remembers accurately is mindfulness. It is the capacity to retain, recollect, and bear in mind that which has been known.

But mindfulness is not confined to past events, let alone distant past events. Present-centered mindfulness is focused face-to-face on something that is arising in the present moment, an ongoing recollection that overcomes the entropy of the mind. The force of entropy leads to disarray, fragmentation, and disintegration of mindfulness, as the mind becomes disoriented, excited, or distracted. Mindfulness means holding everything together, not with grasping, but with presence that can be directed to immediate experience as well as to past events.

Buddhaghosa's definition of mindfulness continues: "Its characteristic is not floating." In our practice of mindfulness, it's very easy to float. When we are not latched on to something, whether it's our body, mind, possessions, or another object of grasping, then it's very easy to simply space out and float. We are so accustomed to compulsively grasping, clinging, identifying with our thoughts, and mistaking them for their referents that when we release our grasp and simply try to be present, we often find ourselves floating—or sleeping! Mindfulness means not floating, not forgetting, and not disengaging.

Buddhaghosa continues, "Its property is not losing; its manifestation is guarding, or the state of being face to face with an object." This is the goal of our practice. We may closely apply mindfulness to whatever presents itself, from moment to moment, in any of the six fields of experience, fully engaged and attentive, as if we were gazing face-to-face with someone. We are not spacing out or grasping but mindfully present. Mindfulness of the tactile sensations of the breath means being face-to-face, from moment to moment, with the respiration. We are not remembering past breaths, and we are not lost or floating—we remain focused continuously on the current sensations of the breath.

Mindfulness can also be prospective. For example, if you must drive to an appointment at three o'clock, remember to leave on time. Bearing a future occurrence in mind, without forgetting, is prospective mindfulness, which is very useful in these practices as well as in everyday life.

Buddhaghosa's definition continues: "Its basis is strong noting, or the close application of mindfulness to the body, and so on." This means that the basis of mindfulness is strongly engaged attention that notes well, without grasping or clinging. Then, in the very definition of mindfulness, he mentions the practice that we are learning. Finally he says, "It should be seen as like a post due to its state of being firmly set in the object, and as like a gatekeeper because it guards the gate of the eye, and so on."[37] Mindfulness focused upon its object is planted like a post or engaged like a guard.

These two authoritative voices from the Buddhist tradition define mindfulness very clearly, with retrospective, present-centered, and prospective modes. Our practice—approaching bare attention, being focused and attentive from moment to moment, and not reacting to whatever is arising—is not yet comprehensive, but it is a fundamental expression of mindfulness.

Introspection

The second key term appearing in the Buddha's discourses on the matrix of vipashyana or insight practices is introspection (Skt. *samprajaña*; Pali *sampajañña*), which is often translated as "clear comprehension." The great bodhisattva Shantideva (eighth century CE) is another wise voice of Buddhism, from the Mahayana tradition. He defines this corollary faculty, immensely important for practicing the four close applications of mindfulness, very succinctly. "In brief, this alone is the definition of introspection: the repeated examination of the state of one's body and mind."[38]

The faculty of introspection is reflexive. While mindfulness may be directed anywhere—to galaxies, electrons, mental states, or to your feet—introspection means attending to phenomena arising within the field of reality that we call "I and mine." I attend to my body, the position of my hands, the sensations in my abdomen, the movements of my mind, and the sound of my voice. Introspection is attending reflexively to the state and actions of one's body, speech, and mind embedded in an environment.

Introspection is an expression of intelligence (Skt. *prajña*) because it is discerning. Given current circumstances, is this mode of comporting my body appropriate or inappropriate? Should I gesture with my hands and smile now? Are the content and tone of my voice too harsh, too soft, or just what's needed? Likewise, as it monitors the processes arising in the mind—attending to thoughts, desires, intentions, and so forth, embedded in reality—introspection asks: Are they suitable or unsuitable? Helpful or unhelpful? Monitoring during meditation may include mindfully attending to the sensations of the breath, while introspection monitors the meditative process. Am I practicing correctly or not? Am I sustaining a flow of mindfulness, or have I fallen into distraction, excitation, laxity, or dullness? Introspection is the quality control monitor for the entire process, repeatedly examining the state of one's body and mind.

Asanga (fourth century CE), of the Mahayana tradition, sums up the two terms "mindfulness" and "introspection," and he is quoted a thousand years later by Tsongkhapa (1357–1419), who found no need to improve upon Asanga's definitions: "Mindfulness and introspection are taught, for the first prevents the attention from straying from the meditative object." In other words, mindfulness is face-to-face, engaged, and present, without losing, floating, or straying. It prevents the attention from straying from its object.

Asanga's definition of introspection follows: "The second recognizes that the attention is straying."[39] Introspection monitors the meditative process and recognizes attentional imbalances: spacing out, laxity, dullness, sleepiness, restlessness, excitation, distraction, agitation, and so forth. It alerts us, "This isn't working; please regain your balance!" With intelligence and will, we can balance the attention. Mindfulness prevents the attention from straying, and introspection recognizes when it has strayed: two key faculties of mind.

In our practice, we are seeking to sustain an ongoing flow of sanity—not losing our minds, not being carried away by obsessive thinking and grasping, and not compulsively equating whatever arises in our minds with objective reality. Conceptualization can be very useful, but the very nature of a flow of discursive conceptualization about reality locks us into constructs that are isolated from reality. Such is the nature of thoughts.

As soon I think of John, I think of something very nice that John did. While I'm focusing on this, I've forgotten the rest of John. Replaying my memory of his actions, I think, "John's such a nice person, and so generous." Fixated upon this pleasant memory—and isolated from the complex fabric of his actual life—my imaginary video clip becomes John: what a jolly good fellow! This is conceptualization, and it can be very powerful. We all use it a great deal. But this conceptualization isolates, freezes, and decontextualizes the actual John, who continues to evolve, embedded in his environment, and does not exist as my caricature.

In this practice, rather than getting caught up in conceptualization, to the best of our ability we simply sustain an ongoing flow of sanity. We practice wholeness rather than fragmentation. Concepts entail fragmentation and isolation, locking on to a construct that is divorced from the rest of reality. The flow of sanity to be sustained is open, attentive, intelligent, and not fixated on any aspect or fragment extracted from the whole. We are open to whatever appears from moment to moment, maintaining an ongoing flow of wholeness and sanity.

GUIDED MEDITATION:
Mindfulness IV

Sustain unwavering mindfulness of all appearances—
monitoring with introspection

Begin, as always, by settling the body in its natural state, imbued with the three qualities of relaxation, stillness, and vigilance. Round off this process by taking three slow, deep breaths and settling your respiration in its natural rhythm, effortless and spontaneous.

With your eyes at least partially open, settle your mind in its natural state. Let your awareness rest in its own space, illuminating all appearances to the six portals of experience in all directions. Allow these appearances to arise and pass of their own accord, without latching on to them or interpreting them. Simply perceive them for what they are, without distraction and without grasping.

With the faculty of introspection, note whenever you have been carried away by thoughts. Let your initial response be to relax more deeply and release all grasping. If you note that you have become spaced-out or lethargic, reignite your interest, freshen your awareness, and pay closer attention. Monitor the balance of mindfulness with introspection, maintaining an ongoing flow of engaged but nonreactive attentiveness to whatever appearances arise in the present moment. ☚

On Maintaining Sanity

The practice of mindfulness is deceptively simple—but not easy to do properly. This method is a direct remedy for the broadly endemic mental imbalance that I call obsessive-compulsive delusional disorder (OCDD). Obsessive thoughts appear continuously, like water dripping from a leaky faucet. Thoughts arise even when there is nothing in particular to think about, and compulsive grasping compounds the problem. Absorbed by our thoughts, we identify them as being true and real, and in so doing we become delusional, very much as if we had fallen into a nonlucid dream. If we weren't so habituated to this bizarre condition, we would be crying for help!

The simple practice of maintaining an ongoing flow of sanity means being present with everything that reality is dishing up to the six senses as perceptions, thoughts, images, and so forth. Being present with these appearances—cognizant and clear, without conceptual superimpositions, and without entering into cognitive fusion with thoughts—is an antidote for obsessive-compulsive ideation. To be present with what is actually occurring is a healthy goal. The point of this practice is to develop our ability to use the mind in diverse ways, instead of being locked into a narrow conceptual framework.

Why not get friendly with your thoughts instead of grasping at them or rejecting them? Apart from states of samadhi, the evidence suggests that while we are embodied, thoughts are never-ending, except possibly in deep sleep or a comatose state. If we closely investigate the primary cause of our torment and grief, we find that it can only be our own thoughts. Disagreeable people, neighbors, and jobs come and go. Married couples separate to end their dissatisfaction. We can distance ourselves from unpleasant situations, but our thoughts are inescapable and not always pleasant. No wonder we often feel harassed by our thoughts—they torment us more than anything else.

There are two primary strategies for dealing with thoughts. The first one is to hunt them down and destroy them like an action-film vigilante. When a thought pops up, blow it away with your samadhi shotgun. If you win the battle against compulsive thinking, then you will be able to think only when you choose to. This constitutes one strategy, and there is evidence that it can work. Of course, since it works via samadhi, when samadhi wanes, thoughts come creeping back like cockroaches.

The second strategy is to be mindfully present with thoughts without being caught up and carried away by them. This, too, is a kind of samadhi, so mindfulness and samadhi are not somehow in opposition: nothing could be further from the truth. What is it that often makes our thoughts painful, unsettled, or anxious? Why do we feel dissatisfaction and low self-esteem? How do our thoughts become toxic? Is the mere arising of such thoughts sufficient to make us unhappy? We all know from experience that a nasty comment is only toxic if we hold it closely and identify with it. A thought becomes particularly poisonous if we lock on to its referent and affirm that the thought represents reality. It's like holding a viper to your throat.

Toxic thoughts can ruin a day or a lifetime, but only if they are closely grasped. To the extent you can cultivate the ability of simply being present with whatever thoughts arise in the space of awareness—without grasping or aversion—thoughts lose their toxicity. Attend to thoughts as if you were in a lucid dream. Having fathomed the nature of the dream while you are dreaming, even your worst nightmare can't faze you. Your very presence in the dream is an imaginary appearance that is immune from harm, and all experiences are simply mental events. There is no possibility of damage to a dream body perceiving dream appearances. Thoughts are not mental afflictions because they cannot afflict.

Prior to the Buddha, many contemplatives saw samadhi as the main goal rather than as a supporting technique. By developing profound samadhi, they silenced the mind so deeply as to transcend thought. When one abides in the formless realm, all thoughts, including the notion of time, have vanished. It seems like the samadhi will last forever because there is no sense of the passage of time. Some adepts mistakenly called this the state of liberation (Skt. *moksha*); the Buddha found that such states, if unsupported by wisdom, pass away over the course of time. His brilliant discovery was that samadhi as an end in itself is merely a delaying tactic. Thoughts that have entered temporary dormancy will return to wreak havoc, just as they have done in the past. But there is a very different result if you can remain present with thoughts, without grasping or aversion, and utilize insight to fathom the very nature of awareness itself. When a thought arises, you'll think, "Oh thought, where is thy sting?"

CONTEMPLATIVE INQUIRY

Throughout this text, I will refer repeatedly to the Buddha's teachings on the matrix of practices of the four close applications of mindfulness. In an oft-quoted statement, he introduces the mode of vipashyana, or insight practice, with the following words in the *Satipatthana Sutta*:

> This is the direct path, monks, for purification of beings, for overcoming of sorrow and lamentation, for overcoming of suffering and grief, for reaching the authentic path, for realization of nirvana—namely, the four close applications of mindfulness.[40]

The four close applications of mindfulness are central to the Buddha's fundamental teachings on the cultivation of insight. He refers to this as a direct path because it leads directly to liberation—the complete and irreversible healing of all mental afflictions. There are no side trips to develop mundane psychic powers, for instance. By recognizing the reality of suffering and its causes, the goal is to irreversibly eliminate the causes.

This is a direct path for the purification of mental afflictions: the internal causes of dissatisfaction, suffering, and pain. The Buddha, sometimes referred to as the Great Physician, offers it as medicine, and structures the Four Noble Truths as a therapeutic intervention. This method for achieving complete healing consists of examining the symptoms, understanding the underlying causes, accepting the prognosis for a cure, and finally engaging in the therapy. This is a direct path for overcoming sorrow and lamentation, for overcoming pain and grief, and for reaching the authentic path.

Reaching the authentic path is a critical consideration, and the word "authentic" is not used lightly. The world's virtues are practiced and promoted by many different types of people; religion has no corner on virtue. Besides Taoist virtues, Roman Catholic virtues, and Jewish virtues, there are secular virtues and even virtues practiced by those with a strong antipathy for religion. Buddhism also presents many virtues to be cultivated. But the Buddha offers something more—a path comprising a sequence of practices leading to the complete and irreversible healing of all mental afflictions that lie at the root of suffering. This profoundly detailed path of spiritual evolution that culminates in the realization of nirvana is extraordinary.

The mental afflictions are often likened to fire. In the *Adittapariyaya Sutta*,[41] known as the *Fire Sermon*, the Buddha says, "The world is aflame" with delusion, craving, hatred, lust, and anger—we're burning up. The term "nirvana" has the connotation of cooling and extinguishing this fire, to reach a state of equilibrium—no longer aflame. The practice of the four close applications of mindfulness is a direct path leading to nirvana.

Stressing Relaxation

The term "mindfulness" is used in a wide variety of clinical settings nowadays, thanks in part to the groundbreaking work of Jon Kabat-Zinn. In 1979, he introduced basic mindfulness practices at the University of Massachusetts Medical School's Stress Reduction Clinic, which he founded. He demonstrated scientifically, and it has been well validated, that mindfulness practices can be extremely effective in overcoming stress and releasing tension, thereby potentially alleviating symptoms of a wide variety of diseases.

I first heard Jon speak in 1990, when he presented his Mindfulness-Based Stress Reduction to the Dalai Lama, and I served as interpreter, together with Geshe Thupten Jinpa. He pointed out that the symptoms of all known mental and physical diseases are aggravated by stress. Even a common cold, let alone a more serious illness, will be much more debilitating when one is under stress. If stress can exacerbate the symptoms of disease, then it stands to reason that alleviating stress and encouraging relaxation will alleviate the symptoms of a wide range of illnesses.

These results have been broadly substantiated, with rapidly growing interest aroused in psychologists and psychotherapists around the world. The application of mindfulness can ameliorate a wide array of human problems in addition to stress. Clinical depression can be overcome if mindfulness practices are introduced during phases of subacute depression. Mindfulness practices can alleviate or prevent cardiac and skin diseases. A very promising preliminary study by neuroscientists Antoine Lutz and Richard Davidson has shown that basic mindfulness practice can be useful in enhancing attention skills.[42] But scientific validation is not the only evidence that mindfulness carries a broad range of benefits; through practice, these benefits can also be realized for oneself.

The path of contemplative inquiry in the four close applications of mindfulness is rigorous and demanding because the Buddha's goal is far greater than the simple alleviation of stress. Although increased relaxation lies along the same trajectory, this is a direct path to the realization of nirvana. Stressed-out people don't achieve nirvana; their stress must be released along the way. When you fully develop the four close applications of mindfulness—unified with shamatha and thereby empowered with finely honed attention skills—you can alleviate the symptoms of a wide variety of psychological and physical diseases. Furthermore, you can heal the mind from its core: this is our goal.

The foundational approach to the cultivation of insight is a perfect paradigm of contemplative science because its explicit purpose is the acquisition of specific types of experiential knowledge. We are not simply investigating reality in general. Whether planets move in circular or elliptical orbits is an interesting question, but not for this practice. Here we are raising specific questions about reality, with the aspiration of gaining experiential insight and knowledge in response.

Three Marks of Existence

Three fundamental questions must be asked as we examine the phenomena we encounter. The answers to these simple but profound questions, pervading the entire matrix of mindfulness practices, are called the three signs, or marks, of existence. Concerning each facet of reality that appears in the ongoing flow of experience, including our own participatory presence in the world, the first question is this: "Is it permanent or impermanent?" Is there anything that is durable and unchanging? Is there anything that once born does not decay? Is there anything that once acquired is not lost? Is there anything that once risen does not decline? Once there is meeting, does parting not inevitably follow? Do any phenomena abide permanently throughout time, or do they persist only momentarily, eventually losing their identity and dissolving?

Without scrutiny, it might seem like a feeling of sadness can descend upon us indefinitely, like a dead weight. But are feelings really permanent and unchanging for extended periods, or are they momentary and variable? Are they stable or fluctuating? Are they solid or evanescent? Contemplating the lack of durability of phenomena, it is easy to understand the answer conceptually as the Buddhist doctrine of impermanence. But a conceptual answer will not have much effect on our lives. On the other hand, penetrating the reality of impermanence through direct experience—backed by the power of samadhi—can be thoroughly life-transforming. Fathoming the impermanent nature of everything you experience will dramatically alter your view of reality.

The second question is quite fascinating: "Is it genuine happiness or unsatisfying?" What are the true sources of happiness and suffering? When we identify a phenomenon as the source of our happiness—a person, situation, organization, job, belief system, scripture, or any appearance to the mind—we think: "It feels good to have this source of happiness. All will be well if I just hold on to it." Is this phenomenon by its nature an actual source of happiness, security, and fulfillment, or is it not? Likewise, when we identify some object or appearance to the mind as the source of our dissatisfaction, we think: "I can't tolerate this situation; if only the source of my distress would go away, I'd be happy." Look again. Is this actually the source of unhappiness? What is the reality of duhkha?

In fathoming the true nature of duhkha, the translation of the term is important. It's easy to misunderstand something I heard in a college course on Buddhism, which was that the Buddha was a pessimist: he thought everything was suffering. Understanding this requires some finesse. What the Buddha actually said was that as long as our minds are dominated by mental afflictions—acting like carriers of a malignant virus, spreading delusion, craving, and hostility, along with myriad derivative mental afflictions, such as envy and arrogance, that corrupt and distort every experience—then nothing will be satisfying. This is why I would define "duhkha" as dissatisfaction.

We have all known various kinds of pleasure aroused by sensory and mental stimuli. When such a feeling occurs, inspect it carefully by probing into its nature with interest but without feeding it. Maintain a high level of attentiveness, remaining focused but without superimposing judgments or preferences. Is this feeling an intrinsically pleasurable one by its own nature? Does it maintain its integrity, remaining vivid the more carefully it is scrutinized, or does it begin to dissolve under investigation?

Finding some person, place, or thing to be truly satisfying, you might think, "Bull's-eye! I've tapped into the wellspring of true happiness." If so, according to the Buddhist analysis, every time you return to that source, it should deliver satisfaction. If it is an actual source of happiness, it should invariably deliver happiness—fifteen times a day or twenty hours nonstop. Can you think of any appearance, person, object, or activity that consistently yields such happiness—a true source of happiness? Or do unsatisfying qualities always crop up over time? That was a delicious fourteen-course meal I had in Australia, but I didn't want a fifteenth course. Investigating the sources of dissatisfaction and satisfaction constitutes an empirical inquiry.

The final question is this: "Self or no self?" What is it that you refer to as "I and mine"? Within all these appearances to your mind, is there something that is inherently your "self"? Is some aspect of your mind—your will perhaps, or awareness itself—the real you? Is some structure in your brain—the prefrontal cortex, hippocampus, amygdala, or pineal gland— really you? Is any element within the matrix of your body and mind the direct referent of the word "I"? Is there anything in your body, thoughts, emotions, and consciousness whose very nature is definitely your own?

Is there anything about your perceptions or feelings that indicates that they are intrinsically yours and bound to you in some ontological fashion? For example, the appearance of a color in your visual field is unique to you because nobody else has your precise perspective. Is this color yours simply because it appears in your visual field? Most of us would say that a color is not ours, and the sounds we hear are not ours either. When events arise in our mental field, are they our own any more than the events arising in our visual, auditory, or tactile fields?

I may think, "My DNA is unique to me." But my DNA is just a particular sequence of molecules. It might be unique, but it's not labeled "Alan Wallace." Unique DNA is like a unique snowflake; neither one is necessarily mine as a result. Even a unique fingerprint is just a pattern until I superimpose the notion "mine" upon it. What really constitutes "I and mine"? Do the words "I" and "mine" have any true referent in reality from their own side, or is speaking of my "self" simply a useful convention?

With myriad aspects of reality to investigate, why should we focus on these three questions? In fact, we have a natural propensity to get all three answers wrong. We instinctively grasp on to the impermanent as permanent, durable, and unchanging. We grasp on to that which is not by nature a true source of happiness, thinking of it as a true source of happiness. Finally, we grasp on to that which is not by nature I or mine, thinking of it as inherently I or mine.

Because of these three ways of fundamentally misapprehending reality, we experience craving, hostility, and endless, unnecessary suffering. The natural world has always been a dangerous place; water and fire devour our homes, cyclones wipe out entire cities, and earthquakes bury tens of thousands. Natural disasters are inevitable, and when government leaders compound these miseries, the devastation becomes tragic. Learning to treat each other compassionately would be a big step toward mitigating our suffering. But the ultimate liberation, according to Buddhism's foundational teachings, is the direct realization of three particular aspects of reality—impermanence, dissatisfaction, and non-self—which eradicates the very root of afflictive mental tendencies and suffering. This is the goal of our inquiry.

Direct Knowledge

It is fascinating that our approach to knowledge does not depend on a creed: "All conditioned phenomena are impermanent. All phenomena tainted by mental afflictions are unsatisfying. All phenomena are devoid of 'I and mine.'" We might memorize this and believe it, but will we suffer any less due to reciting a creed? By asserting, "I'm a believer; I'm a Buddhist; I'm part of this group, and this is my faith," will you suffer less? Perhaps there is more to this than simply having faith.

In the Buddhist understanding, the authentic path is reached by way of direct knowledge—this is what liberates the mind. It makes perfectly good sense because in the Buddhist understanding, the deepest root of suffering is not wrong creeds or lack of faith. The taproot of suffering is ignorance—not only simple lack of knowledge but the misapprehension of reality and the resulting delusional actions.

For example, if I believe I'm Napoleon, my delusion will give rise to a lot of suffering and frustration as people fail to treat me with the deference I expect. Even with a hard-core belief that I am Napoleon, I might practice shamatha meditation, deactivating the conceptual mind that continually reinforces my identity as Napoleon. It is possible that as long as I remain in meditation, all the pretense of grasping on to myself in this delusional fashion would dissolve. I might focus on my breath or bare attention and go into very deep samadhi, or shut down the conceptual mind by focusing single-pointedly on some object. Nevertheless, as soon as I come out of samadhi and reengage the conceptual mind, my Napoleonic delusion will emerge like a hibernating bear, growling, *"Je suis Napoleon!"* Shamatha meditation merely allows the mental afflictions to go dormant, without permanently affecting them.

Permanent change requires the fusion of quiescence and insight. Vipashyana does not put mental afflictions to sleep. By inquiring into the nature of reality, insight becomes the antidote for delusion. For example, you might convince me that this is the twenty-first century, leading me to realize, "Aha! I can't possibly be Napoleon because he died in 1821." Once I see that I'm not Napoleon, whether I'm resting in samadhi or actively engaged in daily life, no thought of being Napoleon will arise. I have seen through my delusion.

The Buddhist claim is that we ordinary sentient beings, who have not reached the authentic path, continuously grasp on to the impermanent as permanent, suffering enormously by projecting far more durability than truly exists upon our selves, our health, our relationships, and our possessions. We grasp on to things that are not true sources of happiness, as if they were, and we recoil from other phenomena as sources of unhappiness, even though they aren't. We take "I and mine" very substantially—setting them in radical opposition to "you and yours"—and gratify our "selves" with compulsive grasping while we protect our territory and possessions with fierce brutality. Could any discovery in the universe compare with a direct knowledge of reality that thoroughly transforms and liberates the mind?

Highest Goal

I'm very glad that I don't have to choose between worldly technology and contemplative inquiry: these are complementary approaches to knowledge. Science and technology are not irrelevant on the Buddhist path. Nevertheless, the differences between these modes of inquiry are utterly essential, and one key difference concerns the purpose of the inquiry. The Buddha says explicitly that the goal of our pursuit of experiential knowledge is to liberate ourselves from grief, pain, and sorrow by healing the mind. We seek knowledge that will lead us to a state of well-being, or genuine happiness, that is rooted in reality rather than in clinging and grasping; such knowledge will also lead us toward nirvana.

To be effective in catalyzing radical transformation, the practice of vipashyana must be fused with shamatha, in a clear and stable mind. Any attempt to practice vipashyana with an unstable mind that oscillates between excitation and laxity is bound to fall short—the mental technology is inadequate for the task. Truly effective contemplative inquiry requires an exceptionally wholesome, ethical way of life and an exceptionally sane, well-balanced mind, with finely honed attention.

UNIFIED SCIENCE

How can a clear, stable mind be attained while embedded in the active lifestyle of a social being? The mind, including attention in particular, is closely conjoined with emotion. We witnessed the vivid manifestation of all kinds of emotion during the three-month Shamatha Project retreats that were held in 2007.[43] When we meditate for eight, ten, or twelve hours daily, powerful emotions are inevitably dredged up. The links between emotion and behavior are complex, and meditative experiences can throw anyone off balance. In a group situation, one person's behavior can catalyze emotions in another person, whose reactions can propagate further disturbances.

In the practice of mindfulness, three pursuits support each other in a unified way:

- the pursuit of a virtuous, ethical way of life
- the pursuit of genuine happiness through mental balance
- the pursuit of wisdom

For me, these three criteria define a meaningful life. What have I done with my life besides contribute to global warming? I would examine these aspects: Have I cultivated virtue and ethics in my life? Have I pursued genuine happiness over mere hedonic pleasures? Have I grown in wisdom by understanding reality as it is?

These three goals—gaining wisdom by understanding reality as it is; achieving genuine happiness and liberation through healing the mind and actualizing its full potential; and leading a virtuous, ethical way of life—are inextricably entangled. The view that they are three facets of a single pursuit is an extraordinary characteristic of Buddhism.

In our quest for contemplative insight, we can consider the pursuit of ethics to be our laboratory because here we test our most meaningful observations about the world. Fine mental balance that is interdependent with genuine happiness is our technology for precise investigation. The four close applications of mindfulness constitute our science of mind, framing our inquiries, recording past findings, and suggesting new hypotheses. Science, laboratory, and technology support each other interdependently.

Leading an ethical lifestyle means cultivating a way of being present and active in the world, especially when we engage with others, that is conducive to our own and others' genuine happiness. We seek to help ourselves and others develop exceptional mental balance, health, and well-being, even nirvana, by acting in noninjurious ways to support everyone's equilibrium, serenity, and good cheer.

Ethics is not optional. It's not the Buddha admonishing, "Be good, or karma will get you." In fact, it is impossible to imagine any significant achievement in mental balance without ethics. If one is leading an injurious lifestyle, thinking maliciously, speaking abusively, deceiving and exploiting people, and perhaps even injuring or killing, these nonvirtues will give rise to a fractious life of discord and unhappiness. In the midst of such suffering and injury to others, one might think, "Perhaps I'm a bit abrasive, and sometimes I use people to meet my needs. But in my meditation, all is well, and between meditations, I do what I must do." For such a person, meditation is a complete waste of time—this way of life undermines any effort to balance the mind.

The acquisition of scientific knowledge is not designed to bring about genuine happiness from within or to purify the mind. Scientific knowledge generates more knowledge, technology, business profits, and a proliferation of hedonic pleasure, but it is largely disconnected from ethics and genuine happiness. The pursuit of ethics, which is certainly important in our society, has typically been affiliated with religion. For a long time psychologists wouldn't even touch ethics, and many still won't.

I recently attended a wonderful conference where the modern movement of positive psychology was a topic. A growing number in the field of psychology have recognized the theme of "authentic happiness," which is an encouraging trend. Positive psychology moves the focus away from investigating mental disease to considering the upside of the ledger: How can exceptional mental health lead to human flourishing?

One presenter described a notion of authentic happiness as consisting of three elements. The first element is simple enjoyment—a pleasant life. Second, by engaging in activities in a state of optimal absorption, engagement, and motivation, one will increasingly experience what psychologist Mihaly Csikszentmihalyi calls "flow,"[44] or being "in the zone," like a marathon runner who is completely immersed in the race and feels no pain. This state has been studied quite extensively and is considered the second element of authentic happiness—a good life. Third, this notion of authentic happiness includes the sense of meaning derived from being part of something beyond one's individual concerns, contributing to a greater cause—a meaningful life. These three things were proposed to define genuine happiness.

Listening to this presentation, it struck me that this view of happiness and human flourishing suffered from a complete absence of ethics. I challenged the presenter: "I can easily imagine a terrorist adopting your view and thinking, 'I am happy to blow people up. I'll train rigorously with fellow terrorists, really entering into the flow. We will achieve our highest goal by converting everyone to our beliefs.' What prevents criminals, racists, dictators, and terrorists from adopting your thinking to justify their actions?"

At first he was dismissive, but then he said, "I believe that we must keep facts and values separate: science is about facts, not values." That statement has never been true in the history of science, and it never will be. Every question we pose to reality is posed precisely because we think the answer has value; meaningless questions are not pursued. Galileo, wondering whether Jupiter had any moons, was asking the question because he thought it had value. He risked his life to promote the notion that the earth goes around the sun, and not vice versa, because he felt it was important. Scientific inquiry always reflects our purpose.

Why would anyone pursue a question that didn't seem important or could not lead to anything good? In fact, such pursuits can be disastrous. In the twentieth century, we developed a great deal of knowledge and technology divorced from benevolent values. Our exponential growth in technological prowess is unbalanced, without commensurate understanding of moral responsibility. I cannot see any evidence that we are more moral now than we were in the time of Copernicus. In his day, if you were wronged, you might settle the score with your sword. Such morality still prevails today, but our weapons are nuclear missiles and biological agents that jeopardize all life on Earth. We seem to have developed ethical amnesia.

The modern pursuit of happiness is largely externalized in consumer mentality and divorced from the aspects of goodness and wisdom. Meanwhile, scientists feel free to assert that they pursue knowledge for its own sake—utterly divorced from ethics. The radical fragmentation of the three pursuits of virtue, happiness, and wisdom in the modern age may be a recipe for disaster. Plato (429–347 BCE) and his student Aristotle, along with many others around the world, recognized that life's meaning comes from an integrated pursuit of virtue, genuine happiness, and wisdom. Perhaps we need to rediscover the ancient wisdoms of the Christian, Jewish, Taoist, Hindu, and Greek traditions.

In contrast to scientific materialism, the Buddhadharma is founded on ethics and requires an integrated approach to the three pursuits of virtue, genuine happiness, and wisdom. It has been known for thousands of years that leading a virtuous, ethical, noninjurious way of life is indispensable for bringing about superior mental balance, including attentional balance in particular. Having achieved mental balance, one is poised to practice vipashyana and radically heal the mind from the inside out.

Buddhism is only one of many modes of contemplative and philosophical inquiry. We can trace the modern scientific paradigm back to Pythagoras, who was the Buddha's contemporary. The dissimilarities between these twenty-five-hundred-year-old traditions of knowledge acquisition have become quite striking with the modernization of science in the last four hundred years. While I have the utmost respect for the fruits of the scientific approach, how much mental balance is entailed? Is emotional equilibrium an essential trait in a brilliant scientist? Does scientific training include the development of refined attention and the power of samadhi? No, these skills are not in the curriculum. I have met scientists who say, "My mind is scattered, my memory's shot, and I can't focus my attention." They might be excellent scientists, but their minds are far out of balance—from the Buddhist perspective, their minds are dysfunctional.

The Buddha's path is a direct, integrated path for the purification of beings. Integration entails the cultivation of virtue and genuine happiness by means of wisdom that can be acquired only by leading a profoundly ethical life and by balancing the mind in extraordinary ways. Contemplative science is a complementary science that does not ignore ethics because it is oriented toward the realization of nirvana.

We have engaged in a practice that I've simply called mindfulness.

A very powerful example of the potential of this practice is given in the historical teachings of the Buddha. During the Buddha's life, there was an Indian seeker of truth named Bahiya, who had many followers of his own. But Bahiya recognized that, like Gautama at twenty-nine, he had not found the liberation he was seeking.

It must have been very frustrating for him to have many followers but still seek the genuine liberation that eluded him. Then he heard about Gautama, known as the Awakened One, and he came to seek the Buddha's counsel. The Buddha recognized Bahiya as a man with very little "dust in his eyes." He offered an extremely brief, quintessential instruction, a Dharma revelation that might have been shared in minutes. Here is the essence of what the Buddha told Bahiya, an accomplished contemplative who was ripe for awakening:

> In the seen, there is only the seen; in the heard, there is only the heard; in the felt, there is only the felt; in the cognized, there is only the cognized.

There is no subjective entity here—no self that is looking out. Attend closely, and see things as they are—unadorned, unelaborated, and unembellished by conceptual imputations, projections, likes, or dislikes of any kind. Let the seen manifest nakedly as the seen, the heard as the heard, the felt as the felt, and the cognized as the cognized. Perceive things as they are, and you will see that indeed, there is no thing here. There is no subject self that is independent from all these appearances.

The Buddha gave him a meditative practice very similar to what we're learning here: "This, Bahiya, is how you should train yourself." Then he described Bahiya's actual realization of this:

> Since, Bahiya, there is for you in the seen, only the seen; in the heard, only the heard; in the sensed, only the sensed; in the cognized, only the cognized; and you see that there is no thing here, you will therefore see that indeed there is no thing there.

No longer reifying the subject as the observer, you simply attend to impressions of mental, visual, auditory, and tactile events, seeing them for what they are. All perceptions, desires, fears, memories, and fantasies simply arise and are recognized as mental events. When you cease reifying yourself, you will then cease reifying appearances to the mind. You will see that since there is no thing here, indeed, there is no thing there. No reified object exists independently, in and of itself. The Buddha continues:

> As you see that there is no thing there, you will see that you are therefore located neither in the world of this, nor in the world of that, nor in any place between the two. This alone is the end of suffering.[45]

Bahiya attended to the words of the Buddha and achieved nirvana right there—he saw right through his delusion. The teaching was just one paragraph, but he was so ripe that he grokked it! The Buddha directed his mind like a guided missile, and Bahiya's mental afflictions were blown away. Those who are very ripe might not need to engage in elaborate investigations if they encounter such powerful words as these—like a finger pointing to the moon. They will see that there is no thing here; then they will see that there is no thing there; then they will see that they are located neither in the subjective world of this, nor in the objective world of that, nor in some borderland between the subjective and objective spheres.

The reified entity "I am" is nowhere to be found, and severing the taproot of this delusion is the only way to end suffering. In practice, it's more difficult than it seems to distinguish superimpositions from so-called real phenomena—the actual appearances arising to the six modes of perception, from moment to moment. The immediate contents of experience, such as sounds, visual impressions, tactile sensations, and thoughts, have causal efficacy and give rise to sequences of results. The imaginary entities that we project upon reality have no causal efficacy in and of themselves. This is an important distinction for mental health professionals because every psychosis entails a conflation of what is imagined to be true with what is true.

Pursuit of Wisdom

Buddhism distinguishes two types of ignorance. One is the ignorance of failing to ascertain some aspect of reality. We weren't paying attention when some feature of reality presented itself, so we didn't get it. This is simple, innocent ignorance, which can be rectified by attending more closely and learning. When we look more closely, we see what is really happening.

The more pernicious type of ignorance, or delusion, actually catapults us into suffering. In active delusion, we project our own prejudices, assumptions, and beliefs upon reality. Then, forgetting that we have done so, we fuse our projections with actual appearances. We hear things that were never said, see things that never happened, remember actions never taken, and so forth. Psychologists call it transference or projection—a marvelously creative mind painting its own reality. Instead of critically comparing our projections, assumptions, beliefs, hopes, and fears with actual appearances, we fuse them together and simply assume that what we perceive is real.

The practice of mindfulness entails a careful examination and surgical dissection of what is being presented by reality from what is being projected by us. Attending closely to this distinction is an act of radical empiricism—we take the immediate contents of experience seriously, no matter how bizarre, intangible, or impossible. Scientific materialism supposes that the natural world consists only of material things and their emergent properties. Here, our awareness is open and unrestricted by any such conceptual blinders.

For example, the immediate contents of experience in the body might be flows of energy coursing along pathways or gathering in certain regions. Just because these phenomena are not validated by modern science, must you be imagining them? Do subtle energies flow or not? Investigate them. What happens to them as you quiet your mind, attending as closely as possible? When we are simply imagining something and we attend with a quiet mind, our projections tend to vanish like mist under a hot sun. On the other hand, when a phenomenon is actually a manifestation of reality, the more closely we attend, the more distinctly it appears.

A central theme in the four close applications of mindfulness is attending to the manifest contents of experience, from moment to moment, in order to distinguish what is really being presented from what is merely projected. We can perceive, acknowledge, and embrace the causal efficacy of all manner of phenomena by seeing regular patterns and associations. When A appears, it gives rise to B, not just once but repeatedly. When A is absent, B never occurs. This is a phenomenological understanding of causality, rather than a metaphysical fixation on mechanistic, physical causes.

A central theme in modern science is called the closure principle; some physicists believe in it passionately, and its influence has spread from physics to biology and many other fields. The idea is that the only causally effective phenomena in the universe are physical phenomena. The physical universe is causally closed—hermetically sealed—and any agent that can actually effect a change in the physical world must itself be physical.

The notion that only physical things are efficacious makes some people feel secure. All ghosts are banished from the hermetically sealed physical universe of science. Even consciousness is reduced to a mere epiphenomenon of the physical activity of neurons. But when you examine the closure principle in light of modern physics, you open a can of worms. Physicality has become extraordinarily elusive. The Standard Model of particle physics describes a virtual zoo of elementary particles,[46] whose masses are said to stem from a hypothetical heavyweight, the Higgs boson,[47] as yet unobserved. Intangible fields, esoteric probability functions, and the inconceivable higher dimensions of string theory strain our everyday notion of physicality to the breaking point.

My favorite modern physical concepts are dark energy and dark matter. It's fascinating that astronomers and cosmologists find the motion of planets, stars, and galaxies throughout the universe to be expanding faster than known physical laws allow. The expansion of the universe is not slowing down but accelerating. There is no physical explanation for this except that there must be a force pulling the universe apart. We have no idea what it is, so we call it dark energy.

Furthermore, in the early history of the universe, matter and energy did not simply disintegrate but formed into stars and galaxies. The universe is bound together far more strongly than known laws predict, given the amount of matter we believe is present. There must be a "missing mass" holding it together, which we call dark matter. The terms "dark energy" and "dark matter" refer to unknowns, which is why they are called "dark." Even these choices of words are telling because the notions are physical. We do not understand why the expansion of the universe is accelerating but rest assured that the universe is really causally closed; these are just the effects of dark matter and dark energy—but we have no idea what these two terms refer to.

According to our current notions of the cosmos, ordinary matter accounts for less than 5 percent of the mass of the universe.[48] Dark matter—not made of atoms—makes up 23 percent and 72 percent is dark energy, whose negative pressure yields the observed expansion of the universe. Philosophers of science speak of a "God of the gaps," when people invoke God to explain the gaps in scientific theories. The current scientific gap amounts to 95 percent of the universe!

Imagine a banker announcing, "We have a little bookkeeping problem. We don't know what happened to 95 percent of our assets. We're going to call it 'dark money'; but don't worry, our bank is secure."

As you can tell, I'm rather skeptical about the notion of a hermetically sealed universe, particularly when 95 percent of it is unknown. Furthermore, I cannot take seriously the notion that mental phenomena, even if we call them nonphysical, have no impact on the body because they so obviously do. It is quite entertaining to see a full 95 percent of the forces and matter in the universe summarily classified as physical. In the mid-nineteenth century, physical meant the chunky stuff, and waves were ripples in the ether. With chunks of matter bumping into each other, everything had a mechanical explanation, including light. In those days, a hermetically sealed universe made good sense, but this hasn't been true for over 120 years.

The world is far more interesting than the closed, classical universe of the mid-nineteenth century. While the extraordinary advances and benefits of the science and technology that dominate our modern world are surely admirable, an ancient, marvelously complementary science—the pursuit of wisdom based upon an ethical way of life that yields genuine happiness—is even more exalted. Such is the nature of our adventure.

GUIDED MEDITATION:
Mindfulness V

Sustain mindfulness of all appearances and projections—
considering everything grist for the mill

Settle the body in its natural state and the respiration in its natural rhythm. Then settle the mind in its natural state, in the mode of open awareness of all appearances. Maintain an ongoing flow of unwavering mindfulness of whatever appears to the physical senses and the mind.

Monitor the balance of mindfulness with introspection. If you see that you have been carried away by distracting thoughts, relax more deeply, return to the immediacy of the present moment, and release grasping. If you see that you have become spaced-out or dull, arouse a fresh interest, focus, and settle your awareness in the present moment.

Carefully distinguish appearances being presented to you from the projections you superimpose on these phenomena. No thoughts are banished, only the clinging to them. As thoughts and projections arise, note them for what they are, without conflating them with perceptual appearances. In the sensed, there is just the sensed; in mental events, there are just mental events. Everything—including projections, when recognized as such—is grist for the mill. ☞

Cultivating Cognitive Balance

Cognitive balance allows us to perceive things as they really are. The critical aspects of balance to be cultivated in these foundational teachings consist of seeing the impermanent as impermanent and differentiating true sources of happiness from false ones. These are enormously important discoveries. We've begun by practicing all-inclusive mindfulness of mental and sensory appearances; now we will become more selective. Out of the four close applications of mindfulness, we will first select the domain of the body and the physical sense fields; next, we will attend specifically to feelings of pleasure, pain, and indifference; then we will attend to events arising in the mental domain; finally, we will attend to the space of all phenomena and their interdependent relationships.

Mindfulness has many practical benefits in ordinary daily life. For example, grasping is common in everyday conversations. While we are engaging with someone, we may be listening to some extent, but often we are caught up in our own emotional reactions, anticipating our next response, and waiting for a chance to interject. Such grasping predisposes us to miss what is being said and to hear things that were never said, particularly when we are familiar with the person and expect them to say predictable things.

Have you ever felt the indignation of being quoted as saying something that you would never say? Everyone has experienced the frustration of making a request such as, "Honey, would you please do this?" But the person to whom we spoke these words never heard them: "You never asked me to do that!" Ronald Reagan was fond of relating a war story of a pilot who selflessly joins his wounded crewman in death, but the story actually came from either the movie *A Wing and a Prayer* or a legend reported in *Reader's Digest*—it was not something that he experienced.[49] He conflated a fictional story with his reality.

Our goal is to cultivate cognitive balance, which is a special term for something very ordinary. Cognitive balance is an absence of both cognitive deficit and hyperactivity. Cognitive deficit occurs when we don't notice something that is being clearly presented to us. For example, we can look directly at a person's face but be so immersed in our own thoughts that we fail to notice his or her expressions, tone of voice, and emotional state. In cognitive hyperactivity, we remember things that never took place or see things that are totally projected. We superimpose concepts on reality and conflate them with what is being presented. Clearly differentiating what is presented from what is projected is the way to overcome cognitive hyperactivity.

For example, when we interpret other people's mental states by reading their facial expressions, we're on thin ice. Paul Ekman, a world-class psychologist and researcher of facial expressions and their relation to emotions, claims that if you become good at reading facial expressions, you can know a lot about the emotions that are being expressed. But he also urges extreme caution because, he says, you cannot know *why* an emotion is manifesting. Ekman has trained agents from Homeland Security, the State Department, and the CIA to recognize facial expressions of deceit, anxiety, fear, suppressed rage, and so forth, which can be done with expertise. But do a person's subtle expressions of anxiety justify detaining and interrogating him? Perhaps he is anxious because he is wearing a turban or because of his government's record for detaining and torturing people without due process. Ekman calls the erroneous interpretation of emotions "Othello's error."[50] In Shakespeare's play *Othello, the Moor of Venice*, Othello kills his wife because he fails to realize that her fear of being disbelieved looks and sounds just like the fear of being caught in adultery—fear is fear.

The practice of mindfulness is designed to bring about cognitive balance, so that we ascertain and engage with what is actually being presented. Mindfulness of appearances arising requires being engaged with these phenomena knowingly, without slipping into cognitive deficit. It also requires not slipping into cognitive hyperactivity by superimposing, interpreting, and projecting our thoughts onto experience. In personal and professional relationships, the ability to attend without the cognitive imbalances of hyperactivity and deficit has enormous relevance. Cognitive balance and emotional balance are closely interrelated.

Untangling Projection from Perception

Take the example of hearing a bird's song. When you hear the sound, you might mentally project an image of the bird. A bird watcher might recognize the song of a particular species, and even know that it appears on page 357 of the *Peterson Field Guide to Birds*. These are projections, and there is nothing harmful about them. Nevertheless, they violate the instruction: "In the heard, let there be just the heard." Our projections draw on memory, superimpose concepts, and classify raw appearances in a framework.

The practice here is to sustain naked attention as much as possible. We let the heard be just the heard, from moment to moment, rather than placing it into a conceptual framework. Nevertheless, when projections occur, the practice becomes all the more interesting. When you hear the sound of a bird and immediately a mental image of a bird appears to you, this too is grist for the mill. Simply be equally present with the sound and the image, as both of them appear and then dissolve back into the space of appearances.

Don't try to inhibit or eradicate mental projections that arise. Notice that the sound of the bird and the resultant mental image constitute a causal sequence. If the sound had not appeared, the image would not have arisen. If this is a regular pattern, we can call it causality. Phenomenologically, this arose and then that arose. This dissipated and then that dissipated. Let everything be grist for the mill, without conflating mental images and other sensory perceptions.

Will there ever be a modern contemplative science, where refined mental perception and introspection become viable modes of scientific inquiry, and many people engage in contemplative inquiry, replicating each other's discoveries? An enormously important concern is the possibility that these contemplative researchers may conflate their projections with what is actually being presented in the mental domain—just as this occurs in the visual and auditory domains.

One of the false starts came from Descartes, who emphasized introspection but stated that anything we detect by means of introspection that is "clear and distinct" should be considered an infallible perception. To the contrary, something may be perfectly clear and distinct while being fundamentally false. Even the direct senses are fallible, especially when strong emotions are involved. When a gun is fired in a crowded theater, witnesses' reports will be wildly incompatible.

The confusion that fuses together perceptions and projections can also occur when we attend to mental events. William James addressed this point, saying that the same fallacies and inaccuracies of perception that we witness in the physical senses can also compromise the results of introspection. How could introspection be immune to such distortions?

For example, we can experience cognitive deficit with respect to our own emotions. Sometimes emotions arise without our awareness—we would flatly deny experiencing them. A person accused of being angry might say, "What do you mean I'm angry, you jerk? I'm not angry at all! Why don't you just shut up?" Such a person might not notice the anger in these words and then insist, "I just felt a lot of energy, and I'm a very direct person." Someone involved in a romantic relationship might express words of love for another person saying, "I care only about you," while actually entertaining only selfish thoughts. Cognitive hyperactivity and projection can also produce hidden desires, mistaken emotions, and veiled thoughts.

Unless the ability to distinguish perception from projection can be honed, the prospects for a true contemplative science are nonexistent. Is the measuring apparatus inherently inaccurate and unable to differentiate observations of mental events from the projections upon them? James recognized this issue with much greater clarity than did Descartes, and he took it as a fundamental challenge. Nevertheless, his vision of psychology 120 years ago held introspection to be the primary means of investigating the mind. He believed that, with refinement, introspection could offer a reliable mode of inquiry. As with all scientific tools, observations must be repeated and verified until a consensus develops.

For about thirty years, ending in 1910, the introspection movement included a number of laboratories in Europe and America run by the likes of Wilhelm Wundt (1832–1920), considered a founder of modern experimental psychology, and his student Edward Titchener (1867–1927), who chaired Cornell University's Department of Psychology, but these research projects collapsed. Now they are merely the historical relics of failure mentioned in the introductions to cognitive psychology textbooks. One of the primary reasons for abandoning introspection as a mode of scientific inquiry was that these labs produced diverse results. The questions posed by researchers were often leading ones, and research subjects often corroborated exactly what the investigators expected to find. With different starting hypotheses, different observations were made.

There are many interesting studies of visual perception, in particular, that show how highly selective and prone to bias it can be. Introspective observation is every bit as prone to bias, exaggeration, and embellishment as sensory observation. Nevertheless, there is reason for hope. Traditions such as Buddhism, which clearly recognized this problem thousands of years ago, have developed techniques to refine mental perception, separating the noise from clear perception. By developing a solid foundation of basic attention skills, one can attend to whatever one wishes with continuity, unwavering mindfulness, and clarity. These skills can be applied to any sense field and any activity, from reading a book or running a restaurant to driving a racecar. If refined attention skills are to be applied to vipashyana investigation, separating the noise from the appearances of actual phenomena is essential. This is a serious challenge, but it promises rewards that are enormously relevant to interpersonal relationships and much more.

Science of Happiness

The fact that we do not have a well-developed science of happiness today is really quite bizarre. We have an embryonic start in positive psychology, but why weren't scientists studying happiness from the beginning, when Copernicus was studying the stars? Of course, medical doctors are doing a pretty good job of understanding the physical causes of happiness and suffering. But a science of happiness focused on its mental causes is not very evident, particularly concerning the means for improving the lives of people who are not mentally disabled.

This lack was demonstrated vividly in 1989, when the Dalai Lama met in California with a group of mind scientists, including a psychiatrist, a philosopher, and several neurophysiologists and cognitive psychologists. The psychiatrist spoke with great satisfaction about the treatment of depression using many different drugs, with more being developed. He described the usefulness of these drugs in controlling the symptoms of depression.

Then the Dalai Lama asked, "Depression may arise for a wide variety of reasons, including a chemical imbalance in the brain, diet, lifestyle, or an angry mind. It could be due to the loss of a loved one. It might not even be personal, but could arise from despair over the state of the world. How do you account for the diverse causes of depression when you prescribe these medications?"

The psychiatrist answered, "It doesn't matter. The drugs work regardless of the causes." He was not suggesting that any of these medicines actually cure depression. Professionals in the field use the phrase "managing symptoms," which might be more accurately called "suppressing symptoms." This strikes me as rather primitive. Of course, many brilliant psychoanalysts and therapists investigate the causes of depression and actually heal people. But drugs alone usually fail to produce a full cure.

The central themes of cognitive balance are to recognize the nature of impermanence, differentiate a true source of happiness or unhappiness from a mere catalyst, and fathom the true nature of existence. By realizing what we are not, we will understand how we actually exist instead of misconstruing our inherent existence. Sometimes it seems that cognitive imbalance dominates our lives. Tremendous suffering comes from grasping on to relationships, people, and things as more robust and enduring than they really are. We mistake actual sources of suffering for happiness and mistake actual sources of happiness for suffering. We reify the self and bifurcate ourselves from others, creating the radical isolation in which all religious, national, and ethnic conflicts are rooted. In cultivating cognitive balance as a foundation for vipashyana practice, our focus is on restoring balance in these three domains of reality.

As important as these three themes are, the Mahayana teachings on the perfection of wisdom transcend them to address the universal nature of our conceptual projections. All events and phenomena are explained as dependently related events—nothing exists independently, isolated from the rest of reality. In the process of reifying, we substantiate and project tangibility onto phenomena that have no existence in and of themselves. Every individual and every phenomenon in the world arises as a dependently related event in an ocean of interrelationships.

The importance of cognitive balance, within which there are various levels, is not a sectarian issue. The teachings of the Buddha, as recorded in the earliest accounts of the Pali Canon, clearly show precursors of the teachings on Madhyamaka, the Middle Way view. Some schools of Buddhism highlight certain facets more than other traditions do. I am delighted to be living in this era, with access to the Zen tradition, which has some unique excellences. The Chan, Japanese, and Korean traditions illuminate certain aspects of the Buddha's teachings in marvelous and unprecedented ways. The Theravadins developed mindfulness of the breath and the four close applications of mindfulness with exceptional richness—these are key strengths. The teachings preserved and highlighted in the Tibetan tradition are utterly extraordinary, not to mention the rest of the world's contemplative traditions.

Of course we can look beyond Buddhism, but it is not practical to follow all religions simultaneously. We must follow a path that genuinely appeals to us, nourishes us, and benefits us. I'm happy to follow my own path as far as it can possibly take me. At the same time, I look at my Taoist brothers and sisters with great admiration. Vedantists, Sufis, Christians, and Jews possess ancient legacies with very rich traditions. By appreciating these traditions, one can occasionally draw from teachings that are compatible with one's own path—this is immensely rewarding. For example, I love coteaching with Laurence Freeman, a Benedictine monk.[51] He's a very devout Christian, and I have learned much from him. We learn from each other in ways that are completely compatible with our respective paths.

Living in today's world, we can rejoice in our historically unprecedented access to a wealth of contemplative wisdom from multiple cultures. While remaining true to our own tradition, we can savor the special qualities that are illuminated with clarity and depth in other traditions. The Buddha himself taught the four close applications of mindfulness as a phenomenological investigation of the constituents of immediate experience. Even the Tibetan tradition includes nothing quite like the mindfulness practices in the Pali Canon and the Theravadin commentaries. These are the clearest, most practical presentations I have seen, and they are unquestionably grounded in experience. I am very grateful to my teachers from the Theravadin tradition for maintaining and transmitting these exceptional practices.

⫸ 4 ⫷
Platform of Shamatha

THE BUDDHA strongly emphasized the importance of settling the mind in a state of equipoise before applying it to inquiry into the nature of reality. Therefore, some preliminary effort in the practice of shamatha will be time well spent. Shamatha requires a balance of three factors: relaxation, stability, and vividness of attention. Relaxation is the primary quality to be cultivated, and it must never be sacrificed for stability or vividness.

Within the Buddha's teachings recorded in the Pali Canon, the shamatha practice most commonly emphasized is mindfulness of the breath, particularly for people whose minds are heavily agitated by involuntary thoughts. Even more than Indians in the Buddha's time or nomadic Tibetans living today, most of us can derive great benefit from such practice, which is ideally suited to our modern lifestyle. The Buddha called this practice "an ambrosial dwelling." The very nature of mindfulness practice helps not only by bringing mental calm and joy but also by boosting our "psychological immune system," making the mind less vulnerable to afflictions.

More generally, the cultivation of shamatha leads to freedom from the five obscurations, or hindrances (Skt. *nivaranas*; Tib. *sgrib pa*), which are (1) sensual craving, (2) malice, (3) laxity and lethargy, (4) excitation and anxiety, and (5) uncertainty.[52] Indian Buddhist contemplatives discovered that these five obscurations are counteracted by the five factors of meditative stabilization: (1) coarse examination counteracts laxity and lethargy, (2) precise investigation counteracts uncertainty, (3) well-being counteracts malice, (4) bliss counteracts excitation and anxiety, and (5) single-pointed attention counteracts sensual craving.

In the *Great Satipatthana Sutta*, the Buddha specifically taught mindfulness of the breath as a shamatha method prior to teaching the vipashyana practices of mindfulness. We will engage in this practice in three phases. The focus of the first session and the primary factor in shamatha is profound relaxation of body and mind. Please find a comfortable position; the supine position is excellent for this practice in particular.

GUIDED MEDITATION:
Mindfulness of the Breath I

Attend to the breath throughout the body—
relaxing and releasing with each breath

A general theme in Buddhist meditation is the progression from coarse to subtle. This applies to settling the body, speech, and mind in their natural states, beginning with the critical theme of relaxing the body. Let your awareness slip into and permeate the entire field of tactile sensations. Swiftly note any areas that feel tense or contracted; breathe into them, and as you breathe out, release this tension. Very importantly, soften the facial muscles, especially around the eyes and the forehead, and soften the eyes themselves.

Throughout each session, periodically check to ensure that tension is not mounting in the face—it should remain as soft and loose as a sleeping baby's face. Let the body be still, assuming a posture of vigilance. Breathe in effortlessly, feeling the sensations of the breath in the lower abdomen, which expands with each inhalation. If you wish, take three slow, deep breaths to round off this initial settling of the body.

Settle the breath in its natural rhythm—effortless, spontaneous, and uncontrolled—noting the sensations of the breath wherever they occur throughout the entire tactile field.

Now settle the mind in a state of equilibrium, the prerequisite for the effective practice of vipashyana. Cultivate an overriding quality of mental ease and relaxation—not driven, aggressive, goal oriented, or grasping. Simply let awareness come to rest within the field of tactile sensations. If your attention is like a wild horse accustomed to roaming at will, gently restrain that stallion, keeping it corralled within the field of tactile sensations arising in the present moment.

Let the attention rove at will, but maintain it within the field of the body and the immediate present. Allow it the freedom to be diffuse, permeating the whole field, or at times to focus on a specific region of the body. Take immediate note when the attention escapes the corral of the body in the present moment and wanders away from tactility, revisits the past, or anticipates the future. In response, relax more deeply, and gently return the attention to the body.

Now specifically attend to those sensations related to the breath. With each out-breath, note any thoughts that may have arisen; relax and let them go. Each out-breath is like a gentle breeze that blows away the dry leaves of thoughts and images. Release everything while maintaining awareness of the sensations of the breath flowing throughout the body.

Relax through the entire course of the out-breath, and continue to release and relax as the breath spontaneously flows in. With each in-breath and out-breath, simply note whether the breath is long or short. Don't try to modify the respiration in any way; having no preference for how the breath should flow, just let it be. The challenge in this phase of the practice is to sustain your initial level of mental alertness, or vividness, while letting your body and mind settle into an ever-deepening sense of ease and relaxation.

If you still feel fresh, you may continue directly to the next session, taking a moment to stretch. ⮌

GUIDED MEDITATION:
Mindfulness of the Breath II

Attend to the rise and fall of the abdomen—
balancing stability with relaxation

Settle the body in its natural state and the respiration in its natural rhythm. Always begin on a fundamental note of relaxation as you let your awareness permeate the field of tactile sensations, observing the sensations of the breath wherever they occur. Relax with each out-breath, immediately releasing any thoughts or mental images that may have arisen.

There is a critical balance to be achieved between deepening relaxation and simultaneously cultivating stability and continuity of attention. Introduce the discipline of directing your attention more narrowly; instead of observing the entire body, focus your attention on the tactile sensations of the rise and fall of the abdomen with each breath. Continue to let your breath flow spontaneously, without any hint of control or regulation.

With each inhalation, arouse your attention, focusing closely on the whole course of the inhalation. With each exhalation, relax deeply in body and mind, releasing any involuntary thoughts, while sustaining mindfulness of the sensations at the abdomen. To the best of your ability, attend to the whole course of the inhalation and the whole course of the exhalation. Arouse your attention with each in-breath, and relax more deeply with each out-breath.

In order to reduce involuntary thoughts and enhance the stability and continuity of attention, you may employ the method of counting breaths. At the very end of the inhalation, just before exhaling, mentally count "one" very briefly. Then relax through the out-breath, sustaining your attention on the sensations of the breath at the abdomen. Arouse your attention during inhalation, attending to the whole course of the in-breath, and just before exhaling, mentally count "two." You can count from one to ten or another number, but keep the counts succinct. Do not fall into mindfulness of counting. The counts are passing road markers, while your attention is focused continuously on the course of the breath.

Periodically verify that the body is relaxed, still, and maintaining a posture of vigilance. Ensure that the breath flows naturally, without impediment. If you find yourself caught up and carried away by thoughts, immediately relax, release all thoughts, and return to the tactile sensations of the breath at the abdomen. If you find yourself falling into dullness or drowsiness, open the eyes to let in a bit of light and focus more closely, taking a fresh interest in the practice. ✎

DEPENDENT METHODS

In his discourse on the four close applications of mindfulness, the Buddha refers to these quintessential vipashyana teachings as the direct path to nirvana. A wide variety of meditations are designed to bring about various personal transformations, mental abilities, and other goals. The specific purpose of the four close applications of mindfulness is the complete purification of all mental afflictions, leading directly to the realization of nirvana.

Vipashyana is not a stand-alone practice. The path to the cessation of suffering asserted in the Fourth Noble Truth is depicted as a pyramid in traditional Buddhism. The foundation of the pyramid is ethics. Resting upon ethics are mental balance and samadhi, constituting a platform. Resting upon this platform is vipashyana, which severs the root of mental afflictions.

The ancient Pali commentaries liken shamatha to a great warrior and vipashyana to a wise minister.[53] The example is given of a wise minister authorized to negotiate with a wayward prince who had fallen under the influence of evil friends, symbolizing the five obscurations. If the minister attempts to admonish the prince by himself, he might be killed. But if he is accompanied and protected by a strong warrior, who first subdues the prince, then the minister can persuade him to change his ways.

Similarly, the efforts of the wise minister of vipashyana are strengthened and protected by the great warrior of shamatha.

Ethical Foundation

It is unrealistic to think that without any development of ethics and samadhi, one could still practice vipashyana and achieve the same result. But how ethical do we need to be in order to create a stable foundation for samadhi? What degree of samadhi constitutes an effective platform for practicing vipashyana? To me, these crucial questions are not raised often enough. Many people practice vipashyana simply to cultivate mindfulness, serenity, and harmony in their lives, which is perfectly fine. There's nothing wrong with using vipashyana methods to relieve stress.

A question was posed to the Dalai Lama, in 1990, concerning the teaching of basic mindfulness practices that were radically decontextualized from the framework of Buddhist theory, without ethics, without samadhi, and not even attributed to the Buddha: Did His Holiness think that teaching these mindfulness practices was a kind of plagiarism? The Dalai Lama answered: "If following these practices helps people to simply alleviate stress, even without the framework of ethics, samadhi, and the larger worldview, this is a good thing." All the Buddha's teachings were given in order to alleviate suffering. Even if people derive only a fraction of the benefit of his teachings, simplified practices can help alleviate their suffering. But then the Dalai Lama added this precaution: "Just don't mistake it for the Buddhadharma." A radically simplified, decontextualized mindfulness practice, without ethics or samadhi, is only one small aspect of the vast framework of the Dharma.

How important is the issue of ethics? To pursue the practice of vipashyana effectively requires proper supporting conditions. For example, if you are sick and take a prescribed medicine, following all the dosage, dietary, and exercise requirements, it may yield a complete cure. If you don't follow all the conditions of the prescription, it may result only in temporary relief.

Is it necessary to take monastic vows and be celibate in order to achieve nirvana? The answer is very clear—no. During the Buddha's lifetime, the monastic lifestyle was specifically designed for people intent on achieving nirvana, but it is not necessary. The Pali Canon describes cases of lay people achieving nirvana. Nevertheless, a very high level of ethics—doing one's best to avoid harming others and trying to be of service where possible—is essential for both lay people and monks.

There's an interesting corollary here. As one's quality of life becomes refined through developing increasing mental balance and samadhi, the mind becomes finely tuned, sensitive, stable, and clear. Then, as insight develops through the practice of vipashyana, one finds something quite remarkable taking place: one becomes increasingly sensitive to one's own mistakes. Even while avoiding any blatantly negative behavior, one becomes acutely aware of the pain caused by one's subtler mental afflictions, insensitive comments, thoughtless acts, and innocent gaffes.

A classical Tibetan analogy says that for an ordinary person, the arising of a mental affliction such as craving or hostility is like a hair falling on the palm of one's hand—its presence is barely felt. On the other hand, for a person who is advanced on the path of developing insight, the arising of the same mental affliction is like a hair falling into one's eye—it is quite intolerable. This suggests that one's standard of ethics becomes elevated and refined along the path. The cultivation of ethics is not simply learning a set of ten nonvirtues to avoid, or even abiding by 253 monastic precepts. The enhancement and refinement of the quality of one's behavior, speech, and mental activity is an ongoing process. Experiences of increasing sensitivity lead to increasing purification and elevation of ethical standards. Becoming a monk or a nun can be helpful and is the optimal way of life for some people, but it is not required or necessary for everyone.

Samadhi Platform

Finally, what degree of samadhi is sufficient? Can one disregard samadhi altogether in favor of practicing vipashyana? Clearly not, or the Buddha would not have described the path as consisting of ethics, samadhi, and wisdom. Learned scholars in the Theravadin tradition debate this point and defend different views. I cannot end the debate. Nevertheless, the Buddha's teachings give us a strong hint, such as in the wonderful account he gave to his followers after he achieved enlightenment. I can imagine a disciple asking, "What was the ultimate reason why—after having achieved high levels of samadhi and finding this insufficient; then undergoing six years of incredible austerities and recognizing that this didn't work either; and finally, with good food and restored health, sitting beneath the bodhi tree—suddenly, you were enlightened?"

At the age of thirty-five—having experimented with all the major methods of his time, endured six years of great asceticism, and accomplished deep samadhi—the proverbial light bulb went on in the Buddha's head. Here is what he told his disciples about what was going through his mind just before he sat down and completed the job of becoming fully enlightened:

> I thought of a time when my Sakyan father was working and I was sitting in the cool shade of a rose apple tree; quite secluded from sensual desires and disengaged from unwholesome things, I entered into and abode in the first *dhyana*, which is accompanied by coarse and precise investigation, with well-being and bliss born of seclusion. I thought, "Might this be the way to enlightenment?" Then, following that memory, there came the recognition that this was the way to enlightenment.[54]

His father was a king performing a ritual spring plowing, and young Prince Gautama was off duty, sitting in the cool shade of a rose apple tree on a hot spring day. Saying that he was quite secluded from sensual desire—an enormously important phrase here—means that his mind was withdrawn, not looking for entertainment, not fantasizing about sensual pleasures, and not engaged with unwholesome things. He had settled his body, speech, and mind.

Then, as a contemplative prodigy, Gautama spontaneously slipped into the samadhi known as the first meditative stabilization (Skt. *dhyana*; Pali *jhana*). (The term "dhyana" gave rise to the names of the Chan and Zen schools.) He achieved this state without meditative training. Why was he so lucky? From the Buddhist perspective, he had already achieved it in many prior lifetimes. Similarly, Plato held that much of the knowledge we seem to acquire in this lifetime consists of rekindled memories from past lifetimes.

The Buddha described this very profound state of samadhi, the first dhyana, as being accompanied by coarse and precise investigation. The mind is utterly controlled and settled in a state of equipoise that is nothing like a trance, in which you cannot think or function. To the contrary, in this state you can engage in general investigations or precise analysis of any subject. Your intelligence and conceptual abilities are fully available, but you are completely free of obsessive-compulsive thinking. This state is suffused with a blissful well-being; it's not ecstasy or teeth-chattering, incapacitating bliss. Being born of seclusion means the mind is withdrawn from the sense fields and compulsive ideation, resting naturally in balance. When the mind is settled in the first dhyana, bliss arises from the very nature of awareness.

At the age of thirty-five, the Buddha remembered his spontaneous experience as a youth. Having recalled it, the thought arose, "Might this be the way to enlightenment?" He was clearly referring to the first dhyana, the first of four stages within what is called the form realm. This state is imbued with discerning intelligence, a sense of blissful well-being, and a highly focused mind. Buddhists claim that a mind settled in such equipoise—with awareness that is malleable, supple, calm, clear, and intelligent—comes to know reality as it is.

Following this thought, the Buddha recognized that this was indeed the way to enlightenment. I am happy to take that statement at face value; he couldn't have said it more clearly. He did not mention the second meditative stabilization, let alone the formless absorptions, in which the capacities for investigation and analysis are dormant. He simply said that the first dhyana was the way to enlightenment.

Vipashyana Method

Very shortly thereafter, the Buddha sat beneath the bodhi tree with an adamantine resolve: "I shall not move from this seat until I have achieved enlightenment," and that's what he did. The first dhyana seems to have been his platform for launching into vipashyana. This ultimately led him to what is called supermundane vipashyana, the examination of the facets of reality that directly liberate the mind.

But first, in mundane vipashyana, one simply investigates certain critical aspects of the phenomenal world in which we live. The Buddha described his experiences during that night's three watches, each lasting about three hours. He might have sat down as the sun was setting, and in the first watch of the night, he settled immediately into samadhi. From this platform, he directed his attention back in time to ascertain the circumstances in thousands of his previous lifetimes. In this first exploration, the Buddha probed the history of his own mind-stream, and he declared that he saw with direct knowledge the vast sequence of his past lives.

In the second watch of the night, he directed his attention panoramically, attending to the mind-streams of other sentient beings. He found that they also had long histories, and he attended to their myriad past lives. Then, still applying mundane vipashyana, he examined the patterns in this massive database of the lives of myriad sentient beings, performing a meta-analysis of their actions and the consequences. The results of the Buddha's analysis in the second watch of that night came to be known as the laws of karma; the Sanskrit term "karma" means action. He saw that actions in one lifetime are like seeds sowed that eventually give rise to consequences in later lifetimes. He observed regular patterns of causal sequences from one lifetime to the next, and his experiential insights into rebirth and karma were significantly different from any of the views that were prevalent before his enlightenment. So recent claims that he simply adopted these ideas from common beliefs of his era are entirely spurious, without any basis in historical fact.

In the third watch of the night, he probed into the reality of suffering and its origins, the path, and the culmination of the path. He directly realized the twelve links of dependent origination, the mechanics of samsara, and the path to liberation. As the sun rose, he achieved enlightenment—the Buddha awakened! His platform was the samadhi of the first dhyana.

There are many methods for achieving the first dhyana, and dozens of them were taught by the Buddha. Bear in mind that in teaching the development of the dhyanas, he truly stood on the shoulders of giants. He was born into a culture with a rich tradition in samadhi. Without attaining the extraordinarily sublime mental balance of the first dhyana, he would have had no platform for developing fully effective vipashyana.

It is interesting to consider whether the Pythagoreans might have rivaled the Indian tradition of samadhi. Pythagoras may have achieved very deep samadhi, and some speculate that he learned it from Indian adepts. Legend says that Pythagoras traveled to Egypt, where he received knowledge of India. The travelers between the Indian subcontinent, Egypt, and the near East included wandering ascetics, who were called "gymnosophists" by the Greeks. These naked *(gymno)* wise *(sophia)* people were probably Indian yogis, highly accomplished in samadhi; this could indicate a samadhi lineage in early Greek thought. It is said that Pythagoras remembered twenty of his past lives, including some as members of nonhuman species. This belief in reincarnation persisted through Plato and into the Neoplatonic tradition.

Nevertheless, the development of samadhi was not in our legacy from the Greeks. Plato and Aristotle were titans in the realms of mathematics, logic, philosophy, and physics, but they were not renowned for their methods of developing samadhi. We have no knowledge of the methods Pythagoras might have employed because the brotherhood he founded was quasi-secret.

The cultivation of samadhi at that time in India surpassed that in China, the Americas, and Australia, as well as in the Jewish tradition. Gautama was born in the best possible place for the practice of samadhi, and he inherited a rich tradition from hundreds of years of contemplative research. The trajectory of shamatha had been explored to the heights of subtlety and the depths of samadhi. The Buddha's second teacher had achieved the highest absorption in the formless realm, called the peak of existence, and Gautama reached it ever so rapidly. The practice begins with many obscurations and hindrances, eventually becoming peaceful, then blissful, and finally giving way to an inconceivable equanimity that transcends pleasure and pain.

The nature of this continuum of quiescence is sweet, calm, and soothing. No wonder people pursued this trajectory for hundreds of years, much longer than the history of modern science. Then the Buddha launched a revolution in Indian contemplative culture by claiming that samadhi does not produce irreversible change, and neither do austerities, physical exercises, or the sheer exertion of will. He embraced the wisdom he inherited, refined it, and formulated it into his triad of ethics, samadhi, and wisdom. The Buddha introduced the fusion of shamatha and vipashyana as the technology to effect irreversible change. The vipashyana mode of inquiry does not have the same sweet ambience as shamatha—it can be unsettling, challenging, and demanding. Of course, the revelations and insights can be pretty exciting, but the task is more like research than relaxation. You may pursue peace in a meditative retreat by practicing shamatha, but the practice of vipashyana is an expedition in the pursuit of freedom.

MINDFULNESS OF THE BREATH

In the Buddha's time, there were myriad methods for developing samadhi. The one he emphasized and taught most often, including in his discourse on the four close applications of mindfulness, is mindfulness of the breath. Here is his metaphor for the great power of this simple method:

> Just as in the last month of the hot season, when a mass of dust and dirt has swirled up, and a great, unseasonable rain cloud disperses it and quells it on the spot, so too concentration by mindfulness of the breath, when developed and cultivated, is peaceful and sublime, an ambrosial dwelling; and it disperses and quells evil, unwholesome states on the spot, whenever they arise.[55]

Imagine India in May or June, before the monsoon hits: sweltering, gritty, acrid, and suffocating. A sudden cloudburst can drench the land and make the air crystal clear instantaneously. Likewise, the Buddha said, the single-pointed, focused attention that is achieved by way of mindfulness of the breath, when developed and cultivated, is peaceful and sublime. This development might not occur overnight, but a sublime psychosomatic state can result from simply focusing on the sensations of the breath.

Sweet Abode

It is crucial to note that this sweet, ambrosial dwelling is not the result of attending to some highly pleasant stimulus. The sensations of the breath are quite neutral: neither disagreeable nor agreeable. When one focuses on the breath and settles the mind to be free of craving and aversion, a peaceful and sublime state arises out of the nature of awareness itself. Balancing and settling the mind in this ambrosial dwelling disperses and quells mental afflictions on the spot.

This practice has enormous potential to improve mental health. If mindfulness of the breath can really subdue unwholesome states, such as hatred, malice, resentment, and greed, it is profoundly therapeutic. The Buddha does not say that by merely focusing on the breath and settling the mind in equilibrium, the virtues of loving-kindness, compassion, generosity, and wisdom will spring forth full-blown. He says that this will allow you to achieve a sublime state of neutrality. You will not be irreversibly free; but temporarily, the mind's unwholesome tendencies will be subdued on the spot, and you'll settle into a state of equilibrium that gives rise to a sense of bliss.

First, you must establish a neutral state of balance, without craving, hostility, and resentment. If you can establish this sense of equilibrium and well-being, your development of virtue is bound to be much more effective. You will be equipped with a platform that can be used to actively cultivate wisdom, insight, compassion, loving-kindness, and all other virtues.

The power of a sense of well-being has been measured by research, over the past ten years, in the field of positive psychology.[56] Rigorous psychological studies have been conducted in which subjects are given an opportunity to engage in an act of kindness, generosity, altruism, or some other virtue. One group consists of subjects who report feeling unhappy, depressed, or anxious. Another group consists of subjects who report feeling happy, relaxed, and cheerful. When both groups are presented with opportunities to be of service to others, the happy subjects are much more likely to extend themselves in acts of kindness and generosity. Simple happiness is a valuable thing.

All-Purpose Vehicle

The instructions for mindfulness of the breath occur many times in the record of the Buddha's forty-five-year teaching career. His quintessential description of this practice was largely standardized and most often unelaborate. The commentaries by Buddhaghosa and others give a much richer picture, but the Buddha's words are quite succinct. In the *Satipatthana Sutta*, the Buddha describes a fourfold sequence of practices for mindfulness of the breath, designed to establish shamatha or meditative equipoise.

In the *Anapanasati Sutta*, the Buddha's primary discourse on mindfulness of breathing in and out (Skt. *anapanasati*), he describes sixteen phases, where the first four phases concern the development of shamatha. The next twelve phases concern vipashyana. Mindfulness of the breath evolves from an exercise for developing attention skills into a platform for probing the nature of reality. Having developed shamatha, we can utilize this extraordinary equilibrium and balance of attention to investigate the nature of the mind itself. The breath is the vehicle for exploring the fundamental marks of existence: the reality of impermanence, the nature of suffering, and the lack of an inherent self. At the culmination of stage sixteen, congratulations—you're an arhat! How difficult could that be?

The *Satipatthana Sutta* begins with anapanasati, but the Buddha teaches mindfulness of the breath only in the first four stages, as a preliminary exercise to develop shamatha and achieve the dhyanas. Even though mindfulness of the breath can be one's sole vehicle to reach liberation or nirvana, this sutra reveals another powerful method. The rest of the discourse concerns vipashyana, the act of inquiry into the central features of reality: impermanence, duhkha, and nonself. The framework of the four close applications of mindfulness is a broader one; it addresses not only the body but feelings, mental phenomena, and the array of interdependencies between all internal and external phenomena. In the larger scope of vipashyana practice, mindfulness of the breath appears at the introductory stage.

The Buddha's discourse to Bahiya consisted of a very short instruction. So little needed to be said to this extremely mature contemplative that the Buddha just gave him a couple of paragraphs. These simple words are profoundly deep. If we could listen to them with Bahiya's ears, then we would achieve nirvana too! The Buddha did not mention the close application of mindfulness to the breath, body, feelings, or mental states. He simply said, "In the seen, there is only the seen."

This quintessential exposition progresses from seeing that there is no reified subject that is separate from the rest of reality to seeing that there is no reified object with intrinsic existence; nothing arises independently of the matrix of existence. There is no evidence for an internal subjective agent or self that is somehow separate from perceived objects—nothing here that is the observer. Seeing this, one turns the attention to see that there is nothing external as an independent object—nothing there. Finally, one recognizes that there is no self between internal and external. The Buddha led Bahiya in a stepwise manner and cut through his delusion on the spot. To use my trivial example, Bahiya recognized that he wasn't Napoleon, and now that he's seen the truth, he'll never imagine he's Napoleon again. He was not using the power of samadhi to subdue his grasping into dormancy. He was taking the bull by the horns, investigating very closely, and seeing for himself that there is no Napoleon anywhere.

When the vipashyana insight into the absence of a self here, there, and in between is fully backed by the muscle of shamatha, it's like a wise minister protected by a warrior. When insight breaks through with the stability and vividness of shamatha, there is radiant clarity and adamantine stability, and the practitioner retains this insight—you absolutely and irreversibly grok it. This is like knowing "I'm not Napoleon," with enough certainty to fully eradicate every habitual pattern of thinking and proclivity for grasping. You're free!

Essential Instructions

The Buddha's primary teachings on the practice of mindfulness of the breath are pointed:

> Breathing in long, one is aware: "I breathe in long."
> Breathing out long, one is aware: "I breathe out long."
> Breathing in short, one is aware: "I breathe in short."
> Breathing out short, one is aware: "I breathe out short."[57]

At first, your mindfulness might not include much finesse. When you begin practicing mindfulness of the breath, your mind is bound to be relatively coarse, and your breath will tend to be long. If your inhalation and exhalation are long, simply note their duration. Continuing to breathe in and out while noting this, you settle down, just as if you were falling asleep. Gradually, as your body requires less oxygen, the volume of your respiration may subside and the duration of each breath may become shorter. Let this occur naturally, without trying to make your respiration conform to your expectations.

The Buddha continues, "'Attending to the whole body, I shall breathe in.' Thus one trains oneself. 'Attending to the whole body, I shall breathe out.' Thus one trains."[58] Now the quality of attention is being enhanced, and a greater continuity of mindfulness is being sustained. This requires more attention than simply noticing the length of the breath. According to all the great commentaries, "the whole body" means the whole course of the breath. A classic metaphor says that the breath is like a horse, and awareness is like a rider trying to stay on the horse throughout the ride—a stable union of rider and horse. In a similar fashion, you mount the breath and maintain a face-to-face encounter throughout the entire course of the inhalation and exhalation.

This approaches what Csikszentmihalyi called the state of "flow." At least on a coarse level, you are mindfully and uninterruptedly attentive to the breath—you're not bucked off your horse. Along with the ongoing flow of sensations of the breath, you maintain a corollary flow of mindfulness of these sensations. When you develop and cultivate a smooth flow throughout the whole course of the breath, you begin to taste that which the Buddha called peaceful and sublime.

Going deeper into the practice, stage four is simply described by "'Soothing the composite of the body, I shall breathe in.' Thus one trains oneself. 'Soothing the composite of the body, I shall breathe out.' Thus one trains."[59] The Buddha is describing a progressively deepening calm in the whole body-mind system, not merely in the physical body. Everything is settling into an increasingly profound state of equilibrium. The breath becomes rhythmic, but not because you are trying to make it so. It gradually settles into a gentle, sinusoidal pattern, with lower volume, simply because you don't need as much air anymore.

Achieving the First Dhyana

The body's energy system is settling into a silky, sweet state of balance. The mind is calm, settling into an ambrosial equilibrium, peaceful and sublime. You are approaching the first dhyana, in which your abilities to think clearly and analytically are available, should you wish to use them for coarse or subtle investigation. This is like a surgeon with a wide variety of tools at hand, from coarse saws for cutting bone to fine scalpels for dissecting the tiniest vessels. Your equilibrium, focus of attention, and sense of well-being enable you to venture into vipashyana, which is the ultimate reason for achieving samadhi. By soothing the whole composite of myriad interdependently arising phenomena that we label "body and mind," this system naturally settles into equilibrium.

A great deal of confusion about the first dhyana has been generated in the last twenty years, particularly in European languages. This is not the result of ill will but of ignorance. People hear sound bites, read short descriptions of the first, second, third, and fourth dhyanas, and they say, "Yeah, I had that one!" Misconceiving the Dharma to fit their own expectations, some people go so far as to redefine classic Buddhist concepts in terms of their own experience. It is crucial to study the authoritative accounts of the dhyanas. What are the causes of the dhyanas, what is their nature, and what are their results? The full picture will not appear in a short passage or a select aphorism. Misinformed people think that a dhyana is something you can score at a weekend retreat, and they boast: "I had this dhyana. Then I lost it, but it came back." It sounds like a missing sock!

Buddhaghosa was not only an exceedingly authoritative commentator and scholar, but he was the chronicler of the first nine hundred years after the Buddha—prime time for Buddhists, especially the Theravadins. In this glorious era, many people achieved advanced stages of the path, all the states of samadhi in the form and formless realms, arhatship, and so forth. Buddhaghosa made no claim to be an innovative philosopher or a contemplative adept. Drawing from the Buddha's teachings, upon which he wrote many commentaries, his masterpiece, *The Path of Purification*, narrates meticulous descriptions of the practices, struggles, and accomplishments of adepts during this golden age.

Buddhaghosa's *The Path of Purification* is a brilliant record of theory and practice in the Theravadin tradition. He includes compelling accounts of innumerable accomplished yogis and arhats from this founding era. He claims that when one has actually achieved the state of the first dhyana, samadhi can be sustained "for a whole night and a whole day, just as a healthy man, after rising from his seat, could stand a whole day."[60] When you enter into and abide in the first dhyana, indicated by the Buddha's experience under the rose apple tree, you can sustain your samadhi for a whole night and a whole day. It is clear that achieving the first dhyana is an exceptional, transcendent state if you can maintain unwavering samadhi for a twenty-four-hour period.

Such an accomplishment is not common. I would love to hear about anyone who achieves this on a weekend retreat. The top neuroscientists will definitely invite him or her into their labs because they have never tested anyone like this, as far as I know. The actual first dhyana—characterized by the sheer power to remain in samadhi for twenty-four hours, little notice of the passage of time, full use of conceptual ability, and a largely nonconceptual repose—is an extraordinary state.

Free of Obscurations

Is the point of this practice to win samadhi marathons? No, the primary reason that the first dhyana is said to be an indispensable foundation for fully effective vipashyana is that it temporarily subdues mental obscurations, or hindrances. This is not irreversible, but your mind is no longer prone to the five obscurations that disrupt the balance of the mind: sensual craving, malice, laxity and lethargy, excitation and anxiety, and uncertainty. With the achievement of the first dhyana, you are free of these factors, albeit temporarily.

This is like receiving the tetanus vaccine, which can prevent the disease for ten years or so. If you get regular booster shots, you can avoid contracting tetanus. Still, your immunity is not permanent, and if the vaccination wears off, you could be infected. In a similar fashion, by achieving the first dhyana, you will be free for as long as you sustain it. If you let it atrophy, you will lose it. If you recognize its profound benefits and modify your behavior, by developing at least a quasi-contemplative lifestyle, you can sustain it.

When you abide in the first dhyana, sensual craving does not arise. Although not eradicated, it is dormant. For all practical purposes, the five obscurations no longer trouble you. Enjoyment of good food, art, music, and the beauty of nature does not lead to craving. You know that these are not true sources of happiness because you have discovered an authentic source. This is not a reasoned deduction but a conviction based on personal experience. Settling in the first dhyana yields a blissful sense of well-being, and everything else pales in comparison. Who would search downstream for a few flakes of gold when they have found the mother lode—the source? Sensual craving no longer occurs, making life much more peaceful. Malice and enmity, which so often arise when someone thwarts our desires, disappear as well. Laxity, lethargy, excitation, and anxiety are banished from the scene by excellent samadhi. Finally, the plague of doubts and uncertainties simply evaporates. Such are the results of abiding within the attentional balance of the first dhyana.

We often deny our potential by thinking, "Even if I tried, I probably wouldn't achieve anything. Maybe nobody's ever done it." Of course, if we don't try, we'll never succeed. Nevertheless, there is value in vibrant, energetic skepticism that challenges us to look more closely. How can we be sure that death entails an absolute termination of an individual consciousness? Was there a continuity of lives before this one? Such important questions challenge our very notions of existence. If there is no continuity, and we are locked into a handful of decades, I can live with that. But if there have been countless previous existences, and this continuum of consciousness cannot be snuffed out—like a Buddhist principle of conservation of consciousness—I'd like some idea of what's in store, before I die.

These questions concerning the nature of the mind, consciousness, and death are sometimes presented as imponderable. Theologians and philosophers call them perennial mysteries. How could you possibly know the nature of death? You can't know anything when you're dead, and until then, you're still alive. German philosopher Immanuel Kant (1724–1804) believed that death is unknowable. More often, the assumption goes unsaid: the mind is just a product of the brain. Many people are quite content with that assumption. On the other hand, if the continuity of consciousness before this life and following it can be determined through meditative experience, this is no longer a metaphysical issue but an empirical one. This Buddhist hypothesis can best be put to the test if one develops excellent samadhi, which is not a common strength in our modern world. India developed a vast tradition of samadhi, which has been maintained by Tibetans and other Buddhist cultures.

In order to be irreversibly free of the mental afflictions, one needs to develop the extraordinary mental health and balance of the first dhyana as a platform for the real work—practicing vipashyana to effect a full cure. The achievement of shamatha still occurs today, especially in the Tibetan tradition, and is virtually equated with the achievement of the first dhyana; this is more accurately called "access to the first dhyana." Achieving shamatha is right on the threshold, where samadhi can be sustained for about four hours instead of twenty-four. Note that these are not precise limits.

Even if you have achieved only access to the first dhyana and not the actual state of the first dhyana, you are equally free of the five obscurations. They can still crop up on occasion, but they're manageable. This means that you can tap into them out of curiosity, or perhaps to transmute them, as is done in certain types of Vajrayana practice. By utilizing the energy of desire and transmuting it, or sublimating it (in Freudian terms), this energy can actually propel you toward enlightenment. In this case, you might not want to remain in the actual state of the first dhyana because you may not be able to give rise to desires at all.

Luminous Glow

The notion of the five obscurations raises this question: What do they obscure? Of course they implicitly obscure buddha nature, but you will not realize buddha nature simply by achieving the first dhyana and becoming free of the five obscurations. They also explicitly obscure something more proximate: the substrate consciousness (Skt. *alayavijñana*). The substrate consciousness is the relative ground state from which the psyche emerges each time we awaken, and into which the psyche dissolves each time we fall asleep. When you access the substrate consciousness clearly and vividly by way of shamatha, it's like falling deep asleep while remaining luminously awake. This state is imbued with three universal qualities: bliss, luminosity, and nonconceptuality.

Everyone's individual psyche is unique, like a snowflake. Your psyche is built from the experiences of this lifetime and is influenced by past lifetimes, genetic dispositions, parenting, cultural values, and language, which make your psyche and everyone else's absolutely unique. But if we melt any snowflake, its fundamental ingredient is simply water. Similarly, when you or anyone "melts" the psyche by using shamatha, and it settles back into the substrate consciousness from which it arose, then the three traits that you or anyone will find, regardless of genetic and cultural background, are that the substrate consciousness is blissful, luminous, and nonconceptual.

The substrate (Skt. *alaya*) and the substrate consciousness are not the same. The substrate is the space of the mind itself, and the substrate consciousness is the awareness of that space. The substrate consciousness is the stem consciousness, whereas the psyche is a configured stem consciousness. Just as a stem cell becomes a specific kind of cell in the body, such as a blood cell or neuron, the stem consciousness becomes configured as a specific individual's psyche, which is precisely what psychologists study. The vast array of our mental states and processes is strongly conditioned by genetics, brain chemistry, diet, exercise, language, personal history, and social influences. Without addressing the precise details here, everyone's psyche has a finite duration, beginning in the womb and ending at death. Death is the end of the story for the psyche. The origin of the psyche is the subject of two primary hypotheses. One view is that the psyche emerges from the brain or is equivalent to brain function—the materialist hypothesis.

Consciousness emerging from a complex network of neurons seems just as improbable to me as an emotion arising from my laptop computer. The brain does have emergent properties—such as density and temperature—and they are all physical and are therefore physically measurable. Mental events have no physical attributes and are physically unmeasurable, so the evidence suggests that thoughts and emotions are not emergent properties of the brain. Any cell, whether a liver cell or a neuron, has descended from a stem cell. But no matter how complex this network of cells might be, it strikes me as mystical thinking to imagine that something as radically different as an emotion or a dream could emerge from neurons. We could just as easily believe in the emergence of a genie from a magic lamp.

The alternate hypothesis is that the psyche emerges not from neurons but from the substrate consciousness. If we develop the requisite skills of observation, we can actually witness mental events and emotions emerging from this dimension of awareness. Nevertheless, this does not eliminate the possibility that mental events emerge from the brain. Many scientists say that introspective observations and neuroscientific observations of the brain are concerned with the same phenomena. They assert that the mind and the brain are the same thing viewed from two different perspectives: inside and outside. This could be true, but so far there is no evidence for it.

Why do we often feel dull and lethargic? What obscures the innate luminosity of the mind's relative ground state? If one of the three fundamental qualities of the substrate consciousness is bliss, why don't we always feel blissful? These qualities are always present, but they are veiled by malice, sensual craving, and the other obscurations. Meditative quiescence is not like being gagged and bound. The mind is settled in a state of peaceful, luminous silence in which you can think at any time. Your abilities to investigate and analyze are on tap, but you are no longer subject to obsessive-compulsive ideation. You can finally switch off the mind's motor-mouth. The five obscurations no longer veil the natural serenity and silence of the substrate. On the other hand, without achieving the first dhyana, the Buddha's assessment is sobering:

> So long as these five obscurations are not abandoned, one considers oneself as indebted, sick, in bonds, enslaved, and lost on a desert track.[61]

In other words, don't be content with such a state. This is like living in a village where tuberculosis is endemic and everybody thinks it's incurable; people assume it's natural to cough chronically and die at the age of thirty-five. A doctor might visit such a community and say, "Please realize that you're sick and there's a cure!" In Buddhism, the typical mind is not considered to be a healthy mind. Don't tolerate mental illness any longer!

✥ 5 ✥
Mindfulness of the Body

MINDFULNESS BEGINS with the body: a composite of many elements, coarse and subtle, material and energetic, as well as real and imaginary. We instinctively associate our body with our very existence—we hold on to it for dear life. Following a pragmatic course, our starting point is the thing many of us identify with most strongly. The practice of mindfulness of the body comes directly from the Buddha's discourses. In the *Parayana Sutta*, he offers a remarkably succinct instruction:

> I will teach the destination and the path leading to the destination. Listen to what I say. What is the destination? The eradication of craving, the eradication of hostility, and the eradication of delusion are what is called the destination. And what is the path leading to the destination? Mindfulness directed toward the body: this is what is called the path leading to the destination.
>
> In this way, I have taught you the destination and the path leading to the destination. That which should be done out of compassion by a caring teacher who desires the welfare of his students, I have done for you.
>
> There are secluded places. Meditate; do not be negligent! Don't have regrets later! This is my instruction to you.[62]

As the Buddha's pithy instruction to a group of disciples reveals, the close application of mindfulness to the body is an enormously profound practice, whose scope extends far beyond this introductory text. As we attend to and scrutinize the various elements of the body, while focusing on the tactile sense, the other senses are irrelevant, so the eyes may be closed. The eyes may also be left open, but without giving any attention to visual appearances.

GUIDED MEDITATION:
Mindfulness of the Body I

Scan tactile sensations in three dimensions—
observing without mental projections

Settle the body in its natural state. Utterly relax with each breath as you settle your respiration in its natural rhythm. Let your awareness permeate the field of tactile sensations, attending especially to the sensations of the breath wherever they arise. You might notice a mental image or map of the body that arises spontaneously, but to the best of your ability, ignore it. Simply attend to what is being presented to tactile perception, in your best approximation of bare attention. Maintain awareness from moment to moment of everything that arises in this field, with no conceptual elaborations or projections. In the felt, there is just the felt.

For a few minutes, narrow the focus of your attention to a small zone of breath-related sensations at the apertures of the nostrils or just above the upper lip. Keep your eyes soft, let your forehead be open and spacious, and disengage the focus of your mental attention from visual perception. Remain engaged with the flow of tactile sensations throughout the course of the breath. Let your mindfulness flow together with the sensations of the breath. Keeping your body as still as possible throughout the session will help to maintain the integrity of attention and avoid fragmentation.

Now, while keeping your visual perception disengaged, redirect your mental attention to begin the process of scanning through the body in three dimensions. Direct your attention to an area an inch or two in diameter on the surface of the crown of the head. Observe whatever tactile sensations arise in the area spotlighted by awareness. Expand this area to a hand's-width field on the crown of the head and focus on tactile sensations there, such as throbbing, tingling, pressure, movement, warmth, or cold. To the best of your ability, observe with bare attention and no conceptualization.

Shift the hand's-width field of awareness slowly over the surface of your skin, starting down the left side of the head, to the ear. Gradually shift the field of awareness around to the back of the head and then continue on to the right side of the head. You may conjoin this scanning with the rhythm of the breath. With each in-breath, stabilize and attend very closely, and as you breathe out, gently shift the attention to the next region. In the sensed, let there be only the sensed, not adding or deleting anything from immediate tactile sensation.

Gradually slip the field of awareness to your forehead. If a mental image pops up, release it and attend solely to tactile sensations. Slip the field of awareness down to the left eye, cheek, and jaw, followed by the center of the face, nose, and mouth, and finally to the right eye, cheek, and jaw. Expand the field to cover the entire surface of the face.

Tactile sensations occur inside the head as well as on the surface. Gradually move the two-dimensional plane of awareness from the face, through the center of the head, to the back of the head. Check carefully, applying close mindfulness. Scan this vertical plane again, moving from the back of the head through the interior to the face, noting the various sensations arising in these planes.

Now expand the field of awareness to three dimensions, attending simultaneously to the sensations arising throughout the entire volume of the head. Attend closely to what you perceive and note also what is not perceived. Set this three-dimensional volume of awareness in motion, stabilizing with each in-breath and moving slowly with each out-breath. Move gradually down the neck, over to the left shoulder, down the arm to the elbow, to the wrist, and to the tips of the fingers. Let the field of awareness leap from the left hand to the right hand like a flame leaping between two torches, moving up from the tips of the fingers to the right wrist, the right elbow, and finally to the right shoulder.

Imagining your torso as a tick-tack-toe grid, move the three-dimensional field of awareness to the upper right side of the chest. As you breathe in and out, focus first on the front sector of the upper right side of the chest. Then scan through the interior to the back sector of the upper right side of the chest and return to the front. Move the field of awareness to the upper center of the chest, from the front sector to the back and front again. Finally, shift your focus to the upper left side of the chest, from the front to the back and front again.

Move down to the middle left side of the torso, scanning in sections from the front to the back and front again. Slip over to the middle center part, focusing on the solar plexus, and then move to the middle right side of the torso.

Scan slowly through the lower right region of the pelvis, the lower center region, and the lower left region. Move the field of awareness down to the left buttock, noting the points of exterior contact with your seat; with each exhalation, gradually move it down the left thigh to the knee, the ankle, the foot, and the tips of the toes. Redirect the field of awareness to the right buttock, moving down the right thigh to the knee, the ankle, the foot, and the tips of the toes.

Focus your attention once again at the crown of the head and take a minute or two to scan from the top of the head through the torso and down the arms and legs to the toes. Scan again from the crown of the head to the toes, moving the field of awareness with each out-breath. Repeat this for a third and final time.

Now instantly expand the field of awareness to pervade the whole body at once, illuminating the tactile field without mental projections or conceptual overlays. In the felt, there is just the felt.

If you still feel fresh, you may continue directly to the next session, taking a moment to stretch. ❦

GUIDED MEDITATION:
Mindfulness of the Body II

Attend closely to the field of the body—
observing solidity, moisture, heat, and motion

Settle the body in its natural state and the respiration in its natural rhythm. Then, like turning on a light to illuminate an entire room, let your awareness illuminate the entire field of tactile sensations throughout the body. Within this field, attend specifically to tactile appearances of firmness and solidity known as the earth element—for example, where your feet or buttocks rest.

Attend closely to the nature of the earth element, observing it nakedly, with no conceptual superimpositions. Examine a tactile region where the earth element is dominant and inspect it very closely, as if with a microscope. Is it solid throughout? How firm and substantial is the earth element? Do you find anything in the appearance of the earth element that is stable and unchanging?

The Tibetan term (*'byung ba*) translated here as "element" also has the connotation of emergence—in this case, the emergence of solidity. As these appearances of solidity and firmness emerge, are they stable or unstable, changing or unchanging, a source of comfort, discomfort, or neither? Is there anything that suggests ownership? Are they inherently yours, or do you simply have a privileged perspective on the tactile field in which these events are arising?

Are there any tactile appearances of the water element emerging within this field from moment to moment, such as a sense of moisture in the mouth? Attend closely to fluidity and moistness. What is the nature of the water element?

Can you detect regions of the interior and exterior of this field that vary from cold to hot? Carefully inspect the nature of the fire element emerging in these sensations.

Direct your attention to any emergences of lightness and motility: the air element. This includes the coarse movements associated with the respiration, circulation, and digestion, as well as more subtle motions, tingling sensations, itching, and vibrations. As you attend to all the subtle and coarse movements within this field, is there anything that suggests ownership, or are these merely emergences of motion, arising within a tactile field to which you have privileged access?

You can observe this field as no one else can, so let the light of your awareness illuminate every nook and cranny. Is there anything beyond the emergences of the earth, water, fire, and air elements that you have not noted? Can you observe the tactile space in which these elements emerge from moment to moment? Observe closely. Is this space presented to you or projected by your mind? We commonly designate this field of tactile sensations with the words "my body." How well does the immediate experience of this tactile field correspond to your conceptual notion of your body?

As you attend closely to this entire field, do you find anything present within it that seems to be unchanging, stable, and enduring over time? Check carefully. Are the appearances within this field by nature pleasant, unpleasant, or neither? Are they true sources of either pleasure or pain? While attending very closely, with as little conceptual overlay as possible, inspect the events within this field. Is there anything here to suggest that these experiences are by nature yours, or that they constitute your "self"? Or are they simply impersonal events arising within the field of experience?

Now rest your awareness in this field, without questioning, and simply attend to whatever arises from moment to moment. Let reality speak for itself. In the sensed, there is just the sensed. ☞

On the Elements

When we closely investigate the experience of human perception, we find that the fundamental physical constituents of reality include the elements of earth, water, fire, and air. When the earth element predominates, we feel solidity. When water predominates, we feel fluidity. The fire element makes us feel hot. The body is suffused with the air element, manifesting as continuous movement and change on coarse and subtle levels. Many of the sensations that emerge are expressions of motion and change. In fact, all experiences include all four elements to varying degrees; at times one element is predominant. Something that combines fluidity with solidity is viscous; if it's also warm and in motion, it includes all four elements.

These elements are not the ones described by modern physics because they pertain to a different domain. We are not investigating what exists independently of experience but the constituents of experience itself, and specifically tactile perception. We cannot see the earth element, even though various optical illusions can be created to give the impression of solidity, such as rocks that look exactly like granite but are made of foam. The eye cannot distinguish heavy from light. Visual perception cannot detect solidity, fluidity, or heat. When seeing a candle, we superimpose heat on the visual impression because we know candles are hot, but we are projecting from memory.

Earth, water, fire, and air are objects of tactile perception. The air element is defined as that which is light and motile. You might say, "Nobody could persuade me that I don't see motion!" If a batter waiting for a pitch couldn't see motion, how could he hit the ball? Motion or motility is an expression of the air element, which is an object of tactile perception. When we feel motion, we know it without looking. Motion seems to be an object of visual perception, and under coarse investigation, of course we see motion. But it gets more interesting if we look closely. When we watch a movie or television, we think we see things moving across the screen. But in fact, nothing moves across the screen. A pattern of dots changing in stepwise fashion gives the illusion of motion. Ordinary visual perception is fundamentally the same. Nothing actually moves across the visual field, yet there is the illusion of motion.

Incorporating space as an element in the practice is a matter of semantics. Space is not simply another element like fire and water—space is fundamental. According to Buddhist cosmogony, the elements of earth, water, fire, and air arise out of space, and they dissolve back into space. This same description also appears in the teachings on the substrate consciousness and the substrate, the luminous vacuity that is the space of the mind. When we fall asleep, the psyche dissolves into the substrate consciousness, and all appearances dissolve into the substrate. In deep sleep, no appearances apart from the substrate manifest. Dream appearances emerge from the substrate and ultimately dissolve back into the substrate. When we awaken, all our sensory and mental appearances arise from the substrate. Whether we are asleep or awake, the substrate is the space of the mind.

INTERNALLY, EXTERNALLY, AND BOTH

Welcome to your body—it might be a bit different from what you had imagined! This is a powerful refrain throughout the Buddha's teachings on the four close applications of mindfulness to the body, feelings, mental states, and phenomena. In the *Satipatthana Sutta,* he says:

> One dwells observing the body as the body internally, or one dwells observing the body as the body externally, or one dwells observing the body as the body both internally and externally.[63]

In this practice, observing the body as the body internally means directing awareness reflexively toward our own body in order to become familiar with it in the immediacy of experience. Our goal is to observe what is actually presented versus what is projected. Bare attention pervades the body like sheet lightning, simultaneously illuminating the whole field and emergences of solidity, fluidity, and so forth. The vipashyana investigations focused on the body are designed to gain a very clear sense that none of these internal organs are imprinted with "I, me, and mine," which is a very transformative insight.

In another session, or between sessions, one dwells observing the body as the body externally, which means attending closely to someone else's body. This is an amazingly powerful practice that is sometimes completely overlooked in modern accounts of mindfulness. If you have a willing partner, you may be able to attend very closely and gaze attentively without making them uncomfortable. Otherwise, without drawing attention to yourself, attend to others very closely, directing your attention outward. Attending closely to the body as the body externally is an insight practice of observing what is being presented versus what is projected. See if you can surgically peel away the layers of conceptual projection, transference, assumptions, likes, and dislikes, and attend to what is actually being presented. Travel offers many opportunities to discreetly observe people coming and going in airplanes, trains, restaurants, and waiting lounges.

In order to attend to another person, you don't have to be clairvoyant, but examining the body externally doesn't utilize tactile perception. We have privileged access only to tactile sensations within our own bodies. Although we can pick up our own surface impressions in contact with someone else's body, we can't detect their internal sensations. Attending to the body of another utilizes inference and empathy in addition to bare attention. Most of the mindfulness practices described by the Buddha, such as contemplating the bodily constituents of organs, blood, bones, and elements, cannot possibly be done with bare attention. These endeavors require active contemplation, not merely passive witnessing.

By attending to our own body with bare attention, the richness of direct perception is very memorable. We will not simply forget the immediate experience of corporeality during daily activities, and we will also remember what was not found in the field of the body. Grokking what it's like to be embodied from the inside out unlocks a database of insight. No medical doctor can perceive this by studying someone else's body. No PET scan or MRI can capture the sensations of another's embodiment. The closest achievement might be the Chinese, Indian, and Tibetan doctors who use pulse diagnosis, detecting incredibly subtle signals from another person's body directly through their fingertips. They don't quite get under the skin, but they come very close.

Drawing from memories of our own body, we attend to someone else's body visually; using imagination and inference, we can see more than we normally would. I can't see much of my own body, whereas my view of your body is better than yours. I've seen myself in a mirror enough to know what I look like. By the power of inference, I can create a basis for empathy in wisdom. This becomes enormously important in the close application of mindfulness to feelings, as well as to mental processes such as fear, anxiety, love, affection, and sadness.

If we have directly experienced the richly textured layers of our own mental states, strong intuitions will arise when we attend closely to another person. By quieting the mind and releasing any expectations, memories, or desires, we can attend to someone else. What fresh appearances are being displayed from moment to moment? With training by an expert such as Paul Ekman, we can become quite discerning in our ability to read other people's facial expressions and strongly intuit their expressed emotions. Having closely attended to our own mental processes and quieted our own mind, when we attend very closely to another person, we will not simply project our own experiences on them.

For example, when my little grandson runs to me with a big smile and his arms outstretched, I surmise that he's a very happy boy; this is not merely projection. But am I drawing a causal inference, like assuming there's a fire when I see smoke, or is there something more immediate that we might call intuition? This is an interesting empirical question, and the answer could be quite subtle. Direct perception, valid intuition, inference, and sheer projection might be four overlapping modes of mentation. But even if the distinctions are a bit mushy, such as the ones that philosopher Ludwig Wittgenstein (1889–1951) called family resemblances, with no hard-cut borders between one and the next, I suspect that different brain mechanisms are involved in perception, intuition, inference, and projection.

Finally, we can dwell observing the body as the body both internally and externally. There are various ways of accomplishing this alternation of attention between internal and external, with the goal of recognizing the profound degree of commonality between our own and others' bodies. The Dalai Lama strongly emphasizes this powerful theme as he travels throughout the world, encountering myriad nationalities, ethnic groups, and cultures. Although he is on many missions, he always highlights the common ground we share. Of course there are also significant differences between groups. We are often inclined to believe that anyone not like us must be inferior, which leads to ideological conflicts, racism, gender bias, bigotry, ethnic cleansing, and religious warfare. Instead, we should focus on our common ground, attending internally and externally while exploring our mutual interdependence.

As It Is

The ancient commentary known as the *Vibhanga* is at least 1,500 years old and is based upon eight hundred years of earlier experience.[64] It explains the phrase "internally and externally" as describing the understanding of a contemplated object as such—naked observation. Observe whatever you are attending to objectively, letting it speak for itself. Peel off the conceptual and subjective overlays projected upon what James called the raw stuff of pure experience. Attend to it as closely as possible, stripping away the embellishments that have been superimposed on perception.

Attend closely to the body internally and externally, without considering whether it is part of your own subjective experience or that of others. Eliminate any notions of "I" internally and "not I" externally. Simply attend nakedly, allowing the bifurcation between an absolutely external object and an absolutely internal subject to melt into a unified experience. Attend simply to what is being presented. In the sensed, let there be just the sensed.

Bear in mind that the five elements here refer not only to the components of the human body. We have some direct experience of the referent of the term "earth element." When we probe closely in a mental biopsy of tactile sensations, the earth element is much more ephemeral than it seems at first glance. Probing into the body, there are elements of earth, water, fire, air, and the space element as the context for the other four. Similarly, when picking up my wristwatch, I sense the earth element, no moisture, a very low gradient of the fire element, and not much motion. If I put my finger into a thermos, I find the water element.

According to the Buddhist hypothesis, everything we experience by tactile perception consists of earth, water, fire, and air emerging within the element of space. When I attend very closely, there is no absolute demarcation between the earth element of my hand and the earth element of my watch. The earth element arises without partitioning itself into my part and the other part. It arises in interdependence, rather than one isolated earth element bumping into another one. The body is embedded in a field of earth, water, fire, air, and space elements. The Buddhist periodic table of elements is much shorter than Mendeleev's.

The differences between copper, iron, gold, and silver are important to a metallurgist, but they are not very useful from a contemplative perspective. When we probe phenomenologically into the world of immediate experience, five elements seem sufficient. Can you observe anything that falls outside these five categories?

We have been discussing the close application of mindfulness to the body's tactile field. We sense the body via more than just tactility, but in my experience the tactile field is quite prominent. For example, if a stone hits me, I'll know it when I feel it, even without seeing it. The tactile sense is home base. The stone's visual shape and color appear secondarily and separate from tactile sensations. A sound might emerge out of the stone's contact with the earth element, and taste and smell might even be invoked. We perceive our bodies by way of all five senses, but the tactile and visual senses are primary. We notice our body visually—or the portions we can see, such as our hands—as shapes and colors embedded within a larger mosaic of shapes and colors. Visual attention cannot identify certain parts as ours. The sound of our voice is embedded in an auditory field, where many sounds are arising. Likewise, the odor of our own body coexists with others in the olfactory field.

The close application of mindfulness to the body refers not only to this bag of skin and its contents; it also implicitly entails attending to the whole environment of our embodied experience. The tactile, visual, olfactory, auditory, and gustatory experiences of the body are embedded in larger fields of experience corresponding to the five senses. Others' bodies and experiences emerge from these same fields, so in attending to the body both internally and externally, we break down the superimposed conceptual barriers that divide internal from external.

This practice is very rich. It can be pursued during formal meditation sessions and in public places such as airports. Shopping malls offer fascinating subject matter. In the *Satipatthana Sutta*, the Buddha provides an instruction on maintaining the continuity of practice between formal sessions:

Again, monks, he reviews this same body, however it is placed, however disposed, as consisting of the elements thus:

"In this body there are the earth element, the water element, the fire element, and the air element."[65]

A practitioner sees his body, under all circumstances, as consisting of the elements earth, water, fire, and air interacting within the framework of space. This aspect of formal practice has an enormously practical import in Tibetan medicine, which is embedded in Indian Ayurvedic medicine.[66] The constitutional model of the body is based on the three humors of phlegm, bile, and wind, which are directly related to the elements of earth plus water, fire, and air respectively. When these humors fall out of balance, we experience illness. Tibetan doctors employ a wide variety of treatments, including dietary regimens, herbal compounds, and moxibustion, to restore health by balancing the elements within the body. The body and the physical world in which it is embedded are understood to consist of the four elements emerging from the space element.

The Buddha's discourses include quite elaborate instructions, well worth reading, on the practice of introspection between sessions and throughout the day. Introspection is not simply a matter of focusing on our mental states. This reflexive awareness, which has a connotation of clear comprehension, attends to the movements of our body, the content and tone of our voice, our mental processes, and all our activities, such as eating and walking. It is mindful awareness of being embodied in the world and of conduct in specific situations arising from moment to moment. It asks ethical questions such as, "Is this appropriate and optimal in my present context?" Reflexive awareness is central to this practice.

Experiential Worlds

Buddhist contemplative inquiry is focused on the world of experience, which is quite unlike the Cartesian world that is split into primary and secondary attributes, a distinction that has been central to physics and modern science since the time of Galileo. These scientists took it as axiomatic that some attributes exist absolutely, as it were, from God's perspective, unrelated to any type of human sensory or mental awareness. In their view, God is absolute, and he sees the entire universe with perfect objectivity. These researchers were intent on leaping out of the goldfish bowl of human perception to see the universe from God's perspective. They used technology, integrated with mathematics, which they viewed as the language of God, in attempting to transcend the limitations of their own physical senses.

Primary attributes are those attributes considered to be absolutely existent, from God's omniscient perspective: things like mass, physical extension, location, and motion. Even if there were no sentient beings in the universe, such things would still exist. A tree would be massive, with location, height, and the power to make ripples in the atmosphere if it fell, regardless of whether anyone detected them or not.

Ours is merely an anthropomorphic perception of the world, by way of such secondary attributes as warmth, color, sound, and taste. According to this view, secondary attributes, such as the warmth or color of a bottle of water, are not inherent in the water and plastic, which consist only of molecules. The warmth is said to be a secondary attribute that arises in relationship to the awareness of someone who is holding the bottle. Colors are not really out there; they arise only relative to visual perception. Sounds are not really out there either; they arise when waves in the air interact with the auditory cortex. Scents are just encounters between molecules in suspension and the olfactory bulbs. Similarly, there is no taste in food—only in the consumption of it.

We might say we were deceived at that marvelous restaurant because there was actually no taste in any of those fourteen courses. Taste arises only in relationship to one's palate, and my gustatory faculty is not refined enough to fully appreciate what that meal cost. I should have received a discount because the food contained only molecules, and the tastes that arose were far too subtle for my mediocre faculties! Only a real foodie could have appreciated the chef's artistry.

Buddhism makes no such distinction between primary and secondary attributes. We are instructed to simply attend to and understand the world of experience. The five elements are described, along with derivative attributes, such as roughness, smoothness, and viscosity, but these are not ontologically different from the elements out of which they emerge. It is not taught that some attributes are absolutely existent and others appear only relative to perception. You will not hear Tibetan lamas discussing primary and secondary attributes unless they have studied European philosophy, because the idea of understanding reality independent of anyone's experience would not be meaningful to them.

The overall theme of the close application of mindfulness is the direct observation of the elements of earth and so forth, as they emerge and dissipate. They are not fixed or unchanging. You can see this for yourself, from your own ringside seat overlooking the field of tactile events in your own corporeality. Is anything ultimately durable? How do suffering and pleasure manifest? Observe for yourself. Does anything in the nature of tactile events suggest a personal identity or ownership, or are they merely anonymous, impersonal events arising in dependence upon causes and conditions? Is the earth element that is inside your body the same as the earth element in the outside world? A central theme of this practice, beyond merely identifying the elements, is to inspect them closely.

One statement by the Buddha has been quoted many times, and people find it quite profound. In the *Samyutta Nikaya* he says:

> It is in this fathom-long body, with its perceptions and its mind, that I describe the world, the origin of the world, the cessation of the world, and the way leading to the cessation of the world.[67]

A fathom is the span of outstretched arms, which is about equal to one's height. The body, with its mind and perceptions, is quite a different starting point from the atoms and molecules of a materialistic worldview. The Buddha's description of the world, the origin of the world, the cessation of the world, and the way leading to the cessation of the world takes place within this psycho-physiological system—the measure of all things. From a physicist's perspective, our bodies are made of stardust, the same stuff that constitutes the universe, and everything is permeated by the background radiation of the Big Bang.[68] We are, in fact, attending to a microcosm of the macrocosm.

An interesting point, which often escapes the attention of physicists who focus professionally on the external world, is that in this fathom-long body, not only are there atoms and molecules, and not only earth, water, fire, and air elements, but there are also perceptions and mind. The practice of mindfulness shows the way to understand the world, the origin of the world, the cessation of the world, and the way leading to the cessation of the world—all inseparable from body and mind.

Self No Self

When you pay very close attention to the body and mind, do you ever observe your self? It is important to note that the Buddha never said there was no self at all. He actually said, "I do not say there is no self." It is foolish to say there is no self because we all are ourselves. What the Buddha was addressing is our unrealistic notion of the self and our mistaken ways of apprehending it, for which I gave the example of thinking I'm Napoleon. Such thinking is obviously delusional.

More commonly, I may conceive of myself as an inherently real entity that possesses a body and mind. The notion that I stand apart from, observe, and control my body and mind is quite unremarkable. I feel I really do exist. If you insult me, I'll be unhappy; if you praise me, I'll be thrilled. You're not judging my body or my mind—it's me you're talking about. I'm the real target of praise or ridicule. I am not my body or my mind, even though I'm closely tied to them and have meaningful control over them: my hand moves at my will, and I think what I choose to think.

When we actually observe the body and mind, what appears is more like the froth on a boiling pot of soup—nothing is stable. Everything emerges and disappears from moment to moment. The body is in constant flux: cells are dying and being reborn; blood is circulating; the breath moves in and out. Similarly, nothing is stable in the mind. Mental events arise in staccato fashion, becoming a dynamic flow of thoughts and images tumbling over themselves in rapid succession. From physiological and mental perspectives, everything is in constant flux. Nevertheless, as I grasp on to my reified self, I seem to change only at a glacial pace. I'm not immutable, and I'm not the same as I was at the age of five, but I'm still me.

This is a description of an individual's actual lived sense of self. The experiential sense of "I am" does exist, and it has real effects. If you praise or abuse me, I will feel happy or sad as a result of grasping on to my sense of self. But the question is this: Does my sense of self correspond to something in reality? Recall my example. If you think you're Napoleon, your sense of being Napoleon will have real influence on your behavior. You will affect a phony French accent and expect people to salute you. The belief that you're Napoleon is definitely real. Wake up! There is nothing in reality corresponding to your sense that "I am Napoleon." There's no Napoleon here.

Likewise, investigate the body, feelings, and mental states as they interact with the environment as a whole. Can you perceive the self or find any evidence that such a self is actually present anywhere in this matrix of psychosomatic and environmental events? Do you see any influence by such a self? Waking up means recognizing "Aha! There's no self in here, no self out there, and no self in between." Does this mean that I don't exist at all? No, that's silly; I've simply realized that I'm not who I thought I was, not that I don't exist at all.

In fact, what the Buddha actually said was, "I do not say there is a self; I do not say there is not a self." He wasn't being coy. In saying, "I do not say there is a self," he refuses to affirm what we now believe ourselves to be. In saying, "I do not say there is not a self," he refuses to say that we don't exist at all. Instead, he says, "Investigate." When you see how you don't exist, it's like the analogy of irreversibly fathoming that you're not Napoleon. Nevertheless, the phrase "I am" will continue to be useful in everyday life. "Where are you?" "I'm over here—not Napoleon, but me." This is like the Zen notion popularized in Donovan Leitch's 1967 lyric: "First there is a mountain, then there is no mountain, then there is."[69]

Having recognized that I am not Napoleon, how do I actually exist? Does the word "I" have any referent at all? On a conventional level, it is certainly meaningful. Somebody is writing this, but is he found inside the cortex, or the heart, or is he nowhere to be found? In a very meaningful way of speaking, of course I exist, but this ongoing flow of arising is always a relative one. As I write this, I'm arising relative to a notion of you, my readers. When I stop writing, my sense of self as an author will no longer arise explicitly. When I'm home alone, I might arise from moment to moment relative to my own mental awareness of being present. If my wife appears, I will arise relative to her. My sense of self is always a relative one, arising in dependent origination. It does not exist as an isolated, self-existent entity, an immutable ego in charge of body and mind.

The Buddha did not refute the existence of the ordinary self, just as he would not have refuted the existence of an ordinary bottle of water, for example. If you examine a bottle of water closely, the bottle of water is not found in the cap, the contents, the empty bottle, or the label. Furthermore, there is no bottle of water apart from these parts. Since the bottle of water is not found among the parts or apart from them, there is no independently existing bottle of water. But in ordinary speech, of course, there is something we call a "bottle of water." We have a conceptual framework in which "bottle of water" means something. Depending on our needs and circumstances, the acceptable characteristics of a bottle of water might include a visibly intact seal, adequate pressurization, a cool temperature, a future expiration date, low sodium content, and a specific brand. The usefulness of the designation "bottle of water" arises relative to our particular circumstances and is found neither within the parts nor apart from them. The self exists in the same way as a bottle of water.

Guided Meditation:
Falling Asleep I

Attend to the breath throughout the body—
falling asleep in a smooth transition

Within the three modes of mindfulness of the breath, in which the attention is focused on the entire body, the rise and fall of the abdomen, or the sensations at the nostrils, one in particular can be very helpful in getting a good night's sleep—full-body awareness. Lying comfortably in bed with your pillow under your head, have a final session in the corpse pose (Skt. *shavasana*), with eyes closed, arms extended thirty degrees to the sides with palms up, legs straight, and feet falling to the sides.

Allow your awareness to diffusely permeate the entire field of tactile sensations, relaxing with every out-breath and simply being present with whatever sensations arise on the in-breath. Breathing out, release all thoughts, images, memories, and expectations and then gently breathe in. Settle in a natural rhythm, like watching the ocean on a pleasant afternoon as the waves flow on shore and drift back. Let the breath be soft and smooth, and simply remain present as you settle into a progressively deeper sense of ease, relaxation, and release.

After some time, you will notice a nebulous, velvety quality that signals the end of your shamatha session. Roll into your sleeping position, preferably on your right side, and fall asleep in a smooth transition. Mindfulness of the breath can be a glorious practice for awakening and liberation, as well as for getting a good night's sleep. Both are very important because if you are chronically sleep-deprived, your chances for liberation are very slim. ☚

❖ 6 ❖
Mindfulness of Feelings

THE SECOND of the four close applications of mindfulness concerns the fundamental nature of feelings of pleasure, pain, and indifference—our deepest concerns. We know many other types and nuances of feelings and emotions, but they are all derivatives and will be investigated in the application of mindfulness to the mind.

HEART'S CRADLE

In preparation, we first cultivate a sense of loving-kindness (Skt. *maitri;* Pali *metta*). Buddhism is pervaded by the theme of lateralization. The left hand represents wisdom, while the right hand represents compassion and skillful means. The practices of mindfulness described here develop the foundation of left-hand wisdom by making the mind serviceable for the cultivation of insight, presence, clarity, memory, and intelligence. The complementary practices of cultivating loving-kindness, compassion, and qualities of the heart develop the right-hand foundation: the capacity for empathy. By learning to attend closely to another sentient being, with a quiet mind and an open heart, we break down the barriers between our suffering and others' suffering. As Shantideva said, we are compelled to attend to suffering wherever it occurs, for suffering has no owner.

In balanced practice, we draw on wisdom to give meaning to our logical assessments. The skillful means of analysis reinforces our holistic vision of the world, invoking compassion. The union of wisdom and compassion is symbolized by the mudra of meditation, in which the left hand cradles the right, with the thumbs touching. Ram Dass's guru, Neem Karoli Baba (d. 1973),[70] described these two aspects by saying that when we look at the world with the eye of wisdom, we see that we are nothing, and when we look at the world with the eye of compassion, we see that we are everything. Of course, there is no reason to look with only one eye, so open both eyes.

GUIDED MEDITATION:
Loving-Kindness I

Radiate and reabsorb loving-kindness—
actualizing the highest aspirations

Begin, as always, by settling the body in its natural state, imbued with the three qualities of relaxation, stillness, and vigilance. Round off this initial settling with three slow, deep breaths. Settle your breath in its natural rhythm while attending mindfully to its sensations throughout the body.

Rise to the subtle challenge of attending to the breath very closely, without any influence from your desires or expectations about the breath. The essence of the practice is to observe closely but without exerting your will or deliberately modifying the breath in any way. Allow the body to establish the breath in its own rhythm and equilibrium.

Let your awareness descend and settle, quietly and luminously present, in the field of tactile sensations. Settle your mind in a quality of ease and relaxation, with your awareness in stillness and yet wide-awake, alert, and vivid.

We have predominantly cultivated the faculties of mindfulness and bare attention, with introspective modes of passive awareness and simple attentiveness. Now, apply your mind to the cultivation of loving-kindness by engaging your faculties of imagination, memory, and intelligence.

First, I invite you to imagine your own flourishing. How do you envision your happiness and the fulfillment of your dreams? What kind of satisfaction, joy, and meaning do you most deeply desire? Visualize your own well-being and the achievement of your highest ideals. Whether you conceive of it as awakening, liberation, actualization, or another term, boldly take the working hypothesis that you do in fact have the potential to realize such a state of flourishing.

In Buddhism we call this potential the buddha nature. Picture this immeasurable reservoir of innate natural resources—pristine awareness itself—as an orb of radiant white light at the heart chakra, in the center of your chest. This orb is quite small, but imagine it to be the wellspring of all virtue and a source of innate joy and happiness that lies in the deepest dimension of your own awareness.

Direct this heart of loving-kindness to yourself with the yearning: "May I find happiness and the causes of happiness. May I find the fulfillment that I seek." With each out-breath, imagine rays of light emanating from the orb of light at your heart, saturating every cell of your body and suffusing every aspect of your mind. With each out-breath, imagine actualizing the fulfillment you seek, here and now.

We certainly cannot find the happiness we seek on our own. We must rely upon others and our natural environment for basic sustenance, friendship, and support in reaching our ideals. In order to find the happiness, well-being, and fulfillment you seek, arouse a sense of loving-kindness and direct it toward the world around you with the yearning: "May I receive all that I need to find true fulfillment and genuine happiness. May the world rise up to support me with all the causes and conditions to fulfill my deepest aspirations."

With each in-breath, imagine the world answering your call to satisfy your innermost desires, giving you all you need to follow your path and realize your highest ideals. With each in-breath, imagine white light, as the expression of the kindness of others, flowing into your body and mind, satisfying every need. With each in-breath, arouse the yearning: "May I truly be well and happy, and may I freely receive all that I need to achieve such well-being."

Realizing the well-being that is your heart's desire will clearly require an inner transformation. We inevitably change from day to day and year to year. How would you like to evolve and transform in order to realize the well-being that is your innermost desire? From what qualities of mind and behavior would you love to be freed? With what positive qualities would you love to be endowed? The Buddha declared that as the potter shapes the pot and the fletcher shapes the arrow, so do the wise shape themselves. As the artist of your own being, in what ways would you love to shape, transform, and purify yourself to realize your highest ideals? Let your imagination play. With each out-breath, arouse the yearning: "May I so transform. May I be liberated and enriched by such qualities." With each out-breath, imagine rays of light once again flowing from the orb at your heart, purifying all obstructions on your path and imbuing you with all virtues to further your progress. Imagine the light of loving-kindness suffusing your entire being with every out-breath.

Now direct your loving-kindness to the world. We all inevitably influence our natural environment and sentient beings near and far. For the sake of your own happiness and fulfillment, envision your best possible offering to the world. From your own talents, abilities, and aspirations over the course of this lifetime and possibly others, what would you most like to give to those around you? What would ensure that your life is meaningful and fulfilled, giving you the deepest sense of satisfaction and no regrets? With each out-breath, let your heart radiate this light of loving-kindness to enrich the world, offering your finest service and the greatest good you can imagine. With each out-breath, arouse the yearning: "May we all find genuine happiness, the causes of genuine happiness, and the fulfillment we seek."

In conclusion, release all aspirations, imagery, desires, and mental objects. Let your awareness rest in its own nature, witnessing the sheer luminosity and cognizance of awareness itself. When awareness illuminates its own nature, this metacognition is the awareness of awareness, which we will explore more fully in chapter 8. ☞

On Aspiration

In the Buddhist understanding, loving-kindness and compassion are not classified as feelings or emotions, although they are commonly accompanied by feelings and emotions. Loving-kindness and compassion are considered aspirations. Loving-kindness is the wish that we may find happiness and the causes of happiness. Compassion is the wish that we may be free from suffering and the causes of suffering. These are heartfelt yearnings, not intellectual fabrications.

When a mother sees her child crying, she doesn't simply feel sad. The emotion she feels along with the child is called empathy. Along with this feeling, she has the aspiration, "May you be free of suffering and the causes of suffering." A mother's compassion for her child is an active aspiration that propels her into action to stop her child's suffering. She will protect, comfort, nurture, teach, and punish as needed, motivated by her compassionate aspiration.

When we actively cultivate the four immeasurables of loving-kindness, compassion, empathetic joy, and equanimity, these aspirations are accompanied by specific feelings. However, when we simply settle in the nature of awareness itself, experiencing sheer luminosity and cognizance within utter silence, this practice will bring us eventually to the substrate consciousness. In the culmination of shamatha practice, settling in the substrate consciousness, no ordinary experience manifests. There is no overt sense of loving-kindness or compassion.

When you arise from dwelling in the silent luminosity of the substrate consciousness and attend to the well-being of another person, you can offer your attention, utterly uncontaminated by selfish motivation, attachment, or aversion. This quality of attention to another person manifests as resplendent, luminous presence. Body language, facial expressions, words, tone, and behavior are clearly and accurately perceived. For the moment, what we attend to is reality. When we bring clear attentiveness to another person, there is a high likelihood of empathy arising.

It might seem as though shamatha, which is luminous, clear, and sharp, is rather distant from loving-kindness, compassion, and warmth. But attention itself is the common denominator of all practices of shamatha as well as the cultivation of loving-kindness and compassion. The Latin root of the word attention means to tend to, as a shepherd watches over his sheep and a mother cares for her child. Attention is precisely what is being trained when we cultivate loving-kindness. We focus first on ourselves—we can be severely judgmental and self-deprecating. Even when we are trying our best, we are often hardest on ourselves. Such merciless punishment is undeserved. Can we start by giving ourselves a break? If so, then we will be able to extend this sense of caring to our children, spouses, friends, and everyone else.

The cultivation of attention via the practice of shamatha establishes a fertile soil in which loving-kindness can thrive. If we plant seeds of insight, understanding, and wisdom from vipashyana practice, they will grow into balanced awareness and a way of life in which we can flourish, free of suffering and the inner causes of suffering. When we understand the nature of reality internally, externally, and internally and externally together, our insight flowers as the four immeasurables. The Dalai Lama often says quite simply, "My religion is kindness."

GUIDED MEDITATION:
Mindfulness of Feelings I

Attend closely to feelings—
observing pleasure, displeasure, and indifference

Begin by settling the body in its natural state and the respiration in its natural rhythm. Settle your awareness for a short while in the space of the body. Settle your mind in ease, inner stillness, and vigilance. Attend especially to the sensations of the flow of the breath.

Let your eyes be at least partially open, with your awareness open specifically to the five sense fields: the visual, auditory, olfactory, gustatory, and tactile sensations throughout the body. Open yourself to the physical world by way of these five sense doors. For the time being, set aside everything in the domain of the mind, focusing entirely on physical sensory perception.

Rest in this approximation of bare attention, mindfully attentive to whatever stimuli and appearances arise from moment to moment. Let your awareness rove freely within the five physical sense fields but always hover in the present moment. Don't drift into conceptualizations about the past or the future; don't entertain cogitations about the present. Remain face-to-face with and mindfully attentive of whatever is arising here and now. If you are drawn to a sound, visual impression, or tactile sensation arising in the moment, be wholly present with it. Attending to sensory impressions themselves is the close application of mindfulness to the body.

Now begin to closely examine feelings of pleasure, pain, and indifference that appear in conjunction with these sensations. Feelings that arise in response to visual impressions, smells, and tastes are often fairly neutral and difficult to engage. Sounds and tactile sensations are more likely to generate feelings. For the practice of vipashyana, deliberately focus your attention on the feelings that arise in relation to sounds in your environment and tactile sensations of solidity, fluidity, warmth, and motion arising from moment to moment within the body. What feelings of pleasure, displeasure, or indifference arise in relation to these sensations?

If you feel any inclination to move while attending to the field of tactile sensations, it is crucial that you not act automatically on first impulse. Instead, notice the feeling that arouses the desire and perhaps the intention to move—it is almost certainly an unpleasant feeling. Simply observe this feeling, letting your body remain still as a mountain. Feelings may arise in response to various sensations in the body. Some areas might feel comfortable, giving rise to a mild sense of pleasure. Some regions might arouse a sense of indifference. But in other regions of the body, a sense of discomfort and even physical pain might arise. Carefully inspect these feelings instead of habitually identifying with the pain and reacting with evasive maneuvers.

Closely observe the very nature of the feeling itself. Inspect it to see whether it is identical to the tactile sensation or a way of experiencing and responding to the sensation. Examine the relationship between the sensory appearance and the associated feeling. As feelings arise in relationship to any of the five physical sense doors, observe how they arise. What is the process of origination? Once a feeling is present, observe carefully how it abides. Are these feelings, about which we care so much, stable or fluctuating? Is there anything in the nature of feelings to indicate that they are by nature "I" or "mine," or are they simply events arising within the fields of tactile, auditory, and visual experience? ☞

On Close Scrutiny

Shamatha and vipashyana are two aspects of any investigation into feelings. Shamatha entails simply being present with feelings, with no questions asked. With a good foundation in shamatha, you can simply be present with a feeling as it arises, touching it lightly. Don't crush it with a sledgehammer or strangle it to death. Rather, see if you can observe it out of the corner of your eye, so as not to scare it away.

For example, someone might speak harshly, and you think, "This behavior makes me uneasy, and displeasure is growing." While listening to this person's offensive speech, your feelings become increasingly active, and you note, "Displeasure has arisen." Simply be present with the feeling, sustaining your awareness of it, without overwhelming it by the force of your scrutiny. With shamatha acting as the basis for vipashyana, you will develop the ability to conduct a close examination over a prolonged period.

The world-famous quantum physicist Anton Zeilinger once brought me into a pitch-black laboratory in Innsbruck, Austria, where he had suspended a single atom in an electromagnetic field within a glass enclosure. By heavily bombarding this atom with photons, we could actually see it floating in mid-air. By tweaking the field, Anton could cause the atom to move. I had never seen a single atom before. Of course, I was only seeing the photons being reflected from the atom, and I could not see the atom without the photons. But this is how we see everything. We never really see anything but the visual appearances stimulated by interactions with photons.

Similarly, with increasing finesse, you will be able to hold an emotion, sustaining it with awareness so that it appears vividly suspended in the space of your mind. Then you can investigate it. Probe it. Let it slip away, then regenerate it. How does it arise? How is it present? How does it dissolve? The Buddha called these processes the factors of origination, presence, and dissolution: they are universal aspects of phenomena.

It is rare for us to scrutinize our feelings closely because we are much more interested in the objects that seem to arouse our feelings. For our survival and procreation, this is probably what we need to do. If something is threatening, fight it or flee. If there is food, grab it quickly. But in order to achieve success in this liberating practice, the close scrutiny of feelings is essential.

INVESTIGATING FEELINGS

The first teaching the Buddha gave, after walking from Bodhgaya to Sarnath and seeking out his five former companions, concerned the Four Noble Truths. The first of these is focused on the reality of suffering. Recognizing the reality of suffering is not normally our first response when we experience suffering. We don't want to understand it or even look at it—we just want to get rid of it. The Buddha gave us a counterintuitive instruction. His teaching went against the grain in classical India 2,500 years ago, and even more so in our modern, materialistic world. When suffering arises, he said to attend to it, investigate it, and understand it. From this careful inspection and close application of mindfulness to suffering, we can begin to identify the actual cause of our suffering. This approach follows a therapeutic model. A doctor begins by conducting a thorough examination of the patient's condition. After investigating each symptom and seeing as much of the picture as possible, the doctor can begin to diagnose the underlying affliction.

Prime Movers

As a characteristic of the human condition, suffering is something we all experience. Suffering is included in the second of the four close applications of mindfulness, but pleasure and indifference are also feelings. We often consider feelings as existing with only positive or negative values. We might say that we can feel either happy or sad; otherwise, we aren't feeling anything. In other words, the zero point is to have no feeling at all. Buddhists say that besides positive and negative feelings, there are neutral feelings. Experiences of feelings and our responses to them—which are inextricably intertwined in the Buddhist understanding—are fundamental characteristics of sentient beings. All sentient beings have feelings of pleasure, pain, and indifference. We care a great deal about our feelings: we want pleasure, we don't want pain, and we relax when we feel indifferent.

When a pleasurable feeling arises or is anticipated, the response of most sentient beings is one of craving. Whether from food, music, personal interaction, tactile sensation, or mental stimulation, we hope for pleasure even before it arises. Once pleasure arises, our natural tendency is to respond with attachment. As sentient beings, we are very sensually oriented, and we direct our senses outward because appearances seem to come from outside us. We experience some appearances with a sense of pleasure, and our natural, deeply engrained tendency is to hold on to anything that feels good. In response to appearances of relationship, food, possession, place, or a song on the radio, suddenly pleasure arises to insist: "Don't change this!" We want to hold on to pleasure; this is called attachment. We act as though the pleasure we experience actually comes from the appearance: "I'm getting pleasure from this, so keep it coming—I like it!"

Craving can also arise when we anticipate pleasure. My car radio has a scan feature, and when I'm out of the range of my favorite stations, the ones that provide me with pleasure, I hit the scan button. In southern California, the radio scans through lots of Mexican stations, but I don't speak Spanish, so no pleasure there. It keeps scanning through talk shows, commercials, rap, and country, all unpleasant or neutral at best. "Give me some pleasure!" Suddenly, out goes my finger, "Ahhhh, the Beatles. Stay there!" Then the song's over, and scanning for pleasure resumes. This is normal behavior, isn't it? If there were inherently good songs, all the stations would play them exclusively; there wouldn't be any bad stations, and you wouldn't have to scan. Everybody who turned on the radio would find pleasure on every station.

We make a fundamental error in thinking that our pleasure comes from the radio, anticipating that a particular station will be pleasurable. We scan through all the stations repeatedly without finding one we like.

This eventually becomes unpleasant, so we play a CD that we have specifically chosen to give us pleasure. Even if the CD has no unpleasant tracks, we skip certain ones we're indifferent toward. We crave pleasure, reach out for sources of anticipated pleasure, attach to our experiences of pleasure, and hold on.

Pleasure is a prime mover for ants as well as human beings. Why are they scurrying around in my kitchen? Have you noticed that ants never sit still? They are perpetually on the move, individually and in congregations. One synonym for a sentient being in Tibetan means one who is on the go (Tib. 'gro ba). Why are we always going somewhere? There is usually something we want, and we are on the go either due to the anticipation of pleasure, satisfaction, and fulfillment or else to avoid pain and discomfort. For example, if mundane pursuits are not delivering the goods, we might hope that pleasant feelings will come from participating in a meditation retreat.

I reached that point at the age of twenty. The goods had been delivered for me: good health, romantic relationship, brand new car, loving parents, and a promising career track. Environmental studies in 1970 promised excellent prospects, and my grades were solid. The University of California, San Diego, located in the town of La Jolla, "The Jewel," was a fine university in lovely surroundings, five minutes from the beach. "Surf's up dude, what more do you want?" Even with everything anyone could wish for, I was profoundly dissatisfied. I imagined a motion picture of my life running forward, more of the same for twenty, forty, sixty years, until I keeled over—The End. Is that all there is? I knew that more of the same was not enough for me, so I gave up, got out, and found a much better world in which to dwell.

The pursuit of happiness is very central in our lives, and it normally gives rise to craving. Of course it is always possible, or perhaps inevitable, that something will interfere with our aspirations. We anticipate that something will deliver happiness, but there's an impediment. Perhaps someone doesn't behave as we want, or something thwarts our desire for food, a job, or personal recognition. When this happens, anger and hostility may arise. If we can identify the culprit that has blocked our desires, we may express our hostility and perhaps violently dislodge the obstruction. When we get what we want, we expect the goods to be delivered. "Happiness at last! Thank you so much. Don't ever change."

Now the clinging takes over. "I'll love you forever, if you keep on delivering the goods for me." We solidify our attachment to the perceived source of our happiness. Then things change, someone starts behaving differently, or we simply get bored, and our source no longer delivers the goods. Once again dissatisfaction and anger arise.

As a young monk in Switzerland in the late seventies, I had one friend who was an older monk, in his early thirties; he had been married, unlike the rest of us. He told us very candidly about the demise of his marriage, which became apparent at breakfast one morning. He was sitting across from his wife with his newspaper up; hers was up, too. As he glared angrily at his wife, behind his newspaper, the thought emerged vividly in his mind, "You are supposed to provide me with happiness, and you're not doing it." I can imagine that his wife was glaring, behind her newspaper, and thinking exactly the same thing. Of course they divorced.

When we grasp on to something, craving and attachment arise. Then something changes, and without warning, a person, possession, activity, or situation seems to become a source of displeasure. Sadness, anger, harsh words, and conflict can easily arise. Furthermore, we might receive a big load of unhappiness. Without justification, someone treats us harshly, rudely, or maliciously, selfishly manipulating and deceiving us, and thereby makes us miserable. Such feelings can dominate our lives.

I have an unfortunate tendency, when I see people being rude or reckless, to feel somewhat morally indignant. But scolding them is generally not a good idea. A few years ago, I was driving through town, and a kid in a souped-up car pulled out right in front of me. He could have waited a few seconds, as there was nobody behind me, but he was so impatient that we nearly collided. I was forced to brake hard, and I was outraged: "Lousy driver!" I muttered as I laid on my horn. Oddly enough, he didn't respond to my indignant honking by pulling over to apologize. He flung his hand out the window in an angry gesture to my moral superiority. We had both made each other unhappy. He had obstructed my desire for polite, cautious driving, and I had obstructed his desire to drive freely.

Feelings of pleasure give rise to craving and attachment, and feelings of displeasure give rise to hatred and malice. But when we're indifferent, we don't feel much at all. We simply cruise along with nothing happening—no pleasure arising, no displeasure arising—and slowly we slip into a stupor. The mind becomes bored, dull, and indifferent to everything.

Three Poisons and Three Virtues

The natural responses to pleasure, displeasure, and indifference are known in Buddhism as the three poisons of craving, hostility, and delusion. These three varieties of feelings are enormously important prime movers, manifesting in the body via the five senses, and also manifesting wholly within the mind. The simple arising of an unpleasant memory can make us extremely unhappy, just as the anticipation of some future pleasantness can make us happy. We can generate these feelings independently of physical sensory input.

Not only are these three feelings directly correlated with the three poisons of craving, hostility, and delusion—they also correspond to three virtues. Why do we feel loving-kindness for another person? The expression of loving-kindness is not the attraction of desire; it is a genuine yearning that another sentient being might find happiness and the causes of happiness. We experience this sublime virtue because we care about other people's happiness. Of course we also care about our own feelings, and our own happiness is not something to be abandoned or neglected. In fact, the Buddha instructed us to cultivate loving-kindness by starting with ourselves. He gave us a tremendous koan: "One who truly loves himself will never harm another."[71] If we have a clear vision of our own flourishing, and if we genuinely cultivate loving-kindness for ourselves, rather than infatuation or self-indulgence, then we will have no wish to harm anyone else. Our own experience of happiness and our empathetic imagination of the potential for others' happiness is the basis for loving-kindness.

In this practice, we also experience suffering and know it directly, by attending closely to feelings internally, externally, and both internally and externally. This strategy is quite magnificent. Get to know the feelings arising in your own body and mind by examining them closely and mindfully. Then direct your awareness externally. Even though you might not be psychic, everyone has the capacity for empathy, and it can be cultivated, refined, and enhanced. By simply attending to other people's facial expressions, body language, tone of voice, speech, and behavior, a lot becomes obvious. As Ekman rightly cautions, the reasons behind feelings can be very complex, deeply embedded in personal history, and unknowable, but the feelings themselves are often quite transparent. There is an element of projection in the empathetic recognition that my awareness of my own feelings is probably similar to your experience. Nevertheless, we may be able to intuit others' feelings immediately, without projecting, and in many cases we may be correct.

Our awareness of feelings in the body and mind ranges from simple frustration and malaise to anguish, despair, and white-hot physical pain, and from simple pleasures to extraordinary ecstasy. As we become clearly cognizant of the bandwidth of our own feelings, we direct our awareness externally. We become vividly aware that myriad sentient beings around us are not simply objects of our pleasure, displeasure, or indifference, but have feelings just like ours. By turning our awareness outward and closely applying mindfulness to other sentient beings, we can empathize with their feelings. When we empathize with another's suffering and we attend closely, compassion arises. The suffering of unpleasant feelings is the very source of the experience of compassion.

Finally, neutral feelings can directly give rise to impartiality and blossom into equanimity toward all sentient beings. The Buddha might have formulated three close applications of mindfulness by including feelings with mental events, making a perfectly good triad. He taught feelings as a separate category because at all levels they are essential to our very survival and we cannot help but care about them deeply.

Body and Mind

Our feelings influence every aspect of our behavior from the moment we are born. If we don't like food, we'll die. If we're not interested in procreation, our lineage will die. Feelings are fundamental to biological evolution, motivating sentient beings' constant search for food, sex, and territory. Feelings move the world, which is why they are our prime focus immediately after mindfulness of the body. Feelings arise relatively independently in the domains of all six senses. The experience of mental happiness can coincide with a sound that is unpleasant, and the mind can oscillate between mental enjoyment and sensory displeasure. One can feel very comfortable physically while one's food tastes awful. Even if the body is in a state of discomfort, it's possible for the mind to be quite content.

I know a young man who is physically devastated by a disease that will require hospitalizations for the rest of his life. Despite some bad days, his attitude is cheerful and buoyant, and his life is highly meaningful. He explains his lightheartedness, admittedly sounding clichéd: "In fact, this disease has been a great blessing to me." Of course, contracting a disease is not fun, but some people seem to rise to the challenge of transformation. This man can give a detailed account of the disease progressing in his body, and yet his mind is extraordinarily balanced. I know many people who are not doing as well despite having excellent physical health. Even though the five senses deliver pleasurable or neutral feelings, the mind can torment us relentlessly.

Bodily pleasure and pain are easy to detect, especially painful sensations. Feelings of indifference are more difficult to discern. Mental feelings of pleasure and pain are also quite easy to detect, but they generally require a stimulus, such as another person's words. Someone might hurt your feelings or humiliate you with a critical remark. Likewise, you can experience pleasure because of someone's praises or by being awarded a full scholarship to graduate school. Mental feelings of pleasure and pain can be extremely vivid, generating a happy smile or an anguished grimace. Neurologist Antonio Damasio studies emotion, which is the broader category in modern psychology that includes feelings. His somatic marker hypothesis states that when we experience a mental state with an affective quality, such as pleasure, pain, happiness, sadness, anger, fear, or disgust, we will feel a correlated sensation in the body.[72] We may be able to pinpoint these somatic sensations in the gut, heart, throat, or head. He claims that the experience of an emotion is always accompanied by somatic, tactile perception. But the sensation and the emotion are not the same, and detecting the difference between the two requires some finesse.

There is an empirically testable claim in Buddhist psychology that a single moment of awareness of around two milliseconds is the shortest period in which you can actually apprehend something. The Buddhist hypothesis is that you cannot detect two stimuli in different fields of experience during a single pulse of cognition. If a sound and a color are both presented, you will not perceive both. The metaphor is given of a monkey in a house with six windows having nonoverlapping vistas, representing the six sense spheres. The monkey can jump from window to window very rapidly, but can look out only one window at a time. This implies that in one fifty-millisecond period you might be aware of an unpleasant physical feeling, while in the next fifty milliseconds, you might be aware of a pleasant mental feeling.

You might also oscillate back and forth, like a football player who scores to win but gets absolutely crushed—the hero's jubilant ecstasy alternating with the pain of a broken collarbone. He cannot experience physical pain and mental pleasure at the same moment, but his mind can oscillate back and forth. Buddhism asserts that the mental generally trumps the physical. Of course, the mental feeling might also be completely congruent with the physical feeling.

Layers of Confusion

Feelings are prime movers, so we are strongly motivated to understand them. When feelings arise, our natural tendency is to identify with them immediately: "My knee hurts, my back aches, and my stomach is upset; I'm happy; I'm bored." These feelings are immediately fused with our identity, and the source of our feelings is attributed to a sensation, person, or object external to us. The first delusion is the fusing of our identity with feelings. We hold our emotions very closely because they are ours exclusively—we're in touch with them. Something in the nature of these feelings makes them seem to be inherently ours. The second delusion is the attribution of our pleasure and displeasure to the appearances themselves. We are happy due to some phenomena, unhappy due to others, and indifferent due to those that bore us.

The close application of mindfulness strips away these delusions. This process is like a surgeon treating a burn victim by removing layers of dead skin until reaching healthy tissue. The dead skin represents all the notions that overlay the sheer experiences of feelings. When we clear away the false projections of "I" and "mine," we do not find the true sources of happiness and displeasure in external phenomena. Instead of identifying with feelings and reacting to them, we take an interest in them, posing questions: "How do these feelings of pleasure, pain, and indifference arise?" Or, as the Buddha asked, "What are the elements of their origination?" By what processes do feelings emerge into our experience from the senses and the mind? Attend closely, investigating the true nature of feelings.

Once feelings are present, how do they abide? Are they solid and inert like a truck parked in the garage of your mind? Are they quick and unpredictable like a hummingbird visiting your garden? Are appearances by nature inherently pleasant, unpleasant, and neutral, or does it depend on how you react to them? Knowing the answer conceptually does not have the same decisive impact as discovering it experientially.

Finally, as feelings arise, persist, and fade away, is there anything about their nature that identifies them as being inherently "mine," or are they simply events arising in the space of experience? Can you allow feelings to arise in the body and mind without holding them closely, being gripped by them, or dissociating from them? The Buddhist hypothesis is that we can indeed be present with feelings without grasping. Feelings of pain, pleasure, sadness, and euphoria can arise in the space of the mind like clouds forming in a clear blue sky, emerging without an owner, and then dissolving back into the space of the sky, which is unaffected by any clouds. Proving this extraordinary hypothesis to ourselves will change how we feel about everything.

GUIDED MEDITATION:
Mindfulness of Feelings II

Scan feelings in three dimensions—
observing without grasping or identification

Settle the body in its natural state and the breath in its natural rhythm. Let awareness permeate the whole field of tactile sensations, attending in particular to sensations correlated with the breath.

Keep your body as still as possible. If you should experience any impulse to move, before moving at all, direct your attention closely to the feeling behind this impulse. It will almost certainly be an unpleasant feeling. Examine the feeling carefully, and see what happens to it under inspection. Does it dissipate, increase, or remain constant? Sustain a strong resolve to remain still; simply observe the feelings arising within the field of the body, without reacting to them.

Focus your awareness more narrowly, to the feelings in a hand's-width field at the crown of the head. Scan through the body in three dimensions, noting in particular any feelings of pleasure, pain, and indifference. Beginning at the crown of the head, with each out-breath, gradually move the field of awareness around the head, from the left side, to the back, to the right side, to the forehead, and down to the chin. Scan through the head, from the face to the back of the head, returning to the face.

Expand this two-dimensional field to a three-dimensional volume of awareness. Observe the feelings throughout the head—pleasant, unpleasant, or neutral feelings—identifying and inspecting them closely. Move the volume of awareness down the neck, across the left shoulder, and down the arm to the elbow. Continue down the forearm to the wrist, hand, and fingertips, observing any feelings that arise, how they arise, how they are present, and how they dissolve.

Jump across to the fingertips of the right hand, continuing up to the hand, wrist, forearm, elbow, and upper arm, and moving across the right shoulder to the base of the neck. Shift the volume of awareness to the upper left segment of the torso, scanning it from the back, through the interior, to the front surface.

Continue scanning the upper center segment of the torso, the upper right, middle right, middle center, middle left, lower left, lower center, and the lower right segments.

Scan from the right buttock down the thigh to the knee, calf, ankle, foot, and the tips of the toes. From the left buttock, move down the thigh to the knee, calf, ankle, foot, and the tips of the toes. Do you experience any sensations as pleasant, unpleasant, or neutral?

Expand the volume of awareness to fill the entire space of the body. Let your awareness move at will, spontaneously. Take an interest in any feelings that arise within this tactile field, observing them carefully, without moving. Are feelings of pleasure, pain, and indifference the same as the tactile sensations of earth, water, fire, and air—or are they something more? What is the relationship between these feelings and the tactile sensations of the four elements?

Observe how feelings arise, how they are present, and how they dissolve back into the space of the body. Precisely how do they dissolve? Can you detect a subject-object relationship whereby the feelings you inspect are altered by your scrutiny? If so, how does awareness affect feelings?

With each out-breath, relax more deeply. When involuntary thoughts arise, release them, letting them dissolve back into the space of the mind. With each out-breath, release any excess tension or tightness in the body. Let your body melt.

Can you simply be aware of feelings arising in the body without becoming immersed and entangled in them? Can you attend without any preference? In short, attend to feelings without grasping or identification. ☚

On Stillness

When a sensation of itching, heat, or cold arises and you do not react, you can simply observe it as an experiment in the laboratory of your body and mind. Will it dissipate without any intervention? What happens to the feeling when you conceptually reinforce it? Try deliberately generating grasping: "An unbearable itch is driving me crazy, and it's getting worse!" Grasping comes quite naturally; we don't need to practice it. On the other hand, without grasping, is the simple awareness of a feeling sufficient for it to fade away? There is a valuable discovery in the act of silently observing a mildly unpleasant sensation that vanishes of its own accord, without any need to tense up, shift, move, or scratch.

Resting like a mountain, we continue to breathe and blink. There is no prohibition against blinking. It is a mistake to struggle against blinking with dry, burning eyes. Let the eyes lubricate themselves by blinking automatically, and they will not become dry. As the eyes settle in their natural state, blinking normally, the gaze should be casual, as if you were daydreaming with eyes open.

It is important to allow the breath to flow naturally, without impediment. When we deliberately focus in meditation, inspecting something very closely, the sheer weight of our concentrated attention can impede the flow of the breath—this is to be avoided. The breath should flow effortlessly, as silky smooth as in deep sleep, even though one might be engaged in a demanding contemplative endeavor. Use introspection to periodically examine the body, verifying the posture, relaxation, and breath.

The suggestion to practice in short sessions of twenty-four minutes, while maintaining the strong resolve not to move, ensures that feelings of discomfort do not threaten one's relaxation. I'm a real softy compared with a teacher such as Goenka. In his ten-day course, he asks people to sit for one or two hours, with a strong resolve not to move—if you move, you have failed to follow the instruction. After sitting for hours and trying your best not to move, the pain becomes intense, and Goenka has no problem with that. The instructions are to inspect without moving, simply bringing bare attention to the pain arising in the body. By following these instructions, thousands of people have experienced breaking through the pain, making practice enjoyable because the grasping is gone.

For a twenty-four minute session, do your best not to take any steps to shift your weight, alter the body, or tense up in any way. Simply regard this practice as an investigation into the nature of feelings. Any feeling can arise, including bliss, but there are often encounters with unpleasant feelings and discomfort. Investigate experientially any feeling that arises. Can you penetrate it with sharp, discerning attention? Can you distinguish between the feeling and the raw, tactile sensations of solidity, heat, cold, motion, and so forth that are associated with it? Are they inseparable or distinct?

The goal of this practice is to differentiate the tactile sensations of the four elements—earth, water, fire, and air—from positive, negative, and neutral feelings. A tactile sensation of solidity might arise in the body due to a big bear hug from your loving grandfather, or due to a pickpocket's lunge. The resulting pleasant or unpleasant feeling is not in the sensation of the earth element itself. Furthermore, the intensity of the sensation does not correlate with the intensity of the feeling. Sensing the light touch of someone's finger on your wallet can be most unpleasant. You might relish a soak in a very hot bath and feel disappointed if the water is only lukewarm, only to happily jump into much cooler water in the swimming pool. There is no direct relationship between the sensation of the fire element and our feelings. Likewise, there is no relation between sensations of fluidity and motion occurring in the body and our feelings. Pleasure and displeasure are not directly correlated with the raw tactile sensations of the elements. Is this merely a conceptual distinction, or can you observe it in your own experience?

GUIDED MEDITATION:
Mindfulness of Feelings III

Attend to feelings in body and mind via all six senses—
observing emergence, persistence, and dissolution

Begin with the practice of shamatha and close mindfulness of the breath in any of three modes: full-body awareness, the sensations of the breath rising and falling at the abdomen, or the sensations of the breath at the apertures of the nostrils. Taking close mindfulness of the breath as your vehicle, keep your body still and maintain a strong resolve not to move.

Whenever a feeling of pleasure, pain, or indifference arises in the body or mind, observe carefully how it emerges, how it is present, and how it dissolves. Once it dissolves, simply return to the breath.

Use this process to closely apply mindfulness to feelings that arise in the body and mind in relationship to all six senses. Attend closely to feelings without identifying with them. Observe their nature—how they emerge, how they persist, and how they dissolve. ☞

Real-Time Mindfulness

A chain of thoughts may be coupled with feelings of happiness or sadness, and sometimes we feel happy, sad, or blue for no apparent reason; it's like a coloration or tonality in the space of the mind. An affective quality or feeling tone can arise unassociated with any particular thought or experience. When thoughts occur without any apparent affective valence, this is called an affective valence of zero, a number whose conception is attributed to ancient Indian mathematicians.

We can attend to thoughts while simultaneously perceiving mental feelings because they are within the same domain. Unlike hopping back and forth between sensory windows, a thought and its associated feeling or tonality appear in a single vista. This becomes especially interesting and quite subtle in the following hypothesis: some events arising in the space of the mind can be observed as they occur, in real time. For example, if you are attending very closely to the space of the mind and whatever arises therein, and I say: "Please visualize a peach," the hypothesis is that the occurrence of that mental image is simultaneous with your awareness of it. It makes no sense to speak of having a mental image of which you are unaware, so there is no lag time between the appearance of a mental image and the awareness of it.

A prime example of this occurs in a dream, when you experience various events while seeing them in real time, with no lag. You might be able to continue watching the dream play out in real time until eventually it vanishes. In the waking state, I would suggest that we apprehend mental images and our own internal commentary in real time. These are objective appearances to the mind, just as the substrate is an objective appearance to the mind, even though it happens to be a vacuity.

On the other hand, the mind has subjective impulses, which do not appear as objects but as modes of apprehension. For example, if I bring to mind an image of a peach, and then the desire to eat a peach arises, the desire does not arise in the same way as the mental image. Desire is more subjective. James stated the empirical hypothesis that by the time we are aware of a desire, it's in the past. This is a subtle distinction, which asserts that our mental awareness of a subjective impulse like desire is always retrospective, so there will be some short lag time.

For example, you might see an attractive dessert, and your desire manifests in response to the visual appearance. Now imagine you're approaching the dessert table, with your eyes focused on a favorite cake, when somebody calls to you, interrupting your attention. In that moment, the desire is gone because the attention is directed elsewhere: "Who called me?" Similarly, if you approach the desserts and see something you like, leading to desire—but remember the practice of attending to desire and mental processes—suddenly, you're fascinated and fully attentive: "Look, it's desire!" Your attention has abandoned the cake and focused on the desire; consequently, the desire is likely to fade. By the time you're aware of the desire, it's gone; it's like seeing the contrails of an unseen aircraft.

The hypothesis is that, when observing subjective impulses such as desire, as long as we are focused on an external object, the desire is strengthened by our attention. As soon as we direct our attention toward the desire itself, we are experiencing what psychologists call "working memory," which is a very short-term memory, lasting perhaps a hundred milliseconds. When we direct our attention toward desire with great curiosity, we disengage attention from the object of desire, ceasing to reinforce it.

This has important implications in a therapeutic context. A person who nurses a deep resentment will not eliminate it by occasionally becoming aware of this emotion. Someone who has a hard time resisting fattening desserts will not solve a weight problem by merely becoming aware at times of the desire for dessert. Desire might be interrupted momentarily; however, as soon as the attention returns to the dessert, the old habit of desire will reappear.

We can investigate subjective impulses for ourselves as they arise, and the prime candidates are desires and emotions. Is it the case that sheer, focused awareness of these impulses is always an exercise in working memory or retrospective mindfulness? Or can we bring real-time, present-centered mindfulness to mental appearances of desires and emotions as they arise?

When you train the attention using shamatha techniques, your awareness of emotions will become increasingly vivid but not to the point of real-time recognition. The dimension of vividness or acuity has both spatial and temporal aspects. Qualitative vividness means high-resolution perception that captures fine details, like high-definition television. Temporal acuity means very rapid observations. Meditation training may enhance your temporal acuity of awareness; nevertheless, according to both James and Buddhism, you can never detect a subjective impulse in real time. The moment you focus awareness upon the desire itself, the desire has passed because you are no longer attending to the object of desire.

Settling the Mind in Its Natural State

Shamatha is the platform for venturing into vipashyana. Mindfulness of the breath is a very good platform for attending to feelings arising in the body via all five physical sense fields. In the shamatha method called settling the mind in its natural state (Tib. *sems rnal du babs*), the full force of awareness is focused on the mental domain. We attend specifically to the space of the mind and the mental phenomena that arise within that domain, to the exclusion of the five physical senses. This is one of the three methods that are highlighted in my book *The Attention Revolution* as central to the development of shamatha, attention, and metacognition.[73] It was also a prominent practice in both three-month Shamatha Project retreats in 2007.[74] In his book *The Vajra Essence*, the great nineteenth-century master Düdjom Lingpa elucidates this practice in an enormously inspiring presentation, embedded in the rich context of a Dzogchen worldview.[75] The classic strategy invites slipping into the substrate consciousness via a profound release and simply being present with the events of the mind.

My favorite image for this practice is of a falcon, like the tiny kestrel, kiting into the wind. The kestrel faces into the wind, remaining stationary with respect to the ground by making subtle adjustments to avoid moving backward or forward. It is in motion while remaining stationary. In a similar way, we face into a steady wind of thoughts, images, memories, and fantasies. If we lose our balance and allow ourselves to succumb to mental activities, then we are drawn forward into the future or swept backward into the past. The practice is to remain motionless like the kestrel, mindfully attentive to every thought but unmoved by anything.

When you're in a busy restaurant and keenly interested in your own conversation, you can't block out the next table's ruckus, but you're simply not interested. Despite all the noise, you don't give it any attention. Sound impinges upon your awareness, but you're focused on your own companions. Similarly, the shamatha practice of settling the mind in its natural state entails attending exclusively to the domain of the mind and whatever arises within it. This space of experience includes all thoughts, mental images, desires, emotions, and fantasies. Although impressions may enter as sounds, visual images, or tactile sensations, give no attention to the five senses—pay them no mind.

GUIDED MEDITATION:
Settling the Mind in Its Natural State I

Attend to the space of the mind and its contents—
observing without distraction or grasping

Begin by settling the body in its natural state, imbued with the three qualities of relaxation, stillness, and vigilance, and round this off with three deep breaths. Settle the breath in its natural rhythm.

Direct your attention to the field of the body and whatever tactile sensations arise within that space. Maintain unwavering mindfulness as you observe sensations arising within the tactile field, from moment to moment; attend to them without distraction and without grasping. Having no preference, whatever feelings arise, simply let them be.

Gently open your eyes, at least partially, and rest your gaze vacantly in the space in front of you, without taking any interest in the visual domain. Rest your awareness in the space between yourself and visual appearances. Keep your eyes open but vacant, while blinking and breathing naturally, as if you were daydreaming.

Now direct the full force of your attention to the domain of mental experience—ideas, thoughts, images, desires, emotions, and aspirations—while paying no attention to the five physical sense fields. To help direct your attention to the mental domain, you may deliberately generate a mental image of a familiar object, face, location, or phrase, such as "This is the mind." Focus your full attention on this mental image. When the thought or image vanishes into the space of the mind, keep your attention focused where it was and observe the next event in the mental domain. No matter what arises within this mental space—a discursive thought, mental image, emotion, or desire—simply attend to it and observe its nature, remaining alert but nonreactive.

With body and mind relaxed from the core and breath flowing effortlessly and unimpeded, sustain unwavering mindfulness of the space of the mind and whatever arises within it. Observe this domain and its contents without distraction, diversion, straying to other senses, grasping, or latching on to anything. Don't identify with thoughts, images, or memories. Don't try to control them, silence them, or sustain them. Simply be present with them as an unbiased observer. Let them be.

It is quite natural to be caught up in thoughts and carried away. Using introspection, note this excitation arising as swiftly as you can. In response, relax more deeply, release all grasping on to thoughts, and continue observing the thoughts themselves.

At times you might find yourself getting spaced-out and the mind becoming dull or lethargic. Immediately note this with introspection and freshly arouse your attention. Focus intently on the space of the mind and whatever arises within it. Let your body be still as a mountain and your awareness still as space, as you observe passing images, emotions, and thoughts. ☞

On the Space of the Mind

The primary instruction for settling the mind in its natural state is to direct the attention to the space of the mind and whatever arises in it, without distraction or grasping. The very essence of the practice is to selectively attend to the space of the mind while ignoring appearances to the five physical senses. We can attend specifically to mental feelings without hunting them down. Choosing an object in this way does not imply grasping—it's simply the act of directing the attention.

We define the space of the body as the domain of tactile events, and we study the body as it is experienced firsthand—not from a God's-eye view or a medical doctor's perspective. The field of tactile experience is distinct from flesh, cells, molecules, and atoms. When you feel an itch, it occurs in the tactile space. Consider the location of phantom limb sensations that sometimes occur following the loss of a limb. The tactile field can persist in surprising ways, even without a material basis.[76]

When we direct bare attention to the tactile field and events arising within it, the contours of this field might be quite nebulous. When we do experience contours, the chances are good that we are projecting them rather than perceiving them. The shape, volume, and dimensions of the field of the body are defined by the tactile events arising within it. The space of the mind is analogous. Do these fields have shapes? How big are they? Explore these questions experientially. As you progress in your ontological probe of the nature of the mind, allow the nebulous to remain nebulous, without trying to superimpose anything upon your observations.

Tactile events are distinct and tangible, and the space of the body is easy to identify. In contrast, mental events are intangible and not located in physical space, while the space of the mind is nonlocal and immaterial. It's not behind the eyes, in front of the eyes, to the left, or to the right. The space of the mind does not need to be visualized—it's already there. Anything you visualize is an overlay upon the preexisting space of the mind, which simply denotes the domain in which mental events arise.

Mental events such as thoughts and emotions are not observable by any of the five physical senses. They are not measurable with technological instruments, which only detect physiological correlates and behavioral expressions. Thoughts appear in the space of the mind. When we see a man in the moon or patterns in the constellations, these phenomena manifest in the space of the mind; they don't appear in physical space. Mental space can be as vast as our imaginations—or as cramped.

Can you easily attend to feelings and clearly observe them arising together with thoughts, memories, and mental images, or are your feelings often hidden, protected, or suppressed? With repeated practice, feelings can be observed with increasing detachment, clarity, and discernment. Contemplative science is not a simple practice for anyone; however, an investment of time in training the attention to become extremely stable, vivid, and sharp in the observation of feelings will yield a rich return for everyone.

Mental objects may be perceived very similarly by multiple individuals, just like the intersubjective objects of the other senses. How can you investigate this? Your mental space is defined as the domain of your direct experience of mental events. This is not a physicist's notion of Newtonian or Einsteinian space that exists independently of experience. Newton spoke of absolute space as it appears from God's perspective rather than human perception. Likewise, when Einstein speaks of space-time being curved by bodies of matter, the phenomenon he describes is not dependent upon personal experience. Even though Einstein rejected the biblical notion of God, he did embrace an abstract idea of God, more like Spinoza's (1632–1677) description: impersonal and unresponsive to prayers. Einstein frequently used the word "God" in a traditional fashion, representing the ultimate perspective; at times, he virtually equated God with nature. Instead of space as God sees it, Buddhists speak of phenomenological space—the space of experience—which precedes any other space independent of experience.

Is the space of your mind susceptible to outside influence? Might it contain events that are accessible to you and others simultaneously? These are empirical questions, and some who work in this field are convinced that it is possible for clairvoyance or remote viewing to occur. Perhaps the spaces of our minds interpenetrate. In order to put these questions to the test of experience, release all grasping on to your own psyche, fixated upon "I, me, and mine." Settle into the vastness of the substrate. Test the range of the laser pointer of your attention in this superfluid state of awareness. The psyche is a tiny cell in which to be confined—the substrate is infinitely spacious.

GUIDED MEDITATION:
Settling the Mind in Its Natural State II

Attend to the space of the mind and feelings—
observing pleasure, pain, and indifference

Settle the body in its natural state and the respiration in its natural rhythm. Focus your attention on the field of the body and whatever sensations arise within it; attend without distraction or grasping.

Let your eyes be at least partially open, with your gaze vacantly resting in the space in front of you. Direct your full attention to the space of the mind and its contents. You may start by deliberately generating a thought or a mental image; as that mental event fades into the space of the mind, keep your attention focused where it was.

Take special note of feelings that arise in the space of the mind. At times, feelings of pleasure, pain, or indifference arise along with images, memories, and discursive thoughts. At other times, feelings seem to arise independently of any thought or image. Attend closely and carefully to the emergence, persistence, and dissolution of mental feelings.

If you have difficulty identifying the arising of a distinct mental feeling, you may begin by deliberately generating one. Vividly recall some unhappy or troubling experience and observe very carefully the feeling that arises along with this memory. Recall a happy memory or fantasy and observe the ensuing feeling. Bring forth a neutral thought or mental image and observe what arises. Whether feelings are deliberately generated or spontaneously arisen, inspect them closely to see how they arise, how they abide, and how they dissolve. ☞

On Observing Feelings

Identifying feelings as they arise, with focused and sustained attention, allows for highly discerning observations. Exactly how do feelings arise? How are they present? How do they dissolve? How is a feeling affected by the sheer act of observing it? Is there an analogy to Werner Heisenberg's (1901–1976) Uncertainty Principle, or can you observe a feeling without influencing it? Does the mere act of observing a feeling invariably make it change or vanish, or do some feelings withstand scrutiny, lingering even under observation?

It is a subtle practice to simply observe without grasping or chasing after feelings. Directing your awareness does not necessarily imply grasping. Any expression of repulsion, attraction, preference, or control constitutes grasping. Any identification with feelings as "I" or "mine" is also grasping. Attending closely to something without grasping is quite feasible.

It is true that attending to the space of the mind and specifically selecting feelings as opposed to internal dialogue and mental images entails a certain type of grasping. In fact, any act of contemplative inquiry in vipashyana is a form of grasping, but this is minor and harmless—not malignant. The subtle grasping involved in contemplative inquiry can do a great deal of good by penetrating and shattering coarse, delusional grasping. Selectively inspecting the nature of feelings can yield highly beneficial insights. Eventually, when one is liberated, there is no more grasping.

The term for grasping is directly related to the Sanskrit and Pali term *nimitta*, meaning a sign, which is defined as an object identified within a conceptual framework. We make sense of the world by grouping appearances into categories. Boundaries between categories are drawn by us—they are not defined by nature, even for material objects. For example, fifteen inches of thorny stem with a bud is called a "rose," and twelve of these make a "bouquet," while placing them in a vase constitutes an "arrangement." To an online vendor, this arrangement, with an insulated box and overnight delivery, is an "Old Flame Special," and we might be pleased to receive such a "gift" from an old friend. Our spouse might be furious at this "proof" of infidelity, the housekeeper might clean up an "accident," and a divorce attorney might label the shattered vase "Exhibit 1."

Even the boundaries between pleasant and unpleasant feelings are quite arbitrary. I am convinced that feelings do not have absolute, inherent tonality. We might think that an arising feeling possesses an intrinsic level of suffering or pleasure, independent of circumstances, but this is clearly false. For example, if a feeling of hunger arises, it exists only relative to past experiences of hunger and to what food we anticipate. Whenever we experience a feeling, it manifests relative to the context of feelings that have preceded it. When we fixate upon a feeling's sign—an object identified within a conceptual framework—we draw upon memory to analyze and classify it as pleasant, unpleasant, or neutral. This reflexive process entails grasping.

The experience of a feeling becomes interesting when you are able to refrain from grasping. Do the boundaries between various feelings begin to fade? Does the distinction between a thought and its tonality become less clear? Is the thought an entity and the tonality its attribute, or is the tonality an entity and the thought its appendage? Does one belong to the other? Does the feeling have a cognitive aspect?

Are thought and feeling in opposition, in the way the Greeks viewed reason and emotion? Should human beings be governed by reason, unlike ignorant animals that are ruled by emotion? Buddhists do not view reason and emotion as opposites but as simultaneous psychological processes. A thought may arise along with a feeling, both focused on the same object. For example, the thought, "That cake looks delicious," may arise together with a feeling of desire—both arising with respect to the cake. There is no absolute demarcation between thoughts and feelings; they arise concomitantly and interdependently. As grasping decreases, what happens to feelings? Do they still arise? How do they arise? These are questions worth investigating empirically.

GROUND STATES

One of the most important questions to be explored, with enormous relevance to our very identity as human beings, is the nature of the ground state of our feelings. Is there a baseline condition underlying all our experiences of feelings? We can clearly feel pleasure by encountering something pleasant in any of the sense fields, including the mind. Likewise, displeasure or indifference can arise from any of the six sense fields. But in the absence of any stimuli to arouse our feelings, what is their ground state?

Habitual Ground State

The Buddhist assertion is that there is a ground state characterized by habitual afflictions. To conduct a thought experiment in this habitual ground state, put yourself in a neutral environment where nothing is pleasant or unpleasant. The perfect case is to seal yourself in a sensory isolation tank, where you float in body-temperature salt water, and it is pitch black and utterly silent. In such a thought experiment, with no stimulation from the environment, you are an isolated body-mind in a tank. What happens to your mind as you float in this silent, dark, solitary confinement? What feelings arise, hour after hour? Chances are good that after a while you will become unhappy and remain so. This feeling might intensify and create a very deep mental imbalance. When sensory isolation tanks were first popularized, there were reports of people who stayed in too long—the results ranged from disorientation to temporary psychosis. These days, sensory deprivation is most often mentioned as a technique for torture.

The habitual ground state is one in which—without any stimulation or catalyst from the five physical senses—the mental afflictions of grasping, craving, and hostility automatically come to the forefront. They appear like cockroaches in a dark room, making you unhappy; they multiply to keep you unhappy. The habitual ground state is characterized by dissatisfaction and even misery, which is why solitary confinement is considered punishment. A prisoner in solitary confinement is engaged in battle with his or her own mind. For an untrained mind that is strongly habituated to mental afflictions, the habitual ground state in the absence of stimulation will be pervaded by these same afflictions. Boredom becomes restlessness, followed by anxiety, craving, and one flavor of unhappiness after another, potentially driving a person to mental instability.

Natural Ground State

On the other hand, there are yogis in India, Tibet, and China who voluntarily live in isolated places, under conditions much like solitary confinement. I recently visited the northern Gobi desert, where a monastery was established in the nineteenth century. In a vast expanse of red dirt like the surface of Mars, utterly devoid of vegetation, was a little mound of black volcanic rock. There the yogis had carved out austere caves, some no more than holes in the side of the rock.

Yogis spend days or months in such holes in the rocks in the middle of the Gobi, which is a terribly harsh environment at best. Accomplished yogis live without food or water for sustained periods of intense solitary confinement. In Tibet, it's not uncommon for yogis to seal themselves into a cave with only a slit for food to be passed through, and they live in the dark for many days, weeks, or months. A monastery that I visited in eastern Tibet was home to fifty-five monks engaged in three-year retreats together in a compound. Over the course of their three years, each of them spent forty-nine days in a pitch-black room. They had plenty of time to observe their minds because there was nothing else happening. I spoke with one of the monks who had completed forty-nine days in darkness during his three-year retreat, and he reported that the time was profoundly therapeutic. At first his mind was imbalanced, neurotic, and unhappy, he said, but by the end of the retreat, his mind was balanced, cheerful, and healthy. I found him to be very bright, friendly, and contented.

The habitual ground state makes solitary confinement a cruel punishment of loneliness and unhappiness. On the other hand, the practice of shamatha leads to a different state of mind called the relative ground state. In the practice of settling the mind in its natural state, you simply attend to whatever arises within that space, without specifically ferreting out feelings. As you spend several thousand hours practicing shamatha, for up to twelve hours a day, everything gradually settles like the flakes in a snow globe. Your attention becomes focused on the mind, your physical senses withdraw, your mind dissolves into the substrate consciousness, and all appearances fade into the empty vacuity of the substrate. This is settling the mind in its natural state—the relative ground state.

Discovering the Substrate

There are two terms that are used to describe the ground of the mind, and I am convinced that they refer to exactly the same experience, although some might debate this. In the Dzogchen tradition, the relative ground state into which the psyche dissolves in shamatha is called the *alayavijñana*, or substrate consciousness. The term "alayavijñana" does not appear in the Pali Canon or in the Theravadin commentaries; however, another term, *bhavanga*, is used instead, which can be translated as "ground of becoming," where *bhava* means to "become" and *anga* has "basis" as one of its meanings. An excellent, scholarly presentation of the bhavanga is given by Peter Harvey in his book *The Selfless Mind*.[77]

I find it fascinating to compare the two Buddhist lineages of Theravada and Dzogchen, which experienced very little contact for hundreds of years. Dzogchen originated in India and evolved on the far side of the Himalayas, while Theravada prevailed in Burma, Sri Lanka, and other areas. Since these traditions had no common language, it seems safe to assume that the Dzogchen accounts of the alayavijñana were developed independently of the Theravadin notion of the bhavanga.

The Theravadin tradition describes two ways in which we access the bhavanga, the ground of becoming, which is the ground state when all the activities of the mind have subsided. We access it naturally and effortlessly both when we fall into dreamless sleep and when we die. The Tibetan Dzogchen tradition says exactly the same thing about the alayavijñana but also maintains that it can be accessed by means of effort and training: upon achieving shamatha, there is vivid awareness of the substrate. In both traditions, the senses are said to dissolve. I think the similarities are striking; these are independent tracks of contemplative inquiry with different names for the same experience.

One of the greatest discoveries concerning the nature of the mind—

not yet confirmed by modern science—is that its natural ground state is blissful. Having released habitual anger, craving, and neurosis, the mind is settled without being suppressed, manipulated, or contrived; and it naturally dissolves into its ground state. The substrate consciousness is simply aware, luminous, blissful, and nonconceptual.

It is an enormously important insight into human nature that the mind with which we normally operate, the one typically studied by psychologists, is characterized by habitual afflictions. As Sigmund Freud (1856–1939) said, psychoanalysis endeavors to take us from an unbearable state of neurosis to a bearable state of neurosis. I believe Freud's limited notion of the possibilities for human flourishing and virtue has seriously impoverished the modern psyche. It would be unfortunate to assume that the habitual ground state and the natural ground state are merely religious dogmas. These are extraordinary claims that can be tested empirically—they are either true or false. The nature of the mind when it settles into its ground state should be the subject of scientific as well as contemplative inquiry.

Freud, as a careful inspector of human experience, made a very germane point in *Civilization and Its Discontents*, saying that there are many circumstances to make us unhappy, but relatively few to make us happy:

> We are so made that we can derive intense enjoyment only from a contrast and very little from a state of things. Thus our possibilities of happiness are already restricted by our constitution. Unhappiness is much less difficult to experience. We are threatened with suffering from . . . our own body, . . . the external world, . . . [and] our relations to other men.[78]

This is true because our psyches are deeply ingrained with mental afflictions—craving, hostility, envy, pride, and the delusion of reification that grasps on to self and other as being absolutely separate—which take all the fun out of life. When habitual afflictions are operative, a person can be miserable despite having a loving family, abundant wealth, beautiful surroundings, and nonstop sensual pleasures. Depression, resentment, and anger are torturers that override all external pleasures. If we are strongly habituated to mental afflictions, then it's no wonder we are primed to suffer—any pleasure must overcome a groundswell of unhappiness.

Relative Feeling

During Palden Gyatso's thirty-three years of abuse and torture in Chinese concentration camps, the days when food was given were the relatively good days, even though the food was revolting. The days with no torture were the best days. When Palden Gyatso was given his freedom, he probably felt a sense of joy that surpassed anything we have experienced. Other people remain dissatisfied even when they possess vast wealth, unrestricted freedom, and extravagant luxuries.

This raises an important ontological issue. Can feelings be measured on an absolute scale that is valid in all circumstances, or do they always arise relative to some context, with no intrinsic positive or negative magnitude or valence? One discovery, replicated many times in positive psychology, concerns the relationship between wealth and happiness. Over the last fifty years, Americans have become wealthier, and we have stuffed our homes and lives with goods and services. Nevertheless, with obvious exceptions, many people have become more affluent together, and there's the rub. When everybody gets wealthier, nobody gets happier, because we value our wealth only on a relative scale.

Closely inspect the nature of pleasant, unpleasant, and neutral feelings. Do they bear an absolute intensity and a positive or negative valence, irrespective of their context? I strongly suspect that they do not and that feelings are analogous to energy in the classical physical model. No absolute quantity of energy can be determined—energy is always measured relative to some arbitrary zero point.

Genuine Happiness

If feelings aroused by sensory stimuli, thoughts, and memories always arise relative to a context, then what constitutes genuine happiness? What is a true source of happiness? The Buddha, speaking as a researcher of happiness and suffering, advised us to examine feelings carefully to find happiness that is not simply relative and not dependent upon pleasurable stimuli.

A clear distinction can be drawn between mundane, hedonic happiness and genuine happiness.[79] Hedonic happiness arises in response to pleasant stimuli. Many of us pursue happiness by seeking pleasant stimuli from friends, families, jobs, homes, possessions, and entertainment. However, as soon as these stimuli are removed, the resultant pleasures vanish too. In Buddhism, these are called the eight mundane concerns: material acquisition and loss, sensual pleasure and pain, praise and blame, and fame and defamation. All such mundane concerns arise due to sensory stimuli.

The Buddha described three sources of genuine happiness. The first one is happiness due to ethical blamelessness. This pertains not to what you get from the world but to the quality of life and conduct that you bring to the world. If you know with confidence that in your interactions with other people you have done your very best not to injure them, and your intent is to treat others decently, respectfully, and honestly, then there arises a sense of well-being and blamelessness. The Buddha called this happiness sixteen times more valuable than mundane happiness derived from sensory stimuli.

Many years ago, when I was living in the San Francisco Bay Area, I was driving home in my little hatchback. I was in the fast lane, in heavy traffic, when the cars in front of me suddenly slammed on their brakes for no apparent reason. I saw the brake lights and hit my brakes, screeching up to the car in front of me without touching it. My satisfaction lasted only an instant—until I was hit from behind. Then another car slammed into the pileup. I suffered whiplash, and my car was crushed like an accordion. When I got out of my totaled car, I felt vividly peaceful and almost happy because I had done my best to avoid injuring anyone else. I would have felt awful if I had crashed into the car in front of me because my mind had been wandering. My neck hurt, but I enjoyed a happy feeling of blamelessness.

The second dimension of genuine happiness and well-being is one that arises through developing exceptional mental balance. A salient example of this is the practice of samadhi. When you achieve samadhi, particularly with the deeply focused attention of shamatha, a sense of well-being arises. Calming the mind and drawing it inward is not the only road to samadhi, which can also be reached by focusing one's spiritual practice on the cultivation of loving-kindness. Over extended periods of cultivating loving-kindness, it will arise increasingly spontaneously, with fewer people excluded. This will definitely lead to a sense of well-being that does not derive from the world but from the quality of awareness one brings to the world. Cultivating the qualities of the heart, emotional balance, and attentional balance create the conditions leading to samadhi and a resultant sense of well-being.

Finally, there is a third aspect of well-being and happiness that arises from gaining insight into the nature of reality. The bliss of knowing reality as it is constitutes a frequent theme in many of the world's contemplative traditions, such as the Taoist tradition and early Christianity. Saint Augustine (354–430) described it as truth-given joy: a sense of well-being that comes from knowing the truth. In his case, he was speaking of knowing God—not just believing or having faith but actually experiencing God face-to-face, with profound realization or contemplative insight.

A good analogy to this is found in the experience of dreams. We have all had nonlucid dreams, and in many of them we feel anxious, uneasy, or unhappy. In fact, about 80 percent of dreams carry a negative affective tone. This is not surprising because when dreaming begins for the ordinary, habitual mind, mental afflictions like craving, anxiety, and hatred come out to torment us. Even worse, in a nonlucid dream we fail to recognize the dream as a dream—we are fundamentally deluded about reality. Freud correctly called the ordinary dream a delusional state, where events are taken as real, emotional responses are evoked, and everything is reified. This fundamental delusion generates craving, hostility, and so forth. The deck is stacked against us in a nonlucid dream. On the other hand, we can be cruising along in an ordinary dream, and suddenly it registers—we're dreaming! A radical shift occurs in a dream when we realize that we're dreaming.

I have collaborated extensively with psychologist Stephen LaBerge, a world expert on lucid dreaming. He has studied lucid dreamers for decades and has experienced well over a thousand lucid dreams himself. A very common experience of people who become lucid and sustain this recognition is to feel a sense of happiness, bliss, or euphoria. This sense of well-being does not occur because the dream is pleasant but because they know the truth about their experience. A truth-given joy arises from recognizing: "This is a dream." If one can sustain this ascertainment, the sense of bliss may continue throughout the dream, regardless of dream occurrences.

This raises a provocative question. What would it be like to be lucid in the waking state? Of course, we believe we are already lucid since we are not asleep. On one occasion, Buddha Shakyamuni was sitting under a banyan tree when a Brahmin named Dona approached him in awe, asking if he was a god. The Tathagata said no. The Brahmin asked if he was a kind of celestial being (Skt. *gandharva*) or nature spirit (Skt. *yaksha*), but again the Buddha denied it. When asked if he was a human, he denied that too. Finally, Dona asked the Buddha if he was neither divine, nor nonhuman, nor human, then what was he? He replied that he was awake (Skt. *buddha*).[80]

This implied that Dona was not awake. The Buddha was also referring to us. We might think we are awake, at least relative to being asleep. But relative to a higher state of consciousness, we are in a nonlucid state right now. There is tremendous joy to be derived from the insight of knowing reality as it is: the joy of awakening.

The application of mindfulness to feelings is an immensely rich practice. Our feelings are so dear to us that to understand them and be released from their grip would be very liberating. No longer holding feelings closely, we can simply be present with them. At first it may seem difficult to examine feelings. Images, thoughts, and emotions flutter in and out, and our feelings about them are just as fleeting. However, with increasing familiarity, this practice becomes easier.

The four close applications of mindfulness are central pillars of Buddhist wisdom. Nyanaponika Thera called them the heart of Buddhist meditation. Monks, nuns, and lay practitioners continue to engage in these practices for years, if not lifetimes. This is a subtle domain that cannot be mastered in a day. It is quite normal—even when we deliberately evoke thoughts, memories, and so forth—to find it difficult to bring forth and attend to an emotion or feeling. Even happy memories vanish quickly. It takes extended familiarization to fine-tune the awareness for careful scrutiny of feelings, and the details of their emergence, manifestation, and dissolution unfold slowly.

By developing familiarity with this process, you learn to attend to feelings dispassionately instead of habitually identifying with them and projecting them upon objects. You become aware that the basis for all these designations is actually your own feelings—not some intrinsic quality of the object. This practice can be very useful when you are engaged in the world. As reality rises up to meet you, feelings of dissatisfaction and pleasure are bound to occur. When they do, if you recall this practice, you can actually observe feelings as they manifest in full force. With increasing familiarization, you can explore the rich abundance of feelings in everyday life, where there is never a shortage.

We are skimming rapidly over a practice that is absolutely foundational—just getting our feet wet in the shallow end of the pool. After this taste of feelings, we will move on to the explicit contents and processes of the mind, the ground of the mind, and finally to phenomena at large.

GUIDED MEDITATION:
Falling Asleep II

Attend to the space of the mind and its contents—
falling asleep lucidly

If you find it very easy to fall asleep, you might experiment with falling asleep while settling the mind in its natural state. Rest supine in the corpse pose with your eyes closed. Then settle your mind in its natural state, and see if you can fall asleep while doing so. People who find it very easy to fall asleep may be able to maintain clarity and lucidity during their descent into sleep: falling asleep wakefully.

Maintaining lucidity as you are falling asleep, you may become aware of the substrate. If you then invert your awareness, you might detect the substrate consciousness as you enter dreamless sleep. If you can maintain lucidity through this process and then emerge into a dream, it might be a lucid dream from the start. This is quite possible for people who find it easy to fall asleep.

For people who find it more difficult to fall asleep, I would emphasize the importance of getting a good night's sleep. This can be facilitated by full-body awareness, mindfulness of the breath, relaxation with every out-breath, and simply releasing all thoughts. ❧

❧ 7 ❧
Mindfulness of the Mind

THE THIRD of the four close applications of mindfulness concerns mental events and processes. Attending to mental phenomena is a subtle practice. Success in observing mental events as they occur is not achieved by trying harder but, counterintuitively, by relaxing more deeply while maintaining the luminosity of awareness.

NATURAL BALANCE

The practice I call balancing earth and wind was a mainstay in the Shamatha Project retreats. The earth aspect entails full-body awareness—letting awareness permeate the entire field of tactile sensations, with special emphasis on the earth element, while attending to the sensations of the breath throughout the body. The wind aspect refers to the practice of settling the mind in its natural state, for in this practice we "face into the wind" of the ongoing flow of thoughts, images, and other mental events, like a falcon kiting into the wind.

These practices can be done in any posture, but the supine position is particularly good for evoking the earth element. Many people find that an upright position enhances clarity of attention. The best position depends on your tendency toward excitation or laxity. If your mind tends toward excitation, distraction, and restlessness, the supine position can be quite helpful. Excitation is overcome by the bodily feeling of profound melting in the corpse pose. A supine position promotes deep physical and mental relaxation, so often lacking in our hyperactive world. On the other hand, when the mind tends toward dullness, laxity, and lethargy, a vigilantly maintained seated posture offers the advantage of enhanced vividness and clarity of attention. Posture is of tremendous value in counteracting both mental excitation and laxity.

The following practice consists of two sessions, with a short break in between. The first session focuses on the earth element; a deep sense of relaxation results from full-body awareness in the supine position, ideal for attending to a large field of contact with the earth element. The second session focuses on the space of the mind and its contents, for which a seated position is optimal.

GUIDED MEDITATION:
Balancing Earth and Wind I

Attend to the domain of tactile sensations—
observing without distraction or grasping

Begin by letting your awareness slip into and permeate the field of tactile sensations, being mindfully present throughout the body. If you notice areas of tightness or constriction, which for many people occurs in the shoulders, the face, the area around the eyes, and the eyes themselves, release this tension as you breathe out. Let your body settle, melting in comfort and ease.

When your body is comfortable, there is no need to move, so remain motionless. Stillness supports the coherence of attention— movement fragments it. Even in the supine position, mentally adopt a posture of vigilance: body straight, arms to the sides, palms up, and shoulders relaxed. This is a posture for formal meditation, not napping or daydreaming. Assume this posture only for meditation, and the association will become habitual; vigilance overcomes laxity.

Conclude the initial settling of the body by taking three slow, deep breaths—breathing down into the lower abdomen, then expanding the diaphragm, and finally breathing into the chest. Release the breath effortlessly, while mindfully attending to the sensations of the breath throughout the body. Repeat this three times.

Relax progressively with each breath, releasing muscular tension on the out-breath. Release any thought, image, or memory immediately, letting everything go with each out-breath. Allow your respiration to settle without intervention or control. As your relaxation deepens, you may become aware that the body is effortlessly breathing itself.

Settle the mind in a sense of ease. Set aside all concerns about the past and the future; even if they are legitimate concerns, they do not require action right now. Give yourself permission to release all thoughts—there is nothing whatsoever that you must think about. At ease, and without a care in the world, let your awareness rest quietly, permeating the field of tactile sensations.

As sensations correlated with the breath arise and pass throughout the body, let your awareness rest in a larger space that is motionless. From this larger space, attend to the subspace of the tactile field; even as tactile events come and go, let your awareness remain still.

The very essence of awareness is to illuminate. Let your awareness naturally and spontaneously illuminate the entire field of tactile events, especially the sensations of the earth element. The supine position offers solid contact under the legs, torso, head, and arms. Let your awareness hug the earth like a motionless ground fog in a meadow.

While resting your awareness in the field of the body, let it illuminate the tactile sensations that arise, including tingling, pulsing, warmth, motion, and all sensations correlated with the breath. Relax deeply and let go with each out-breath. With each in-breath, gently arouse your attention and take a fresh interest in the tactile field.

Attend to the tactile domain and whatever events arise within it without being distracted by thoughts or impressions from other sense fields. Sustain an ongoing flow of unwavering mindfulness, noting especially the sensations associated with the respiration wherever they most distinctly arise in the body. Without grasping or preference, remain luminously present with whatever arises in this field. Witness even strong tactile feelings without desire or aversion—don't identify with them. Let your awareness be as still as space, your body as still as a mountain.

If at any time you discover with introspection that you have fallen into distraction or excitation, relax more deeply, allowing your awareness to descend silently into the field of the body and return to the tactile domain. If you find the mind growing dull, arouse a fresh interest in the practice and focus your attention.

Take a moment to stretch, maintaining mindfulness, and continue directly to the next session. ✎

Attend to the space of the mind and its contents—
hovering in the present moment

Settle the body in its natural state and the respiration in its natural rhythm. As a preliminary exercise to stabilize the mind and calm discursive thoughts, you may find it helpful to count twenty-one breaths—a very brief count at the end of each inhalation.

With your eyes at least partially open, rest your gaze vacantly in the space in front. Direct your full attention to the space of the mind and whatever arises within it. Some mental contents seem to be relatively objective, such as dialogue, music, and images. Other mental events are experienced as subjective impulses of desire, emotion, and other states.

Maintain a deep sense of ease in body and mind as you focus your attention on the mental domain. You may wish to maintain a deliberate, peripheral awareness of the breath by attending closely to the space of the mind and its contents with each inhalation and then relaxing deeply with each exhalation. Sustain an ongoing flow of unwavering mindfulness, illuminating the domain of the mind and attending to whatever arises without distraction or grasping. With no preference for fewer thoughts, different emotions, or particular states of mind, simply remain luminously and discerningly present.

Observe thoughts and other mental events along with the space in which they arise. Mental events arising from moment to moment are their own reality—they may not correspond to anything independent of your mind. Attend to them without becoming entangled, slipping into the past, or anticipating the future. Let your awareness hover in the present moment. ☛

RELINQUISHING CONTROL

There is a close relationship between shamatha and vipashyana. Development of the physical and mental relaxation, stability, and vivid attention of shamatha is an essential prerequisite for finely honed, mindful probes of the body, mind, and other phenomena. Attempting to practice vipashyana with a mind that is scattered and dull is unlikely to produce transformative changes. Although this is an important reason for combining shamatha with vipashyana, their relationship is deeper.

Shamatha is indispensible in the investigation of the human need for control. In the practice of vipashyana, a central theme is deeply probing the nature of personal identity: How do we conceive of, grasp on to, and reify our "selves"? Is there any basis in reality for our concepts of identity? In addition to such self-conceptualizing, there is also an active sense of ego that declares: "I am." This reified sense of self often manifests as the need for control. We exercise control over our body, mind, possessions, and even other people—our reach may be vast. Some people seem intoxicated with power, expressing the drive to validate themselves: "I have control and power over others, extensive wealth, and a large dominion, so I am worthy." We all would like to think of ourselves as being of value—not worthless. Control is central to this self-concept. Feeling helpless and out of control is most unpleasant.

In the practice of shamatha, especially in mindfulness of the breath and settling the mind in its natural state, we deliberately give up control. It is easy to control the breath to some degree—holding it, breathing deeply or shallowly, or regulating it rhythmically. The breath is quite malleable, and, within certain constraints, our respiration responds to our faintest desires. The human tendency is to control whatever we can, especially when we are attending closely. Instead, in this practice we are developing a nonfluctuating flow of clear attentiveness to something that is readily controllable—without deliberately influencing it.

The notion that quiet, rhythmic breathing is preferable can very easily affect the breath, even without conscious control. In a recent retreat, having received these same instructions, one person tried to impose regularity on his breath, thinking that correct breathing is rhythmic and deep. When I said, "Breathe as though you're deep asleep," another person recalled observing people who were deep asleep, and he tried to duplicate the shallow breathing he noticed. All such forms of control over the breath, no matter how well motivated, are to be avoided in this practice. The instruction is to release all intentions—just let the breath be.

Everyone is gifted in one way or another, with diverse educations and practical skills, but we are all massively overqualified for the practice of following the breath. No problem-solving skills, imagination, or artistic abilities are needed to relax the mind, release thoughts, and attend closely to the breath. Nevertheless, it is quite challenging to release all vestiges of control when full attention is focused on the eminently malleable respiration. The breath is influenced by the subtlest of preferences and expectations.

In the shamatha practice of mindfulness of the breath, we voluntarily relinquish control of the breath. We do not actively probe into our sense of personal identity, challenge the existence of an independent self, or eradicate reification, but our usual sense of being in control is 95 percent unemployed. We could control many things—move about, speak, think various thoughts, and so forth—but we choose not to. In attending to the breath without controlling it, we still control something: we constrain our attention from roving among myriad objects in the other sense fields, anticipating the future, and remembering the past. Control is exercised by focusing the attention on the breath and deliberately releasing thoughts and distractions.

Furthermore, if our faculty of introspection detects that the mind is falling into excitation or laxity, we exert control by taking countermeasures. If the mind is falling into distraction, our first line of defense is to relax more deeply and then return to the meditative object. When introspection detects dullness, we exert control by arousing fresh attention. The ego's role in this practice is limited to selecting the object of attention, maintaining this selection, and taking countermeasures against excitation and laxity. This is a limited job description because the vast majority of things that we could be doing and controlling have been eliminated.

Ego Unemployment

The practice of mindfulness of the breath is deceptively simple. At first it appears to be flat and uninteresting, but the dimensions and layers of this practice are subtle and nuanced. To a very large extent, we are practicing egolessness by relinquishing control of everything except the focus and quality of our attention. We are deliberately seeking not to influence the object of our attention.

This skill can be useful in daily life, whether we are raising children or engaging professionally, whenever we slip into what Jewish existentialist philosopher Martin Buber (1878–1965) called "I-It" relationships. When we attend to friends, colleagues, or strangers simply because we want something in return, we are manipulating and controlling them for our gratification—as if they were objects. On the other hand, the ability to give someone the full quality of attention that we are cultivating here—close, stable, vivid attention without control—can be very helpful. One of my favorite quotes comes from my dear friend Father Laurence Freeman, who says, "The greatest gift we can give to another person is our attention."

Of course, if a person is hungry, we should give him or her food not merely our attention. But without first paying attention, the chance that we can provide people with what they truly need, whether it is food, clothing, shelter, or companionship, is almost nil. If we studiously avert our gaze from a homeless person, this lack of attention guarantees we will not help. If we give our attention, there is the possibility of exercising wise judgment. Shall I offer something here? What would be of greatest benefit? These are personal choices that will not even be considered if attention is not given first. When we attend to a person or situation skillfully and closely, with no urge to control, sustaining awareness of what is actually present with clarity and stability, we can penetrate the reality of the situation. We will not react habitually by thinking of how to benefit ourselves. This very useful skill can be cultivated with a simple practice—mindfulness of the breath.

In the practice of settling the mind in its natural state, the object of attention is also something over which we can exert some control. There are many things we commonly do with our minds that seem almost effortless. If I say, "Please visualize a peach," or "Remember where you lived when you were ten," you can do so immediately. The mind really is under our control to a certain extent, at least in terms of thoughts and our focus of attention. When we bring the force of vigilant, clear, unwavering, discerning awareness to the space of the mind and its contents, it is very easy to react by suppressing a thought or diverting the attention. Nevertheless, in this practice we relinquish control over the mind and its contents, just as we did with the breath. We are simply present with whatever appears.

Are we directly challenging the delusional sense of self, the autonomous "I" that's in charge? Not yet. This is still shamatha, which is being developed as a foundation for efficient and effective vipashyana. Are we exerting any control when we attend to the space of the mind? We are exerting control over our attention, just as we do in selectively attending to the breath. In this case, we are selectively attending to mental events from among the six domains of experience. This is an act of will, so our reified sense of self is still being employed. As we settle the mind in its natural state, observing mental events and the space in which they arise, if attention starts to slip into laxity or excitation, the remedies are the same. The primary remedies for all shamatha practices are to relax when we detect excitation and arouse the attention when we detect laxity. This necessarily entails some exertion of will and effort, which will probably be done with a sense that "I am." The reified sense of self is exerting itself by selecting a domain or an object of mindfulness. We are exerting our will to balance the attention—but nothing more.

Attending closely to the space of the mind and its contents without preference, even though nothing could be easier than generating or inhibiting thoughts, is not easily accomplished. The challenge is even subtler than attending closely to the breath without modifying it, allowing the body to breathe itself with no sense of being in charge. Bring to the mental domain this same quality of awareness, utter nonattachment, nongrasping, and nonpreference, and simply attend to whatever comes up without influencing it in any way. This is a tall order, but it is the quintessence of the practice. Attend luminously and discerningly, recognizing wholesome thoughts, unwholesome thoughts, mental afflictions, emotions, and the gamut of mental events. Observe them with such a loose sense of relaxation that they continue to arise unhindered.

Opening the Pandora's box of your mind and allowing free associations to flow, you do not care whether acrid fumes are billowing or iridescent butterflies are lofting into your field of consciousness. The space of the mind is wide-open, and you are simply present with whatever manifests in this space. It is a demanding challenge to relinquish control and maintain a spacious awareness regardless of what arises. The ego, the reified sense of "I am," is quick to jump in and reassert control, starting with preferences: "This thought needs a little bit of editing, that one's not appropriate, and some thoughts are completely improper—I won't allow those!"

Whatever comes up, whether vulgar or sublime, coarse or subtle, unpleasant or pleasant, observe the complete homogeneity of your thoughts. The Dzogchen literature calls this the view that everything is of one taste (Skt. *ekarasa*). It is certainly possible to actualize this view—it is not an asymptotic progression stretching to infinity. Observation without preference is not achieved by trying harder to eliminate preferences but by releasing more completely and relaxing more deeply, deactivating habitual grasping at progressively subtler levels. Whatever appears has no owner or controller; it simply manifests, plays itself out, and dissolves back into the space of the mind.

Our practice is one of egolessness. Without actively probing into the ego to see whether such a reified entity actually exists, the sense of "I am" has been virtually idled. At the same time, we are developing stability and vividness of attention, along with the enormously important faculty of metacognition. With introspection, we can do more than remember or deduce the nature of mental events—we can directly observe them as they arise. Relinquishing control is the essence of the practice.

Bashful Maidens and Circling Ravens

When we first attempt to observe the mind, we often find that the sheer act of closely observing mental events causes thoughts, memories, and images to vanish on contact. We try to observe without influencing, but every time we inspect something, it seems to disappear. The problem is that the phenomena we seek to observe are being overcome by the intensity of our inspection.

The classic metaphor used to describe this problem is at least a thousand years old, and it concerns a "bashful maiden" and a "playboy," to update the terms. A bashful maiden strolls in a village courtyard where she is spotted by a playboy on the prowl. His intense, penetrating stare makes the bashful maiden very uncomfortable, and she quickly slips away. The playboy is advised to try a more delicate approach, perusing maidens with a sideways glance rather than a direct gaze. Like the bashful maiden, your thoughts, images, and memories are easily overpowered. The solution is to relax more deeply, like a skillful playboy who avoids frightening maidens with an overbearing manner, charming them instead with nonchalance.

As you become more adept and the practice is going well, the lovely metaphor of the navigator and the raven may apply. In the Book of Genesis, Noah first sends a raven and later sends a dove to determine whether the floodwaters have receded.[81] Navigators in ancient India also brought caged ravens on long sea voyages, releasing them to locate the nearest land. Ravens are smart birds. When released, they circle higher and higher, looking for land, because they cannot survive in the water. If they see land, they head for it. The navigator simply watches the raven circling upward without losing track of it. In this metaphor, the raven flies as high as it can without detecting land in any direction. In order to survive, it has only one choice: to return to the ship from whence it came.

Similarly, when you are settling the mind in its natural state and a discursive thought circles up like a loosed raven, simply observe it passively, without trying to affect it in any way. Watch it carefully and it will play itself out, circling back down again. Having manifested in the space of your mind, the thought has nowhere else to go, just as the raven must return to the ship. When you become very relaxed and attentive in this practice, you can clearly observe a thought's genesis, emergence, culmination, stimulation of another thought, and dissolution back into the space of the mind. As you engage in this practice, there is a sequence of thoughts but no active agent—thoughts just happen.

If Descartes had practiced settling the mind in its natural state, he might have come to different conclusions. He said, "I think, therefore I am," but if by this assertion he meant that there needs to be an autonomous thinker for thoughts to occur, he was mistaken. In this practice, it becomes perfectly clear that thoughts just happen, and they do not require an active agent. The practice is to simply observe the phenomena in the space of the mind. When there are no phenomena, observe the space from which they arise, in which they manifest, and into which they dissolve. This constitutes a robust foundation for the close application of mindfulness to the mind itself.

GUIDED MEDITATION:
Settling the Mind in Its Natural State III

Attend to the space of the mind and its contents—
observing arising, abiding, and dissolving

Settle the body in its natural, ground state and the breath in its natural rhythm. For a short while, let your awareness permeate the field of tactile sensations. Be present with the earth element, grounding your awareness, while attending to the tactile events associated with the breath arising in this field, observing without distraction or grasping.

Now, with your eyes open and gaze vacant, direct your attention to the field of the mind and whatever arises within it. Sustain an unwavering flow of mindfulness, without distraction or grasping.

Attend to the space of the mind and its contents without preconceptions, simply observing whatever arises in this domain. Maintain the relaxation, stability, and vividness you have developed in shamatha practice, and use this platform to closely inspect the nature of mental events.

Notice immediately as a mental event arises. Observe closely the factors that influence the origination of thoughts, images, memories, and all other mental processes. How and from where do these phenomena emerge?

You might become aware of a mental event only after it has arisen. Once it is present, carefully monitor how it abides. Does it have a location, or is it in motion? Is the nature of this phenomenon changing or stable?

All mental events eventually come to an end—witness their demise. Do they suddenly disappear or gradually dissolve and fade away? Must they be destroyed, or do they disintegrate by themselves?

Out of habit, you might find yourself caught up in a thought or other mental activity. Without rejecting it, let that which entangles you become your object of meditation. Simply relax, release your grasp, and maintain your awareness of it. Observe the thought without grasping or distraction. ☞

On Creativity

In addition to their long-term benefits, both shamatha and vipashyana can be useful in enhancing creativity, ingenuity, and everyday problem solving, which are important whether we are meditators or not. When I was a physics student studying advanced mechanics, our professor gave us a horribly complicated problem. After staring at it for hours, I couldn't even see how to begin solving it. I understood the question, but with no way to approach it, frustration set in—I was getting nowhere. So I dropped it, went into my meditation room, and practiced mindfulness of the breath, without considering the problem at all. In the midst of this, the light bulb went on, and I saw exactly how to tackle the problem. I didn't have the answer, but I knew how to break it into simpler problems, which eventually led to the solution.

Whether the problem is an intellectual exercise or an interpersonal issue, a rigid, fixated mind is unlikely to discover a creative solution. By dropping the problem, we do not entirely forget that a solution is needed. When the mind melts into fluidity—having released all grasping—there is a deep, spacious mode of awareness in which connections are formed more easily. Without conscious effort, a solution often comes to mind in a spark of insight.

The shamatha practice of settling the mind in its natural state is a marvelous technique for doing exactly this, and mindfulness of the breath also works very effectively. Moving out of a relatively rigid mode of operation, the mind releases fixed ideas, grasping, clinging, and anxiety. The psyche gradually settles down toward the substrate consciousness. This might be called a superfluid state because it has no internal resistance—it is nonconceptual, luminous, and blissful. But the psyche and the substrate consciousness are not mutually exclusive states: they are intimately intertwined. The substrate consciousness manifests as the psyche, providing a basis from which all subjective mental processes arise, during both waking and dreaming states.

As our awareness gravitates toward the substrate consciousness, we approach a superfluid state of awareness saturated by deep knowledge that is implicit rather than explicit. Moments of inspiration give rise to flows of intuition and creativity. By tapping into this wellspring, we can use insight to resolve practical and interpersonal issues, even when they are not explicit. I would love to see scientific studies of the elusive mental faculties of intuition and creativity, hard to define but enormously important, and their relationship with practices such as mindfulness of the breath and settling the mind in its natural state. Can engaging in these practices enhance the ability to find intuitive and creative solutions to problems?

Settling the mind in its natural state will open up Pandora's box like no other practice I know. It is perfectly legitimate to approach this practice with a specific, personal motivation. As a manager, parent, gardener, or cook, a situation in your life might call for greater clarity, a fresh perspective, or creative insight. Pose the question, go into the practice, and see what your substrate consciousness dishes up. It's bound to be interesting!

Sometimes too many insights can be disruptive. After four years of doctoral studies at Stanford, having completed my exams but not my dissertation, I felt compelled to escape academia for the wilderness. With my mentor's permission, I began a six-month winter retreat, practicing settling the mind in its natural state in the splendid solitude of the Sierra Nevada mountains. The problem was that there was a dissertation to be completed, and I involuntarily dragged it into the retreat. It was exasperating to be taking a break from my doctoral studies while my mind kept coming up with one creative idea after another. Finally I learned that when a creative thought came up, it was better to make note of it to avoid perpetuating the distraction. In between sessions I could flesh it out. Much of that material became my secondary dissertation, published as *The Taboo of Subjectivity*. This was not planned; it just came up so relentlessly that I had to write it down.

MIND ZONE

The practice of settling the mind in its natural state can be approached in a multitude of ways with various motivations. One might use it to achieve shamatha, settling in the substrate consciousness to develop stability and vividness of attention. In shamatha, we simply attend to the object of mindfulness without posing questions. This is a mode of stabilizing and clarifying attention rather than one of inquiry.

Question of Intent

Vipashyana always entails questioning, which is what distinguishes it from shamatha. We may ask highly complex questions that are analyzed in detail using discursive thinking. We may also ask very succinct questions, without any discursive cogitation. Investigating how thoughts and other mental events arise does not call for an extended analysis; instead, simply observe carefully.

Before learning to meditate, the most closely related experience I knew was bird watching. When you are listening to a bird's song or trying to differentiate one type of sparrow from another, you are looking for very specific features, such as a trill in the song or a spot on the wing. You pose a question and focus your attention without discursiveness. With a sharply focused attention, the answer becomes clear: "It's a Wilson's warbler, not a yellow warbler." A naturalist does not employ undirected awareness but engages in a very discerning mode of inquiry.

When questions probe very deeply, the investigation becomes ontological. What is the nature of mental events that arise? How do they exist? In what ways don't they exist? Is an agent required to generate these thoughts, or do they just happen? These are empirical questions with answers to be found. When such questions are being posed, settling the mind in its natural state becomes a vipashyana practice. But sometimes, even without overt questioning, by simply bringing bare attention to the domain of the mind and its contents, unsolicited insights can arise spontaneously—even deeply transformative ones.

The mode of inquiry that the Buddha teaches in the vipashyana practice of the close application of mindfulness to the mind is to investigate the origination, mode of abiding, and dissolution of mental events. How do they arise? When they are present, are they stable or fluctuating? How do they dissolve? First we observe mental events in ourselves, "internally." Then we observe them in others, "externally," by observation of behavior, inference from experience, and intuition, which can give us insight into others' minds. Even without knowing a person, it is possible to accurately detect restlessness, anxiety, unhappiness, and anger—we're not simply guessing. We can improve our accuracy if we have gotten to know the person well and refined our powers of observation.

Settling the mind in its natural state as a shamatha practice can be a preparation for the close application of mindfulness to the mind as a vipashyana inquiry. These two go together like a hand and glove. We don't say, "Now I will attend to everything arising in the mind except feelings, which I will ignore." We are more inclusive. The spotlight fell first on feelings because they are the driving forces perpetuating the misery of samsara as well as propelling us toward virtue and enlightenment. Whether we are meditators or not, feelings are enormously important.

All in Mind

Now we move to the grand arena of the mind, which includes all types of thoughts, feelings, emotions, mental states, and psychological processes.

Joy, surprise, fear, anger, and sadness are all grist for the mill. In both the practices of settling the mind in its natural state and in the third close application of mindfulness, our focus is on the domain of the mind and everything that arises within it.

As Damasio demonstrated, certain emotions have strong correlates in somatic experience. We may feel our hearts filled with joy or our guts wrenched in fear—feelings arise in the space of the body. Nevertheless, in these particular practices, we do not deliberately give attention to somatic experiences. They are legitimate features of experience, but we do not attend to them. When thoughts, emotions, and mental images appear, positive, negative, and indifferent feelings will naturally arise. In this practice, we maintain our focus on the mental aspect of an emotion or feeling. Although a correlated somatic experience might arise in the body, we do not attend to it. The best approach is to simply let it be. Don't try to prevent or suppress it. Keep your attention in the mental domain.

In the shamatha practice of settling the mind in its natural state, we focus on mental events. By sustaining this focus, the mind becomes progressively more collected. Samadhi means total collection of the mind—a gathering of all mental forces. With the attention focused on the mental domain, less awareness is directed to the other five fields of experience, which eventually grow dark. Continuing along this trajectory to shamatha, the senses and mind dissolve, and only the awareness of the empty vacuity of the substrate consciousness remains. This will not occur if you deliberately alternate between the physical and mental domains. Similarly, if you are paying close attention to your body and mind, you will not fall asleep. You cannot be asleep and vividly aware of your physical body at the same time.

The following practice consists of two sessions with a short break in between. The first session focuses on the earth element and the second on settling the mind in its natural state.

GUIDED MEDITATION:
Balancing Earth and Wind II

Attend to the domain of tactile sensations—
resting awareness as still as space

Ground yourself in the earth element, melting in a supine posture of comfort and ease. Settle the body in its natural state: relaxed, still, and vigilant. Be present with the earth element, with the body as still as a mountain. Let your awareness permeate the field of tactile sensations, attending to whatever arises without distraction or grasping.

Settle the breath in its natural rhythm, releasing tension with every out-breath. Give up all control, allowing the respiration to flow effortlessly at its own pace. Mindfully attend to the sensations correlated with the breath throughout the body, while releasing any preference or influence.

Settle the mind in a sense of ease. Release all concerns and thoughts about the past and the future. As sensations of the breath arise and pass throughout the body, let your awareness rest in a larger space that is motionless. Attend to the tactile domain without distraction from other sense fields, without grasping, and without preference. Sustain an ongoing flow of unwavering mindfulness, remaining luminously present with whatever arises. Let your awareness rest as still as space.

Sitting up slowly and mindfully, take a moment to stretch, and continue to the next session. ☞

Attend to the space of the mind and its contents—
inspecting for "I" and "mine"

Settle the body in its natural state and the breath in its natural rhythm.

With eyes open and gaze vacant, settle the mind in its natural state. Attend to the space of the mind and its contents without distraction or grasping. Experience the ongoing flow of heterogeneous thoughts, images, and memories, without responding by grasping or being distracted into an imaginary future or a remembered past.

As you examine the events arising in the space of the mind, you might feel ownership toward some thoughts. Other thoughts might seem to occur without any sense that you caused them—you are simply a witness. Examine these mental events to see if there is anything in their nature that differentiates some thoughts as being inherently your own. Investigate closely what makes some mental events seem to be yours, while others simply occur.

Remain as inactive as possible, avoiding any intervention in the space of the mind. Quietly witness whatever arises there and notice also when nothing arises. To the best of your ability, do not deliberately generate any thoughts, images, or mental activity. Observe the mind carefully to see how mental events arise, abide, and dissolve, inspecting closely for any suggestion of "I" or "mine." 🕭

Acting Intentionally

In the ancient descriptions of the progression of shamatha practice found in the Pali Canon and Theravadin commentaries, a distinction is made between the bhavanga, the ground of becoming, and the various mental activities that emerge from it. This kinetic mental activity is called *javana*, which literally means "running," and denotes the whole array of associative mental activities linking sensory perception with memories.

When we are deep asleep, the javana consciousness is dormant, disappearing into the bhavanga. If we are suddenly aroused from deep sleep, sensory perception emerges from the bhavanga, followed by a stream of various thoughts, desires, mental images, and emotions. These mental events and associations constitute the javana consciousness, and it is impelled by wholesome, unwholesome, and neutral volitions. It is during the crucial phase at the climax of the perceptual process that karma is said to be accumulated.

Buddhaghosa used the simile of a man sleeping beneath a tree who is awakened by a falling mango to illustrate the process of perception and the role of the javana consciousness.[82] The initial moments of arousal, adverting to, and examining the fallen mango correspond to the initial moments of the perceptual consciousness arising from the bhavanga. Actually consuming the fruit corresponds to the javana consciousness and the accrual of karma.

When we attend carefully to the gamut of mental processes, we see that defilements, or mental afflictions, soon make their appearance. In the Buddha's teachings, they are said to come and go like visitors. When afflictions visit our minds, the consequences for our behavior, other people, and our environment hinge crucially on the presence or absence of grasping.

Engaging correctly in this practice, we open wide Pandora's box. This is like the free association that might be encouraged in psychiatric analysis, but here we don't need to report; we simply observe whatever comes up without grasping. Practicing this for six or more hours per day over an extended period, things that you would never imagine will appear to your mind—they might shock you. People sometimes say, "When I said that, it wasn't really me talking." In our experience, certain types of thoughts, images, and desires do not conform to our idea of who we are—they just happen.

The instruction for this practice is to perform no editing whatsoever; nevertheless, we may harbor concerns about uninhibited free association. What if a malicious, dishonest, or depraved thought should manifest in our mind? Shouldn't highly negative thoughts be censored? From an ethical perspective, it seems irresponsible to allow afflictive thoughts and emotions to arise, wreaking mental havoc. Won't this accrue negative karma?

Crux of Karma

A critical distinction must be observed. The Buddhist term karma means "action," and it refers specifically to intentional action. Volition lies at the very crux of karma. When we take intentional action with body, speech, or mind, karma is accrued. In the Buddhist understanding, karmic imprints are stored in the substrate, or the bhavanga. There are wholesome, neutral, and unwholesome acts of body, speech, and mind. No preordained list has been commanded from on high—this is completely empirical. If the immediate consequences and ultimate repercussions of an act of body, speech, or mind are conducive to the flourishing of oneself and others, then the act is called wholesome or virtuous. Acts that have no impact are ethically neutral, whereas those whose consequences undermine our own and others' genuine happiness are called unwholesome.

In Buddhism, the notion of karma is embedded in the theory of the continuity of consciousness across lives. Seeds sown in one life can germinate and manifest in a future life, and in this life we can experience the fruition of karma from past lives. This theory can be tested empirically, but it requires a lot of time. The full fruition of an act comes when a karmic seed stored in the continuum of subtle mental consciousness germinates and ripens, manifesting as sickness, good fortune, or some other event in our lives. Whether this occurs later in this life or in a future life, we judge the seed to be wholesome or unwholesome by its fruits.

Applying this to mental activity, the simple arising of an angry, unwholesome, or evil thought is not the same as engaging in an activity—it is merely to witness an event. With no intent to actually carry out the deed, no karma is accumulated. Intent makes the crucial difference. A prosaic analogy is to imagine sitting in your car across the street from a bank and seeing masked men run out with bags of money. The fact that you witnessed a robbery does not make you an accessory to the crime. Similarly, if you witness the arising of an ugly mental event— without identifying with it or enacting it—then nothing unwholesome has occurred.

On the other hand, if you see robbers running with stolen money and you willingly offer your services as their driver, then you're an accessory to the crime, whether your offer is accepted or not. Attending to events arising in the mind, the existence of grasping is crucial. Do you identify with these events and invoke your intentions? If volitional action is taken, karma is accumulated.

Along with unwholesome mental states and karmic processes, for which intention is crucial, there are mental afflictions, which distort our perception of reality—we fail to see clearly. If I attend to Jack with attachment, then my perception of him will be biased toward the positive. I'll minimize any negative qualities he might have and exaggerate the positive ones. This can give rise to further attachment. On the other hand, if I see Joe with aversion, then I'll screen out his positive qualities, discount the neutral ones, and exaggerate any negative aspects. This can give rise to increased aversion, anger, or hatred.

In both cases, I perceive inaccurately due to my mental afflictions and biases. The epistemological result of distorted perception is fundamental misunderstanding. The experiential impact of mental afflictions like craving, hostility, delusion, pride, and envy is their defining characteristic: they disrupt the mind's equilibrium. Prior to the arising of a mental affliction, you may have been poised and calm, with a relatively balanced mind. When an intruder like anger or resentment enters the house of your mind, its force perturbs your balance, and ease is overcome by affliction. The universal effect of mental afflictions of all sorts is to disrupt mental equilibrium.

Let's imagine Jack did something really awful to me, and recalling this event, resentment starts to build. My mind returns repeatedly to Jack's deed, for which he never apologized, and angry thoughts arise. Insofar as I grasp on to and identify with these thoughts, my experience is disturbed and unsettled. Ruminating on Jack's past actions and how much I dislike him, my anger can easily infect other relationships. I might become irritable with someone else who is quite innocent. The mental afflictions are called poisons because their effect on the mind is toxic.

In the initial practice of settling the mind in its natural state, all sorts of thoughts will come up. When thoughts arise that could be unwholesome or unethical, we don't identify with them and engage our intentions: we simply observe them. Even when a strong mental affliction arises, if we don't grasp on to it—if we simply witness an orphan arising in the space of the mind—it will dissolve of its own accord. We discover in this process that the mind can actually unravel its own twists, tangles, and distortions, by mindfully resting in its natural state. It is crucial to attend very closely, intelligently, and discerningly, being utterly present—but without identification, grasping, aversion, suppression, or dissociation. In the process of observing our own mind without grasping, we can actually watch the mind heal itself. The mind's knots and contortions loosen up and dissolve into the space of the mind.

The extraordinary practice of settling the mind in its natural state is both diagnostic and therapeutic. Observing the mind, we sometimes see impulses, desires, emotions, and memories that carry strong emotional charges. Whether they are positive or negative, we allow free association to occur, and we explore deeper and deeper layers with diagnostic detachment. At the same time we can watch the mind heal itself. The mind becomes increasingly balanced as the practice deepens. Dredging the psyche, we shine the light of awareness on subconscious mental processes, memories, desires, and emotions. In free association, that which was suppressed or subconscious becomes conscious—fascinating discoveries await!

Substrate Consciousness

The bhavanga, in the early Pali literature, or alayavijñana, in later Sanskrit texts, is translated as the ground of becoming or the substrate consciousness. This is the dimension of consciousness from which the psyche springs each time you awaken, enter the dream state from deep sleep, or emerge from shamatha meditation. If you have been under general anesthesia and it wears off, your psyche emerges from the substrate consciousness. The psyche is an umbrella term referring to the array of mental states and activities we experience whenever the mind is active. When the mind goes quiet, what remains is the substrate consciousness.

Realms Apart

The substrate consciousness underlies the psyche, which is being dredged in this practice. It is deeper than the Freudian notion of the subconscious, which is still within the psyche, but different from the collective unconscious of Jung. Collaborating with quantum physics pioneer Wolfgang Pauli (1900–1958), Jung developed the notion of the *unus mundus*, or one world: a unitary, fundamental reality from which all formations of mind and matter emerge. Archetypes and synchronicity are cited as evidence that everything springs from this singular source. In Buddhism this is called the form realm (Skt. *rupadhatu*), and it is not confined to one person's continuum. We each have a psyche and our own substrate consciousness, which is not collective—it is the repository of our individual memories and imprints. However, if we slip into the substrate consciousness by way of shamatha, it is possible to access a deeper dimension of existence that is indeed a collective one.

The form realm is not individuated but collective and archetypal. This domain is more fundamental than our human constructs of mind and matter in the physical world. It is encountered by achieving shamatha, which gives access to the first dhyana: the entrance to the form realm. If you bring your mind to a state of further refinement, you can slip from the first dhyana into the progressively subtler second, third, and fourth dhyanas, still within the form realm.

Roger Penrose, one of the most brilliant mathematicians on the planet, has described the reality of mathematics with tremendous insight. He is very much inspired by Pythagoras and Plato in positing a purely mathematical dimension of reality that may be related to what Buddhists call the formless realm. George Ellis is another fine mathematician who argues that mathematical discoveries are just as real as physical or biological discoveries. Mathematical truths are discovered by using extremely rarefied ideas to venture conceptually into a realm of existence that is purely mathematical.

Consider the notion of the holographic universe that I've written about extensively in my book *Hidden Dimensions*.[83] Mainstream physicists suggest that all our experiences of galaxies and atoms are an illusory holographic display manifesting from an underlying ground. This ground transcends the display, and it holds the seeds of all appearances we can observe. From the Buddhist perspective, the underlying ground is the form realm. In Buddhist cosmogony, our everyday physical world emerges out of the form realm, which in turn emerges out of the formless realm. The form realm is like the domain of geometric forms that Plato theorized, and the formless realm may be associated with pure numbers and algebra.

It is fascinating that first-rate scientists like Pauli, Penrose, and Ellis have arrived at the notion that the more one investigates the nature of physical reality, the more mathematical it appears to be. Probing deeply into the nature of matter, it is not found to exist in and of itself. Instead, there are only mathematical abstractions, such as fields and probabilities, out of which the chunky stuff seems to materialize. Jung and Pauli's elegant theory of the *unus mundus* lies untested after forty years because nobody has a means to test it. On the other hand, Buddhism does offer methods of empirical verification. The form realm, which bears a strong resemblance to the *unus mundus*, can be experienced for yourself.

By achieving shamatha, you have access to the form realm. Pushing further to actual achievement of the first dhyana, your mind dwells there, as the Buddha said of his own experience. You have made your mental home in the form realm. Beyond this first echelon lie increasingly subtle domains of experience. At the limit of the form realm, in the fourth dhyana, it is said that advanced practitioners can remain in samadhi for days without even breathing.

Settling the mind in its natural state begins with the ability to observe the mind with stability and clarity. It's like getting a brand new telescope, which must be mounted solidly and focused accurately to obtain a clear image. Only then can you begin to make reliable observations, such as looking for moons around Jupiter. Our instrument is the practice of observing without distraction, intervention, distortion, preference, or aversion. When this ability becomes stable and clear, we can pose questions about the events arising in the space of the mind. Are they lingering and stable or momentary and effervescent?

Another interesting question is whether the mental events arising in the space of your mind are under your control or not. At first blush, they seem to be. If you want to think of a peach, you can do it in a flash. Clearly, our thoughts are controllable to some extent. On the other hand, can you simply decide that no thought shall arise for the next sixty seconds? Try it. Do your thoughts abide by your decision? If thoughts arose against your will, who was it that generated them? Is that even a meaningful question?

When you seem to be in control of your thoughts, is this simply an illusion? Are thoughts personal or impersonal? Is there something inherent in your thoughts that makes them intrinsically yours? Can you observe thoughts and mental images without affecting them, or are they inevitably modified, embellished, or destroyed by the sheer act of observing them? These are profound questions. Can you develop a lighter touch, like a biologist who learns to use a microscope very carefully so as not to injure a delicate, living specimen? This would be a handy skill.

Nature of Freedom

While some of these questions might seem esoteric, the question of free will is central to everyday life. Modern writers have produced many tomes on free will, but in the Sanskrit, Pali, and Tibetan literature this is not a fundamental concern—there isn't even a term for it. Free will and moral responsibility are certainly debated by nontheistic philosophers, but these become key issues when you believe in a God that created and governs the universe. Would an omnipotent God preordain some of His creatures to live on Earth for a short time and then sentence them to eternal damnation for actions they were powerless to prevent? If we can be consigned to hell for our sins, the existence of free will is critical. No free will means no responsibility. If your PC crashes, it's silly to punish it. If a robot helps you, it's useless to reward it. You can disassemble, repair, or replace a machine, but you can't punish or reward it. If we are simply programmed biological robots, then the notion of moral responsibility with reward and punishment makes no sense.

Since Buddhism does not operate from a theistic framework, free will does not pose such a dilemma. But even nontheists say we have free will, including prominent philosophers of mind like John Searle, Daniel Dennett, and Owen Flanagan. At the same time, these writers are reductionists, holding that human beings are merely biological organisms, and that mind, will, intention, and consciousness are nothing more than emergent properties of the brain. They assert that free will entails the ability to imagine some fortunate outcome in our future. We set goals to survive, flourish, and lead productive lives. Bearing our goals in mind, and understanding the consequences of our actions, we freely choose what to do and what not to do. When an impulse arises, we examine the consequences of our actions and choose the best response. Wisdom increases as we develop a clearer sense of the consequences of our actions and the nature of our flourishing. Such behavior is sensible, grounded, and wise, but I cannot imagine how a biological robot could manage it.

Owen Flanagan, who is a good friend, declares: "We are animals. Get over it!" If there is no other dimension to human existence, we will eventually understand everything about the mind in biological terms. It is an interesting hypothesis, but it seems peculiar to postulate the existence of free will while simultaneously reducing everything to matter and its epiphenomena. It certainly seems reasonable to think that we are biological organisms, and perhaps nothing more. If so, consciousness terminates at death; our actions are governed by the laws of physics, chemistry, and biology; and the notion of an agent who exercises free will is absurd. If we are biological robots, then everything we do is determined by physics and biology. Darwin contradicted some of his predecessors by saying that biology is not teleological—organisms are not designed to fulfill a purpose. Natural selection and random genetic mutation result in evolution but not in order to reach some preordained goal.

We humans have the sense of behaving with purpose, but teleological explanations are not accepted in mainstream physics, biology, or chemistry. If we are biological robots, there is no such thing as free will. Some people say so unequivocally, such as Daniel Wegner, in his book *The Illusion of Conscious Will*.[84] He claims our free will is illusory. Most Christians believe we have free will—God's gift to humanity. We are free to choose to accept Jesus as our savior or not and free to submit to God's will or not. We make our choices, so we are morally responsible; therein lies the practical appeal of the concept of free will. A Buddhist asks instead, "Who is it that makes choices, free or otherwise?" If there is no inherently existing self, there is no owner of free will, and no supernatural agent calling the shots. In Buddhist practice we simply attend to what arises, without imputing agency or ownership.

The Buddha's teachings do not address the topic of free will; instead, they point out the extent to which we are not free and how we may become freer. Liberation, enlightenment, or awakening is an aspiration, not a description of our current situation. Buddhism takes a refreshingly phenomenological approach to this topic, avoiding the metaphysical baggage. We need not invoke God, and we are not constrained to a biological mechanism. Neuroscientists who assume that we are merely biological robots have no clue how the brain produces mental phenomena. This is their "hard problem."

The phenomenological approach begins with the world of experience. When we venture out into the world, our mind encounters visitors like irritation, impatience, and arrogance. Perhaps we must complete a very important task, far too important to be delayed by the slowpoke ahead of us. We're not aware of our impatience; we're acutely aware that an inefficient person is causing us to be delayed. "Hurry up!" we grumble. In such a moment we are not free. We are acting impulsively and habitually due to our subjugation by mental afflictions. Our mouth is a puppet, manipulated by mental afflictions into saying things we may later regret. The effects ripple on and can escalate into conflict.

Craving works the same way. When an attractive object appears, craving arises, pulling us like a dog on a leash. The extremes of addiction are tragic. Where is the freedom of a person addicted to nicotine, alcohol, or methamphetamine? Obsessive thrill seeking, gambling, shopping, and eating can become deadly traps. When a mental affliction dominates our mind, we are completely fused with it. Our very sense of identity is controlled by desire, hatred, or ignorance. Where then is our freedom of will? Experientially, it's nonexistent.

It's not that we are never free. When mental afflictions are not active, we can investigate and initiate actions that will bring the greatest benefit to ourselves and others. Using our intelligence, generosity, kindness, and empathy, we can engage in thoughtful, helpful behavior. The Buddhist tradition makes no ontological assertions about free will; the issue is purely experiential. Under which circumstances are we more free and under which circumstances are we less free? We experience a broad gradient of freedom.

At the extreme of psychosis, the afflictions are so powerful that there is virtually no freedom. I have observed such people to be quite miserable, with little control over their thoughts and behavior, and no real freedom. I have also known people with exceptional degrees of sanity. Even after thirty-three years of torture, Palden Gyatso declares, "I feel no hatred for those who tortured me." We spent many hours together, and I saw in him no trace of desire for retaliation. Despite tremendous adversity, he is free to feel love and compassion instead of hatred and resentment, and he is dynamically motivated to help his fellow inmates.

I translated for Palden Gyatso at the first Tibetan Freedom Concert, in San Francisco in 1996, and we sat in the VIP tent with world-famous musicians and activists. The huge lunch buffet included beautiful platters of delicacies and a mound of strawberries two feet high. Palden Gyatso is a wiry little monk with a big appetite, and he piled his plate high. As I was eating next to him, I noticed his eyes filling with tears. He explained, "My friends who are still in the concentration camps have so little to eat. They're always hungry, and I have a feast in front of me." He was free to feel compassion without resentment, and free to engage in passionate activity to restore human rights without hatred or vengeance.

His Holiness the Dalai Lama has been abused and ridiculed by the Chinese Communist government for fifty years now. And yet only on the rarest of occasions does he express any sense of irritation at the occupiers of his homeland. Most often he says, "We are brothers and sisters; let us live in harmony." That's real freedom!

The spectrum of freedom ranges from the slavery of psychosis, through the dungeons of addiction, the everyday traps of craving, hostility, and ignorance, the subtle snares of spiritual materialism, and into the realms of exceptional mental well-being and complete liberation. Freedom from domination by mental afflictions allows one to make wise choices based on compassion, kindness, and foresight. One has no inclination to act otherwise. In this view of freedom, there is no notion of an independent ego standing outside the matrix of causality and acting freely without constraint by causes and conditions. Instead, wisdom, compassion, and other virtues are cultivated to reduce the dominance of mental afflictions, which no longer compel harmful behavior. When the mind is completely freed, all mental afflictions are eliminated, and one acts purely out of reality-based compassion. According to a Buddhist notion of free will, the most realistic impulse that a person can experience is compassion.

Most of us live somewhere in the spectrum between psychosis and enlightenment. How can we progress toward greater freedom? There are many applicable practices, but settling the mind in its natural state is utterly superb. This practice enables us to become increasingly aware of mental impulses as they arise. If a desire arises and we are mindlessly captivated by its energy, it might lead to our own and others' detriment. If our intentions are unwholesome, we might take actions that generate negative karma. Instead, if we can observe the arising impulse of desire before being seduced, we can avoid becoming ensnared.

When we rest in the space of awareness, seeing wholesome, unwholesome, afflictive, and nonafflictive mental impulses manifesting, our goal is to observe them in their birthplace. Insofar as we are able to notice these impulses as soon as they arise, we have the opportunity to make wise choices. Bringing knowledge, experience, and intuition to bear, we can anticipate the consequences of our actions. When a potentially harmful impulse comes up, we can simply allow it to dissolve. As we become increasingly familiar with the gamut of mental events, without acting on any of them, we develop a panoramic awareness of mental processes.

People who have never meditated sometimes imagine that meditation doesn't generate insight into the ordinary mind; they think the goal is to achieve a blissful state of consciousness. Nothing could be further from the truth. Opening Pandora's box will unleash much more than angelic choirs. Besides joyous mystical states, you can trigger ancient traumas, disturbing emotions, repressed desires, and bizarre fantasies. Your task is to remain present with whatever is dredged up, be it vulgar, ridiculous, or sublime. Recognizing mental events arising before they take control will enable you to be present with them and to make healthy choices.

Cultivating this ability on the cushion, you become increasingly skilled at recognizing mental processes arising during daily activities. In social interactions, work, and play, opportunities for wiser choices appear more frequently when you are able to maintain awareness of your own mental space.

Real freedom can be experienced. There is no presumptive agent who stands apart from the mind, making decisions to act. There is no supernatural entity within the system of interactions of the body, mind, and environment. There are simply natural impulses of compassion, wisdom, intelligence, mindfulness, and concentration—a vast array of helpful, neutral, and afflictive mental processes. Activating our wisdom, judgment, and compassion, we cultivate wholesome thoughts and release unwholesome ones. Many options appear for consideration. When we make a decision and take action, it is conducive to our own and others' well-being. This is real freedom.

Freedom is not a reward at the end of a long tunnel to nirvana or enlightenment—we can develop it now. Modern philosophers debate whether we have free will or not, but freedom is not framed as a binary choice in Buddhism. Instead, freedom is seen as a dynamic process to be cultivated. Experientially, it's obvious when the mind is in the grip of a powerful emotion—psychologists call it a refractory period. A mind overwhelmed by anger or craving sees reality through a very narrow slit. With a limited perspective, poor decisions are made. At such times, we are not free.

This practice is to maintain mental spaciousness, never collapsing into narrow views or familiar ruts, while gradually cultivating a sense of freedom. Even when visited by mental afflictions, we don't have to give them the keys to our house. By simply recognizing them as they arise, we can cultivate antidotes such as loving-kindness and compassion. When we are able to act most beneficially for ourselves and others, then we are truly free.

⊰ 8 ⊱
Mindfulness of Phenomena

THE FOURTH close application of mindfulness concerns the Sanskrit term *dharmas*, which in this context simply means all phenomena—it's wide-open. You might hear an internal dialogue, see mental imagery of two people talking, feel emotions about their relationship, and sense somatic resonances in the heart, all arising as entangled experience. Mindfulness of phenomena is all-inclusive.

SPACE BETWEEN

As we progress from coarse to subtle phenomena, the profound nature of experience becomes increasingly fascinating. Nothing is excluded as sounds, visual images, and somatic memories arise stochastically, like disjointed bubbles. We seek to identify the precedents and the causal nexus out of which our experiences arise. When we attend to the entire matrix of experience, we are observing what the Buddha called dependent origination. All phenomena are dependently related events arising in a network of mutual entanglement.

Bahiya was asked whether there is a real internal subject who is observing, called "I." If you try to find this subject, it is not to be found. Furthermore, is there any real, substantial, and self-existent object externally? Nothing can be found. We observe internally, externally, and then both internally and externally, and we see only the display of a matrix of dependently related events in which the demarcation between inside and outside has vanished.

The following practice consists of two sessions with a short break in between. The first session focuses on the earth element in full-body awareness, and the second focuses on the space of the mind, from which mental events emerge. Utter ease and relaxation are essential for this practice to be truly beneficial. The supine position is ideal for the first session of settling awareness in the body, but a seated posture is fine if you can remain thoroughly comfortable.

GUIDED MEDITATION:
Balancing Earth and Sky I

Attend to the domain of tactile sensations—
monitoring with introspection

Settle the body in its natural state: relaxed, still, and vigilant. Settle the respiration in its natural rhythm. Let your awareness settle in the field of the body, securely embraced by the solidity of the earth element.

With each out-breath, release excess tension in the body, which softens and begins to melt. With each out-breath, release any thoughts of the past, present, or future. There is no need for cogitation. This time is a gift of freedom. Allow yourself the luxury of resting silently in the body's nonconceptual tactility.

Savor the freedom from obsessive flows of thoughts, compulsive grasping, and fixation upon thoughts. Maintain a silent vigil, clearly mindful of whatever sensations arise within the tactile field.

Let your breath be as effortless as waves washing on the shore. Arouse your awareness with each inhalation. Relax in body and mind throughout the entire course of the exhalation, and continue relaxing as the next breath flows in. Monitor this process with introspection, taking remedial steps when your attention falls into laxity or excitation.

Sitting up slowly and mindfully, take a moment to stretch, and continue to the next session. ☞

Attend to the space of the mind—
focusing on intervals between thoughts

Settle the body in its natural state and the breath in its natural rhythm. For a few minutes, attend to the space of the body and tactile events without distraction or grasping.

With eyes open and gazing vacantly into the space in front, attend to that space rather than to any visual object, color, or shape. Is this intervening space something or nothing? If it is something, what are its characteristics?

Direct your awareness to the space of the mind and whatever arises within it. At first, focus on the foreground experiences of thoughts, images, and mental events. Attend to them closely, observing how and whence they arise. When they are present, are they located to the left or right, above or below, near or far? How do they persist? How do they dissolve or disappear? Carefully observe the events arising in the space of the mind.

Now focus your attention on the space of the mind: thoughts arise from, are present within, and dissolve into this substrate. When a thought arises, observe the space from which it manifests. When a thought is present, rather than focusing on the thought itself, focus on the space in which it abides. When a thought subsides, focus on the space into which it dissolves. Focus in particular on the intervals between thoughts.

The primary object of mindfulness is the space of the mind rather than its contents. Use periodic introspection to ensure a vigilant posture and spontaneous, unconstrained breath. If you find yourself becoming spacey or dull, arouse your attention and focus closely on the object of mindfulness. If you become caught up in thoughts, release, relax, and return to the space of the mind. ☞

On the Ground

The sequence of the four close applications of mindfulness progresses from coarse to subtle. Tactile sensations in the body are subtle but not terribly difficult to observe. Bodily feelings of pleasure, pain, and indifference are more subtle than tactile sensations but still relatively tangible. Mental feelings are less straightforward and more challenging to observe—they can be elusive, bashful maidens. Mental phenomena such as thoughts and images certainly have coarse aspects; however, by continuing to sustain unwavering mindfulness of mental events, previously hidden layers of nuance are revealed. Sharpening the attention increases qualitative vividness, the detection of rarefied events, and it enhances temporal acuity, the detection of very brief events. Phenomena of increasingly subtle intensity and fleeting duration become manifest.

The preceding practice directs mindfulness to the ground of the mind. In the Sanskrit term *alayavijñana*, the *alaya* is the substrate and *vijñana* is consciousness. In the Dzogchen tradition, these two aspects are fully revealed in the achievement of shamatha, when the psyche's subjective sensory and mental processes dissolve into the substrate consciousness, and objective sensory and mental appearances dissolve into the substrate.

Resting in shamatha, awareness is the substrate consciousness, and the object of awareness is the substrate. The conceptual mind is quiet, so there is no sense of separation between awareness and its object. This is the experience of the unity of the substrate and consciousness. Rather than metaphysical dogma, this is an experiential report from the front lines, enormously useful in illuminating one's practice.

The term "alayavijñana" is not found in the Theravadin tradition, which uses the term "bhavanga"; this ground consciousness, or ground of becoming, is not depicted in two aspects. The Gelugpa tradition of Tibetan Buddhism speaks simply of a subtle continuum of mental consciousness rather than the alayavijñana. However, in Dzogchen the two aspects are described, and it seems to be an excellent phenomenological description of experience in this practice.

Examining the two aspects of substrate and consciousness, the substrate is the space of the mind: the field in which appearances arise. Not only mental appearances, but all visual, auditory, olfactory, gustatory, and tactile appearances arise from this source. All perceptual and conceptual phenomena appear within the substrate, and they all dissolve back into the substrate when we fall asleep and when we die.

The word "space" is used in a wide variety of ways. In mathematics, the term is used for purely abstract notions, such as physicists' concept of Hilbert space. There is also the Einsteinian notion of space that is warped by matter. In this context, we are using the word "space" to denote a domain or a field, such as a stage on which actors might perform a play. This word is simply being used to indicate features of actual experience.

One way to become more aware of the space of the mind and develop a sense of its scope is to attend closely to the events arising within it. For example, if you visualize Mickey Mouse in front of you, he is appearing in the space of your mind because there is no physical basis for this image. Moreover, your visual perceptions of objects that do have a physical basis also appear in the space of your mind. Simply noting the extent of the space in which mental events occur lets you make inferences; even subtler is the observation of the space itself. Conduct a phenomenological examination of your experience. Pay close attention to pauses, interruptions, or gaps in the flow of thoughts. Scrutinize those blank spaces—reading between the lines—and the space of the mind will become increasingly evident.

CREATING REALITY

My mantra is James's quote, "For the moment, what we attend to is reality." Brilliant mathematicians such as Ellis and Penrose, who have focused on mathematics day after day for decades, truly live in a world of the mind. For them, mathematical phenomena are as real as anything else. Some even say that notions like matter and energy are merely derivative of mathematics—which alone is real. The idea that everything emerges from an underlying archetypal reality is credited to Plato, whose attention was largely devoted to the mind and mental phenomena. In Plato's theory, the ideal forms are real, whereas the sensory phenomena of the physical world are derivative and illusory: shadows on the wall of his allegorical cave. In contrast, Plato's student Aristotle focused his attention on the sensory phenomena of the world, and he wrote extensively about many subjects, including physics, biology, and mental phenomena. For Aristotle, mathematics was an abstraction to be teased out of real phenomena, like matter, forces, space, and time.

Pursuant to James's radical idea, these two orientations toward reality might have resulted from what the two philosophers paid most attention to. Bertrand Russell (1872–1970) describes these two views in *A History of Western Philosophy*:

> In philosophy ever since the time of Pythagoras there has been an opposition between the men whose thought was mainly inspired by mathematics and those who were more influenced by the empirical sciences. Plato, Thomas Aquinas, Spinoza, and Kant belong to what may be called the mathematical party; Democritus, Aristotle, and the modern empiricists from Locke onwards, belong to the opposite party.[85]

Over the last two millennia, philosophers and scientists have fallen into two camps: those like Plato who attend to the inner world of ideas, and those like Aristotle who attend to the outer world of matter. Hardcore scientific materialists are most comfortable in the world of classical nineteenth-century physics, where fields are physically real and matter is chunky. Much of biology, and neurobiology in particular, is unwittingly embedded in a materialistic worldview that has been rendered obsolete by quantum mechanics.

Leading physicists such as Zeilinger assert that we can know nothing about the world independently of our systems of measurement.[86] John Archibald Wheeler (1911–2008), by all accounts one of the most brilliant theoretical physicists of the latter half of the twentieth century, coined a pithy aphorism stating that information is primary rather than matter and energy: "Its from bits."[87] He asserted that the worldly aspects of matter, energy, fields, space, time, and mind are derivative conceptual constructs manifesting out of information. Having acquired information by making measurements, we then construct our notions of subatomic particles, wave functions, force, mass, and consciousness.

Andrei Linde, a brilliant physicist at Stanford, emphasizes the same theme.[88] He recommends we stop assuming that awareness is an emergent property of matter. Since all our knowledge of the world comes from perception, perhaps awareness is more fundamental than matter or energy. If the primal element is information—which can only come from experience—then we must start with the world of experience. We can be informed only about a world we measure. Heisenberg said that what we observe is not nature itself but nature exposed to our method of inquiry. In other words, we cocreate our universe. We have not dreamt it up from nothing—that would be solipsism. But the universe appears to us in response to our specific modes of inquiry.

During the past four hundred years, modern science has systematically focused on objective external phenomena, such as energy, fields, and particles. Given this orientation, scientists are inevitably drawn to the assumption that something material and objective, such as the brain, gives rise to the immaterial epiphenomena of the mind. Studying the mind externally by observing behavior and neural functions allows certain inferences to be drawn, but it's a poor substitute for direct observation of the phenomenon under investigation. What is missing from the scientific study of the mind is a rigorous means of observing the subjective reality of the mind itself.

Not in Your Head

In this practice, we direct our awareness inward to observe mental phenomena in their natural environment, yielding information that is unobservable externally. With a different mode of inquiry, nature arises in a different way. As we direct awareness to the space of the mind and its contents—using rigorous methods unknown to modern science—something new becomes real for us: the space of the mind that constitutes the ground of all experience.

The Buddha's teachings are quite compatible with the notion that the categories of mind and matter are derivatives of information. In fact, everything that informs us arises in the space of the mind. All that appears to us—conceptually and perceptually—arises from the space of the mind, is present in the space of the mind, and dissolves back into the space of the mind. No perception, no thought, and no information whatsoever could appear without this substrate.

When you attend to the space of the mind—observing the intervals between thoughts or the space from which a thought arises, abides, and dissolves—do you perceive something or nothing? Is it large or small, bright or dark? Does it carry an affective quality, such as peaceful emptiness or potent fertility? Is it possible for information to manifest in the space of the mind from outside one's own continuum? Of course, the space of the mind does not remain empty indefinitely. Appearances arise like a fireworks display, and then they dissolve back into this same space. Even between displays, I would suggest that this space is not black. Any color we imagine is likely to be a superimposition based on our notions of vacuity or empty space.

Where are the boundaries of the space of the mind? Is it vast and unbounded, or are there distant borders? If your eyes are closed, this space might seem to be rather small and localized inside your head, which is why the eyes remain open in the practice of settling the mind in its natural state. You can experiment with keeping your eyes closed or open to various extents, observing your experience of the space of the mind. Does it seem more spacious with the eyes open? Everyone's experience is different and has its own validity.

Allowing the eyes to be open and the gaze vacant—not looking at anything—undermines the tacit belief that the mind is inside the head. The ruling assumption in the popular media, as well as in much of the psychological and neuroscientific literature, is that all our sights, sounds, pleasures, and anxieties are located within our brains. It is easy to imagine that we can watch our mind by closing our eyes and seeing a virtual screen that displays mental images. But there is no homunculus, the "little self" that watches the screen.

The scientific explanation for the subjective experience of pleasure involves an activation of the left prefrontal cortex, accompanied by increased blood flow. The sense of sight is accompanied by an activation of the visual cortex with specific neural correlates for colors, patterns, motion, and so forth. Hearing is characterized by an activation of the auditory cortex. Fear and anxiety are correlated with activation of the amygdala. While these subjective mental states and processes are being experienced, oxygenation of blood in the brains of subjects can be observed using fMRI.

But what can we say about the actual nature of these observed correlations between subjective experiences and activity patterns in the brain? The top neuroscientists are quite candid—they do not understand the relationship. They can observe patterns and correlations but cannot explain how subjective reality emerges from the brain. In fact, there is no evidence that qualia (the subjective properties of experience, such as the perceived color red) actually occur inside the brain. Nevertheless, this untestable metaphysical assumption pervades the modern scientific view. The popular media depict images of brains lit up in multicolored patterns associated with some experience, such as pain, and commonly use the words "mind" and "brain" interchangeably. These journalists boldly presume that the mind-body problem has been solved, and they simply use the two terms synonymously! But it is absurd to say that a computer-colored image of the blood flow in a region of the brain is an observation of pain.

There is no technology for objectively measuring the presence or absence of pain. If you visit a neurologist and complain of severe pain, you may be asked to rate your pain on an eleven-point subjective scale defined by this series of faces (see figure 1).[89] But the doctor has no way of verifying whether you are telling the truth. Similarly, if you report feeling depressed, anxious, or happy, there is no instrument to objectively measure these feelings in your brain or any part of your nervous system, even though certain parts of the brain are commonly activated during such experiences.

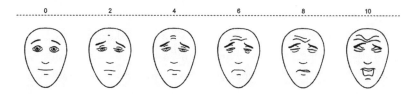

FIGURE 1. Faces Pain Scale – Revised (FPS-R).
Used with permission from IASP

I am sure that William James observed his mind quite a lot. So did Descartes, which is why he could not simply dismiss thoughts as being derivatives of matter. He took thoughts and matter very seriously, and he reified them both. On the other hand, modern materialists reify the material world but dismiss the entire subjective world of the mind as an illusory epiphenomenon. What they attend to becomes their reality. We need not become Platonists or philosophical idealists, and it is not necessary to abolish the notion that there is an external world independent of our minds. But we do need to compensate for spending so much time looking outward, seduced into media-driven materialism. As we pay attention to the mind, it will manifest with increasing clarity.

There are two complementary experiential orientations that I find extremely useful in observing the mind. The first is to attend to the foreground, which is what James did. At the beginning of his book *The Principles of Psychology*, he defined psychology as the study of the mind. He was interested in a fairly long list of mental phenomena: perceptions, thoughts, images, emotions, desires, memories, fantasies, and all contents of immediate experience. Such things can be classified as foreground mental activities. Psychologists have extensively studied these processes; many valuable discoveries have illuminated their nature and enabled therapeutic treatments.

As we attend to the foreground of mental events arising, they become our reality. We may overlook the fact that these events occur within the context of a particular space, from which they emerge and into which they dissolve. For example, in a theatrical performance, an actor with commanding presence might completely captivate the audience—all eyes are focused on her. During her performance, most people pay no attention to the stage and props; however, a professional stage designer is always aware of the stage.

The second experiential orientation in observing the mind is to attend to the background. When you first attend to the space of the mind, you might think this space is empty. As you attend to it repeatedly, this space becomes your focus. Observing it day after day and month after month in meditative concentration, the space of the mind becomes increasingly real. Eventually, the space of the mind might appear to be more real than the events arising in it. The sky is durable and unchanging compared with ephemeral phenomena like rainbows and lightning. The background is relatively constant from one session to the next, but it is not static or immutable. In fact, sometimes it seems pregnant with potential, a field in bloom, or an effervescence about to explode! This space is not an empty nothingness—it's not flat empty. Such qualifiers point to a paradox: emptiness is full.

Absurd Reduction

The Buddhist hypothesis and description of the substrate differs radically from mainstream materialist assumptions concerning the source of mental phenomena. Some highly intelligent writers on the philosophy of mind assert that qualia—colors, smells, feelings, thoughts, and the immediate contents of the mind—do not exist! Such a bizarre claim defies my understanding. How can someone be thoughtful enough to conceive that we are mindless robots without relying upon his or her mind to do so? Waving off such inconsistencies, a hard-core materialist is convinced that all life is reducible to biology. If nobody can explain subjective experiences of mental images, thoughts, feelings, colors, and smells in the language of biology, these things must not exist. Such a mind, fixated on a single source of truth, refuses to see any conflicting evidence.

The more sensible position, accepted by many scientists and philosophers such as Searle, is that of course qualia exist—but not in the way we think. There are subjective perceptions of ideas, sights, and sounds in our immediate experience, but the overriding assumption is that they are strict functions of brain activity. The methodology of scientific materialism dooms any alternative. Having never developed a sophisticated first-person science of mind, the scientific community dogmatically holds that all subjective experiences of qualia emerge from complex configurations of neurons.

As the reductionist theory goes, brains contain complex arrays of neurons, which are assemblies of molecules, which are combinations of atoms, and ultimately, elementary particles. The particles in your brain are the same as those in a football. It just so happens that these ordinary particles are arranged in extremely complex configurations, and as a result of interactions with the environment, various perceptions, thoughts, and emotions emerge. This hypothesis strikes me as bizarre, utterly lacking in explanatory power, and impossible to test empirically, even while it is almost universally assumed in neuroscience and psychology research labs around the world. It makes the brain sound like a magic lamp: Rub it and a genie will appear! There is no explanation of how the genie arises, and no evidence that it actually arises from the brain. In fact, the entire domain we are observing—including perceptions, thoughts, feelings, and all the phenomena of subjective experience—is invisible to science; no technology exists for detecting qualia. Perhaps it is true that images, colors, smells, tastes, thoughts, memories, and the entire array of mental phenomena simply emerge out of neuronal interactions. But I see no evidence for this hypothesis, only a dogmatic assumption, compounded with a cognitive deficit that stops many people from observing their own minds with scientific rigor.

Stage of Experience

Buddhism has a different hypothesis: all mental phenomena emerge from the substrate during waking experience, dissolve into the substrate when we sleep, and emerge again when we dream. The substrate is something that can be observed and explored experientially. It is the source of all appearances, the space in which they manifest, and the medium of their dissolution.

For example, when you look at a rose and see red, the subjectively red quale exists only in the substrate. The redness you perceive is not in the molecules of the rose, even though the petals reflect some wavelengths of light more than others. As photons are emitted from the rose to your eye, they can be characterized by their energy, but there are no red photons. Photons hit the retina and launch a sequence of electrochemical events culminating in activities of the visual cortex, but there are no red neurons and no red locations in the brain. Neural events occur in physical space, but the perception of redness occurs in the space of the mind, specifically in the visual subspace.

When you are dreaming, you can see the color red even with no photons entering your closed eyes. The redness you see is not in physical space—it's a mental appearance. The space of the mind is like a master illusionist that can take on any appearance in a dream, from the color red to a close friend who speaks to you; it can take on the form of any sound, scent, thought, or tactile sensation. When the dream is over, these appearances dissolve back into the holographic ground of the substrate.

The scientific pursuit of a God's-eye perspective has given us good explanations for what occurs in physical space, but it says nothing about the subjective reality of phenomena. Beginning instead with the actual experience of perception, we see that everything arises in the space of the mind. We can choose to attend selectively to the visual or auditory subspaces, or we can focus on mental phenomena and ignore the other five senses. We can also simply allow awareness to illuminate everything, and the demarcations between subspaces will fade away.

Furthermore, rather than attending to a visual object, for example, we can attend to the visual space in between ourselves and the appearances of objects. As we maintain our focus on this intervening space, are we attending to something or not? It's not nothing; it could be described as empty and peaceful, but not flat or dark. Anything could manifest within this space; it is an experience of the substrate, even if filtered by the psyche's conceptualizations. Of course, we can also attend to the entire space in which visual appearances emerge like actors on a stage. These appearances occur within the substrate, and the space we attend to is nothing other than the substrate.

Ingrained in us since childhood is belief in the fundamental existence of matter, energy, space, and time. In the classical view of a chunky universe, we seek to acquire information about these four realities and various derivative qualities, and reality returns bits of information to us. As we focus our telescopes, microscopes, MRI scanners, and other instruments upon space, time, matter, and energy, we derive information, knowledge, and understanding. Wheeler says we have it backward. He asserts that information is more fundamental than our humanly conceived categories. People define space, time, matter, and energy, just as we define what is real. We define these concepts in diverse ways; the dictionary offers many definitions for the adjective "real." These notions are not self-existent, awaiting discovery by a brilliant researcher. We construct them on the basis of information drawn from our measurements, analyses, and interpretations. Space, time, matter, and energy are all derivatives of information, which is primary. Information—that which informs—is the contents of the mind.

Waking perceptions are correlated with, but not entirely dependent upon, phenomena occurring in physical space. When you see red, the visual cortex undergoes a very specific process, which probably occurs each time you see red. Cognitive neuroscientists are investigating the complexities of the visual cortex and finding phenomena correlated with seeing faces, vertical lines, horizontal lines, colors, motion, and other visual phenomena. This is excellent science, but it can measure only correlations with actual subjective perception; correlation is not equivalence.

Furthermore, cases of localized damage to the brain have resulted in alteration, impairment, or elimination of certain types of perception. Such losses are sometimes permanent, leading to the conclusion that these perceptions are localized in the brain. Nevertheless, it is increasingly recognized that to a limited extent a damaged brain can reconfigure itself to perform a missing function—this is called "neuroplasticity"— and it challenges the assumption that perceptual phenomena occur in specific locations within the brain. A more cautious view is that perceptual processes are merely correlated with physical brain processes: the relationships between perception and brain activity have yet to be demonstrated.

Dreaming has been studied by researchers like LaBerge and his mentor, William Dement, who founded the first sleep laboratory, at Stanford University. The brain is very active during dreaming, perhaps even more so than in the waking state. Brain scans of subjects dreaming of visual imagery show visual cortex activation similar to that in waking visual perception. There is neural activity in the auditory cortex when we dream of sound. Based on his extensive research into lucid dreaming, LaBerge formulated an insightful aphorism describing the nature of experience that is worth contemplating: Waking experience is dream experience with physical constraints, while dream experience is waking experience without physical constraints.[90] When you perceive a rose in waking experience, photons are being emitted from a physical structure that is independent of the perceiver. When you perceive a rose in a dream, there are no photons, and the rose can appear in any color. In a lucid dream, you can change a red rose to blue, black, or chartreuse if you wish because there are no photons to constrain your imagination. You can freely paint an artistic creation on the canvas of your mind. Dreaming constitutes a vivid demonstration of the independence of sensory space from physical input.

The ancient practice of dream yoga is designed to enhance your ability to transform dream appearances until you recognize that everything can be transformed—the only limit is your own imagination. In the dream state, there is nothing objectively present to constrain appearances. In the waking state, various physical processes constrain appearances arising in the substrate. By attending closely to this substrate, it becomes more real than the ephemeral phenomena appearing in it. The illusory nature of reality is a theme that pervades the Buddha's teachings, from the Pali Canon to Mahayana, Vajrayana, and Dzogchen. The Buddha, recognizing this illusory nature, was awake. The rest of us, not recognizing, are not as awake as we think. Therein lies our challenge.

GUIDED MEDITATION:
Mindfulness of the Substrate I

Attend to the space of the mind—
observing the domain of mental events

Settle the body in its natural state and the respiration in its natural rhythm. Allow the awareness to come to rest in the field of tactile sensations for a short time. Observe this tactile field and whatever arises within it without distraction or grasping.

With eyes open and gaze vacant, direct your awareness to the space of the mind and whatever arises within it. For a little while, focus your attention on mental events, such as discursive thoughts, dialogue, and imagery. Attend to the mind's contents without distraction or grasping.

Now shift your focus from the foreground to the background. Pay special attention to those spacious intervals that manifest between explicit thoughts and discrete mental events. Observe the space from which mental events arise, in which they are present, and into which they dissolve. Focus on the background space: the domain of mental events. ☞

On Practice Space

I encourage you to conduct your own research on the results of practicing in various environments. Tibetan yogis are especially attracted to places with an enormous amount of open space and distant vistas. I have greatly enjoyed meditating in the high desert of the eastern Sierra Nevada range, where the views extend to peaks sixty miles away. The ability to direct the attention to such distant points gives a very expansive feeling to the intervening space.

In such a spacious environment, allow your awareness to come out, with your eyes open and your gaze resting vacantly in the space in front of you. The experience in a vast space is very different from that in a tiny room. Gazing up at a clear night sky studded with stars is a wonderful way to experience the sheer enormity of space.

It is important to distinguish between the contents of a space and the space itself. Colors and shapes constitute the contents of visual space. These are aspects or representations of ordinary phenomena in the visual field. Attending to the space of the mind means attending to that space from which all such contents emerge, in which they are present, and into which they dissolve; it is the space that lingers in between discrete events.

HEART-MIND

The Sanskrit and Pali term that is generally translated as "mind," *chitta,* also means "heart." In the *Anguttara Nikaya,* the Buddha says this of the heart-mind:

> I know of no other single process that, thus developed and made much of, is as pliable and workable as is this chitta.

He is suggesting that among the six modes of perception, the one capable of extraordinary enhancement is mental perception. Visual, auditory, olfactory, gustatory, and tactile perceptions can be enhanced to some extent through training; however, mental processes can be significantly developed, refined, and transformed. You will notice that the Dalai Lama wears glasses. I think it's safe to say that he's an exceptional meditator, but this has not eliminated his need for glasses. Another extraordinarily realized Mongolian lama named Senge Rinpoche, whom I met in Tibet in 1992, was quite hard of hearing. It was very embarrassing to have to shout at a lama, but it was the only way to communicate. His meditative prowess had not strengthened his hearing. The simple point is that meditative ability enhances the mind, but it doesn't necessarily enhance the other senses.

The Buddha continues:

> Monks, the chitta that is thus developed and made much of is pliable and workable. Monks, I know of no other single process so quick to change as is this chitta.

If you refine the mind, it becomes pliable and workable, and it can do extraordinary things. All phenomena are impermanent, but some are more quick to change than others. The mind's capability for rapid change is unsurpassed. Here is the famous statement:

> Monks, this chitta is brightly shining, but it is defiled by adventitious defilements. Monks, this chitta is brightly shining, and it is free from adventitious defilements.[91]

The mind's inherent nature is luminous, but it is obscured or veiled by temporary, adventitious defilements, such as craving, hostility, lethargy, and excitation. Mental afflictions arrive like visitors; they don't stay permanently, but linger awhile and then leave. When visited by afflictions, the mind's inherently luminous nature is obscured.

In the final two statements, the Buddha summarizes the essence of the path. The nature of the mind is luminous, but this is not always evident. It is obscured and covered by defilements—mental afflictions. Simply remove the obscuring, adventitious defilements, and the innate luminosity of awareness will be perfectly clear for all to see. This quote from the Buddha is recorded in the Pali Canon, and similar statements are attributed to him in the Mahayana discourses.

In the Theravadin tradition, this use of the term "chitta" refers to the bhavanga, which is naturally luminous. The bhavanga is the naturally pure and undefiled state of radiant mind from which the javana consciousness arises. There is debate between some Theravadin schools whether the javana consciousness literally emerges from the radiant bhavanga, but it makes good sense experientially to say that it does. Resting in the bhavanga, you observe mental events arising.

When the Buddha says that all things issue forth from this brightly shining mind, his words are consistent with ordinary English usage. Everything that occurs to you occurs in your mind; furthermore, you observe everything with your mind. We can use the word "mind" to denote both the domain in which mental events take place and the awareness that observes these events.

Subtle Evidence

Does the mind, as we subjectively experience it, have any location, size, shape, or mass? It's hard to answer these questions because they don't fit the subject. Such questions are perfectly reasonable in regard to material things, but they are meaningless relative to the mind. The natural conclusion is that the mind does not have physical attributes, so it cannot be located in physical space. Asking where the mind is located doesn't make any more sense than asking, "Where is beauty?" or "How big is justice?" Beauty and justice exist without physical attributes in a different category from physical objects. If the mind itself has no spatial dimensions, then assigning it a location would constitute a category error—ascribing impossible properties to an object.

There is another more interesting way to describe the attributes of the mind. In mainstream Tibetan Buddhism, specific states of consciousness are correlated with subtle energies, known as *prana*, or *chi*, experienced in the body. Despite the fact that modern medicine has no language to describe it, this energy is manipulated by acupuncturists around the world to help many people with a wide variety of disorders. Whether it is the Chinese model of chi and the meridians running throughout the body, or the Indian concept of prana with the various chakras and channels, these descriptions of the body's subtle energies are not mere superstitions. Prana is just as real as emotion, thought, and desire, yet all these are currently invisible to science. Prana is physical, but it is not composed of matter. It is located in physical space, and it interacts interdependently with the physical body. Similarly, an electromagnetic field is physical and travels through empty space, but it is not material.

The traditional Indian Ayurvedic and Tibetan medical systems assert that states of consciousness are correlated with, but not identical to, specific types of prana flowing in the body. Various forms of prana are involved in diverse functions, such as digestion, evacuation, the movement of limbs, and mental processes. When the mind is in the waking state, prana is said to gather in the forehead chakra, located in the middle of the brain. In the dream state, prana descends and gathers in the throat. In dreamless sleep, prana descends to the heart. The heart chakra is strongly related to mental awareness, most specifically to the substrate consciousness. Traditional Tibetans consider the energy of mental consciousness to be located in the heart—when referring to their minds, they point to their hearts.

Awareness of Awareness

The practice of awareness of awareness was taught by the Buddha. He called it *vijñana kasina*, which entails focusing on the nature of consciousness. Awareness of awareness was one of ten objects of meditation the Buddha taught, known as the ten *kasinas*. This practice is described in Tibetan Buddhism under various names, including shamatha focused on the mind. The fifteenth-century master Tsongkhapa teaches that the practice is to focus directly on the sheer luminosity and cognizance of awareness itself.

GUIDED MEDITATION:
Awareness of Awareness I

Attend to the cognizant luminosity of awareness—
inverting on inhale and releasing on exhale

Settle the body in its natural state and the respiration in its natural rhythm.

With eyes open and gaze vacant, attend to the space of the mind and whatever arises within it, without distraction or grasping. For a short while, focus on the foreground events arising within this space, attending to them with unwavering mindfulness.

Now attend to the background: the space of the mind. This is the space that manifests during the intervals between thoughts; it is the space from which thoughts and other mental events emerge, in which they are present, and into which they dissolve.

As you attend to the space of the mind, note that there is an experience distinct from the appearance of the space of the mind: the awareness of that appearance. As a preliminary exercise, maintain a peripheral awareness of the in-breath and the out-breath. During the course of the inhalation, invert your awareness, drawing it in from the space of awareness and all objects appearing to awareness. Draw your awareness in upon the very experience of awareness itself. The experience of knowing that you are aware may be the most certain knowledge you can have. Rest in this knowing of knowing. With each inhalation invert your awareness upon this luminous cognizance, taking no interest in any appearances to the mind, thoughts, imagery, or sensory perceptions.

With each exhalation, relax from the core, utterly releasing your awareness without latching on to any object or mental appearance. Sustain the thread of awareness of awareness as you profoundly relax and release the mind. Whatever thoughts come up, release them immediately, especially with the out-breath, and rest in the ongoing, silent flow of awareness of awareness.

Arousing and inverting your awareness with each inhalation overcomes laxity by enhancing the vividness of awareness. Relaxing and releasing with each exhalation overcomes excitation by stabilizing the flow of awareness of awareness. Experiment to see whether it is more effective to breathe through the nostrils, the mouth, or both. Let the breath be unimpeded, effortless, and spontaneous.

Employing introspection, if you find yourself caught up in thoughts, relax, release them, and return to the awareness of awareness. If you find yourself becoming spaced-out or dull, arouse and refresh your attention. ❧

On Being Aware

When you are simply aware of the subjective experience of being aware, is this occurring in real time or in working memory? We might expect that attending to awareness would occur in working memory, much like attending to an emotion or desire. As soon as you attend to a desire, the desire vanishes because you are no longer attending to the object of desire. According to the Buddhist understanding, a single moment of awareness cannot take itself as an object because that moment would have to be subdivided. Therefore, the shamatha practice of awareness of awareness is a retrospective observation.

Even so, one can be aware of a moment of awareness a mere tenth of a second ago. The preceding one-hundred-millisecond pulse of awareness can be observed in a kind of working memory. Simply being aware of awareness doesn't redirect attention away from any object, resulting in homogeneity from moment to moment—a continuous awareness of the preceding moment of awareness. The experiential sense is one of dwelling in a flow of awareness of awareness. It feels like real-time awareness of a moment of awareness because each moment is so similar to the preceding moment that it doesn't matter. For all practical purposes, you are aware of awareness in a working memory that approaches real-time observation.

The essence of this practice is to take no interest in anything but awareness itself. Visual, auditory, and mental images appear, but you are not interested. As soon as any thought arises, release it immediately without commentary. Don't pounce on it, push it away, or restrain it; simply let it go, like a child releasing a balloon. You are interested only in the sheer occurrence of awareness. Being aware is a process like knowing rather than a thing to be known. Knowing happens, and we can be aware of it. Once you have learned the method, it becomes clearer and easier through practice.

The classic commentaries mention the oscillating motion of inversion and release of the attention as a preliminary exercise. Conjoining this oscillation with the breath is something I have taught for a number of years as an introductory technique. Although you are doing something to control awareness, this form of grasping is a benign one. Alternating between inversion and release of the attention is highly effective in overcoming both laxity and excitation.

Once you learn to allow your attention to flow between intensified and loosened states, then you can disengage from the breath and oscillate at any rhythm you find comfortable. Like a child's swing that travels farthest when you draw it all the way back, the more intensely you focus the attention inwardly, the more profoundly you can release it outwardly. Without ever grasping on to a subject or an object, simply sustain the flow of awareness of awareness at all times. Settling into a natural rhythm of concentration and release, you become absorbed in a smooth flow.

Approaching what is called the fourth stage of attentional development,[92] you never disengage from the object or forget the meditation, but rest in an unbroken flow, minute after minute. At this point you may wish to move into the next phase, which is allowing the attention to swing without pushing it anymore. Finally, center your awareness where it always was—right in the middle—without inversion or release. Rest in utter simplicity, sustaining the flow of sheer luminosity and cognizance of awareness. Breathe naturally, without holding the breath, and this practice will take you all the way to shamatha.

SIGN OF MIND

Calling it shamatha without a sign, Padmasambhava (eighth century CE) teaches the practice of awareness of awareness in his text *Natural Liberation*,[93] which I translated with Gyatrul Rinpoche's commentary and guidance.[94] A sign here refers to any object that you can identify in the context of a conceptual framework. It appears when you direct your attention toward something, whether it's tangible like a rock, intangible like thoughts and images, or abstract like the square root of minus one, justice, or beauty. When you point the finger of your mind at something, directing and focusing your attention, you will come up with a sign. In this practice, "without a sign" signifies not attending to any object. Don't point your finger—retract it. Even without directing your attention, awareness is present. Rest your awareness in its own space that precedes any directionality; let it illuminate its own nature.

The Sanskrit and Pali word for "sign," *nimitta*, has different meanings depending on context. It appears in the *Samyutta Nikaya* in a remarkable statement by the Buddha:

> In this manner, monks, the wise, experienced, skillful monk abides in happiness here and now and is mindful and introspective as well. What is the reason for that? Because, monks, this wise, experienced, skillful monk acquires the sign of his own mind.[95]

This passage is an explicit reference to the sign of the mind or consciousness—it's not a visual image. Generally speaking, a sign refers to the distinguishing feature by which one recognizes or remembers something. One acquires the sign of one's own mind by ascertaining the essential features, namely, luminosity and cognizance, that distinguish awareness from everything else. In this mention of acquiring the sign of mind, the Buddha is referring to the foundation of achieving shamatha as a prerequisite to vipashyana. Upon the basis of meditative quiescence, insight meditation becomes practical.

If you were an astronomer with a new telescope, you would inspect the mirror and lenses carefully before relying on their accuracy. Having cleaned, lubricated, and calibrated the instrument, you could make reliable observations. Similarly, if mental perception is your primary instrument for investigating the nature of reality in order to acquire insight that will liberate your mind irreversibly, then you should optimize this instrument. The mind is actually the primary tool in all scientific inquiry. Telescopes, microscopes, and MRI scanners are powerful extensions, but all research is conducted with the mind. It seems bizarre that three hundred years passed from the time of Copernicus until the scientific study of the mind began with James and Wundt. That's like using a telescope for three hundred years without ever inspecting its mirror. Does it distort appearances? Are the lenses rose tinted?

The Buddha's approach seems more sensible, which is to develop the mind as a rigorous platform for definitive contemplative inquiry—in order to gain direct, experiential knowledge of reality. First of all, investigate the mind itself, ascertain its distinguishing features, and learn how to recognize awareness. This is what occurs in shamatha. But what is the sign of the mind?

Clearly Knowing

Philosophers of mind, neuroscientists, and psychologists employ diverse definitions for consciousness—there is no consensus whatsoever. Without an objective means of detecting consciousness, they find it hard to agree on a scientific definition. Buddhism offers an enormously useful definition that is purely phenomenological and experiential, with no metaphysical baggage. Scientific materialists, theists, and atheists alike could adopt this definition: consciousness is that which is luminous and cognizant.

Only consciousness, here synonymous with awareness, illuminates phenomena and makes them manifest: this is the first distinguishing feature of consciousness. A light bulb is not by nature luminous. It may spray out photons, but a light is bright due to awareness. Photons are not bright and have no color, except to visual perception. Without awareness, the sun's radiation would be invisible. Awareness alone illuminates all appearances of form, sound, smell, taste, tactile sensations, emotions, thoughts, memories, and desires. It illuminates every sensory object from mind to matter and every idea from algebra to ethics. These things only appear due to the luminous nature of awareness.

The second quality of consciousness or awareness is cognizance. If you gaze at the palm of your hand, for example, there will be appearances of flesh colors, lines, and shapes. In addition to these appearances arising, something else occurs: you know it's a hand. You recognize its color, shape, and position, and you can report on this knowledge.

The two aspects of luminance and cognizance may operate simultaneously, but they occur independently. At times you may perceive very brilliant appearances but make no sense of them. For example, if you were radically disoriented by a drug, your awareness might be flooded with vivid sensations accompanied by profound confusion. This is how James describes the appearances of the world to an infant:

> The baby, assailed by eyes, ears, nose, skin, and entrails at once, feels it all as one great blooming, buzzing confusion; and to the very end of life, our location of all things in one space is due to the fact that the original extents or bignesses of all the sensations, which came to our notice at once, coalesced together into one and the same space. There is no other reason than this why "the hand I touch and see coincides spatially with the hand I immediately feel."[96]

On the other hand, let's suppose you have spent up to five thousand hours in the continuous practice of shamatha to the point of impeccable stability and vividness. Directing this awareness upon the luminous vacuity of your own substrate consciousness with intense interest, almost nothing appears. But you may know what you are observing with a high degree of certainty.

This widely accepted Buddhist definition is a phenomenological one that is useful in practice and ascertainable in experience. The words are easy to understand conceptually. The purpose of this definition is to distinguish consciousness from everything else, like a finger pointing to the moon. Knowing that the defining characteristics of consciousness are luminosity and cognizance, you can search for it. Is there something that illuminates appearances? Is there an experience of knowing? Can you rest your awareness in sheer luminosity and knowing and attend only to this? The nature of this practice is to release any interest or focus of attention and simply rest in an ongoing flow of cognizant luminosity. The Buddha suggested that an important prerequisite is to know the nature of awareness by acquiring the sign of mind, calibrating your instrument for investigating the nature of appearances to awareness.

Visualizing Mind

The practices described here are not dependent on visualization techniques, but many other methods are taught that do include the generation of mental images. For example, you might focus upon a depiction of the Buddha, such as a colorfully painted Tibetan *thangka*. Examining this image very carefully over an extended period, drenching your visual awareness in it, you become quite familiar with it. To some extent, you have memorized the image in detail, and know the color of the robes, the hand emblems, and the other symbolic elements. Eventually, you can mentally replicate the visual image. People who work with imagery professionally, such as artists, architects, and designers, often gravitate to the generation of mental images. For some, this can be exceedingly effective.

Generating a mental image involves a very useful element of grasping because while you are literally holding on to the image, you are not superimposing any concepts of ownership or personal preferences. Developing stability by means of holding on is referred to as tying the rope of mindfulness to the object. The goal of mindfulness is to remain attached to the object, not allowing the mind to fly away like a loose kite. This is one way of practicing shamatha.

Düdjom Lingpa recommended that people with agitated nervous systems and strong mental afflictions should not approach the practice of shamatha by attempting to focus on a mental image. As long as one is submerged in the turbulent ambience of society, attempting such visualizations may be counterproductive. For such people, he advocated settling the mind in its natural state. Rather than trying to forcefully constrain a jittery mind, one should release this energy.

The Buddha himself called mindfulness of the breath the best practice for people who are highly discursive. This soothing practice allows them to release mental chatter, obsessive thoughts, and compulsive reactions. Mindfulness of the breath is taught in various ways, but the Theravadin tradition does not employ visualization. Instead, it is taught that mindfulness is placed like a gatekeeper at the apertures of the nostrils. One simply attends to the sensations there, without allowing awareness to move inside the nostrils or outside the body.

In the Sanskrit texts that were translated into Tibetan, there were generally visualizations to accompany mindfulness of the breath. One might visualize a white light moving along with the breath, which offers a clear mental image to hold on to. This is taught because people have found it to be beneficial. Although there are many classic techniques, mindfulness of the breath does not require any visualization at all. One can simply attend to the tactile sensations of the breath.

Imagine a point in your life when you decide: "It's shamatha or bust." Having investigated numerous methods, you are drawn toward mindfulness of the breath. In a conducive environment with the requisite supports, you persevere in practice for months on end. As you continue to focus on the tactile sensations of the breath, they become subtler and subtler. You discover deep stability and intense vividness as you attend to progressively subtler images. Utilizing only the sensations at the apertures of the nostrils, you can travel far along the path to shamatha.

Shining Brightly

Arriving at the substrate consciousness, the experience is luminous without being veiled by dullness, lethargy, or sleepiness: the mother lode of luminosity and cognizance. According to the Pali Canon, the bhavanga is the undefiled state of radiant mind, synonymous with the Buddha's "brightly shining mind." This naturally luminous mind is undefiled because all mental activities, including anger, boredom, active compassion, and so forth, have gone dormant. It might seem like throwing out the baby with the bathwater. When everything goes dormant, this includes wholesome mental states such as loving-kindness, generosity, and compassion. But the dirty bathwater included craving, hostility, envy, and all the mental afflictions.

With all mental processes dormant, what remains is a naturally pure, undefiled state. The afflictions have gone quiet, though not irreversibly so. The sheer radiance of awareness of the substrate consciousness manifests because it is no longer veiled by mental activities. You rest in this state of consciousness while in dreamless sleep; your dreaming consciousness emerges out of it, and the contents of your dream emerge out of the substrate. Operating in dream mode, you mentally see, hear, think, and experience emotions, but the substrate is naturally pure and undefiled.

In the Theravadin tradition, the bhavanga is the mind's naturally pure state, but it is normally inaccessible and manifests primarily during deep sleep. We tap into this state multiple times daily; however, in falling asleep we generally lose clarity, and the ground state is veiled by dullness and sleepiness. The naturally luminous nature of the mind is hidden like a light in a box.

In stark contrast to this is access to the bhavanga via shamatha, which cultivates increasing luminosity and vividness of attention. With all mental processes dormant, there remains an exceptional degree of luminosity: the ground luminosity of the substrate consciousness. In the practice of shamatha, we make adjustments when the mind gets a bit dull or excited. We modulate, refine, and balance the attention to cultivate a vividness that becomes progressively clearer and sharper, in both temporal and qualitative aspects. Vividness reaches a crescendo upon attaining shamatha. Lo and behold, at the end of the tunnel, luminosity meets luminosity!

Ordinarily when we fall asleep, dullness overpowers our innate luminosity; this is why, on awakening, we can't remember what it was like to be deep asleep. To unlock the power of the natural purity of the bhavanga, the mind must be fully awakened by development. The ultimate task of shamatha is the full activation of the mind's radiant potential.

Zero Point

The bhavanga is known as the natural, unconfigured state of mind, the ground state or substrate consciousness from which the ordinary mind emerges as a configured state. When we operate out of waking consciousness, it is heavily configured for a specific gender, ethnicity, language, and personal history: the psyche studied by psychologists. When we fall asleep, it becomes unconfigured once again.

The bhavanga is also the final experience of a person's life. In the Pali texts, the state of consciousness of the ground of becoming is called the "falling away" mind. When you are dying, your gender-specific, species-specific psyche is dissolving and falling away; you are losing your mind. As the brain gradually shuts down, it is no longer able to support the generation of thoughts, memories, sensory perceptions, feelings, and so forth. Finally the EEG lines go flat, and a neuroscientist would declare that consciousness has ceased because the brain is no longer generating it; with neurons no longer functioning, there is no emergent feature of consciousness. Of course, if you are studying the mind by way of neurons, this conclusion is preordained by your methodology.

On the other hand, if you are investigating from the inside out, then you might actually die lucidly, analogous to falling asleep lucidly. If you can rest in the ongoing flow of awareness, you might observe the thinning out of mental processes and the falling away of the physical senses, thoughts, memories, emotions, and desires. Everything falls away and dissolves—but not into nothing. An extraordinarily daunting Buddhist principle that is analogous to the conservation of mass-energy in physics is that consciousness cannot be destroyed. Your psyche can withdraw into the bhavanga, and you will have lost your identity as male or female, old or young, fat or skinny; all your personal history will be dormant. If you die lucidly, observing your specific psyche dissolving and falling away, you will know what it's like to be dead. You can rest in the bhavanga and know you are there.

The dress rehearsal for death is learning how to fall asleep consciously, the opposite of the normal process for most of us. Watching yourself lose your mind as you fall asleep, you can observe the process of withdrawal of the physical senses, thoughts, memories, and images, while you slip consciously into the bhavanga. Without training, at best you may retain some fraction of your waking clarity, but it is possible to witness this falling away and maintain lucidity in deep sleep. On the other hand, if you approach the substrate consciousness via hundreds or thousands of hours of shamatha training, you have enhanced the vividness and polished the clarity of your mind to a fine state. Accessing the substrate with this powerful instrument, you will encounter the source of all luminosity.

In Nagasena's famous dialogue with King Menander, he likens the bhavanga's radiance to the sun's luminosity. The naturally pure and radiant ground state when consciousness is turned upon itself instead of toward the senses also forms the basis for karmic processes in daily life. The luminosity characteristic of the ground of becoming is also that which illuminates all ordinary phenomena. When the mind is not activated in dreams, physical sensations, thinking, or problem solving, whether due to falling asleep or brain damage, then consciousness returns to this ground state.

Normal mental functioning is like a light that can be switched off. Perception via the eyes, ears, and other physical senses, as well as mental perception of thoughts, images, emotions, and so forth, is subject to interruption. If you are blinded or damage your auditory cortex, the corresponding appearances will no longer be illuminated. The ability to think and remember can be destroyed by dementia. Even the sense of physical pain can be disabled by disease, resulting in great risk of injury. On the other hand, the substrate consciousness of dreamless sleep has a radiance that is said to persist whether or not it is obscured. This important hypothesis could be tested empirically if any neuroscientist were so inclined. I can suggest several experiments that could be performed, but the first-person perspective would have to be taken seriously.

All Configurations

The first verse of the *Dhammapada* contains one of the most frequently quoted aphorisms of the Buddha: "All phenomena are preceded by the mind, issue forth from the mind, and consist of the mind."[97] One interpretation of this statement is that the mind here refers to the bhavanga.

All phenomena means all appearances. This doesn't mean that all galaxies in the universe somehow emerged out of our minds. The Buddha is saying that all appearances in our world of experience are preceded by the mind. Awareness underlies everything else, and it exists even in deep sleep, when virtually nothing appears.

We commonly say that someone in dreamless sleep is unconscious, but this is nonsense for a person who is experiencing lucid, dreamless sleep. Buddhism holds that consciousness can never be eliminated, even under general anesthesia. It's just that people ordinarily have a very low level of luminosity and cognizance while they're asleep. Many of La-Berge's subjects have achieved lucidity in dreamless sleep, which demonstrates that one can be conscious in deep sleep. The Buddhist view is that, even in a comatose state, although consciousness is greatly diminished, it isn't completely absent. All phenomena are preceded by the mind, and the awareness of the bhavanga is like the pilot light on a stove. It's always lit, though unseen until activated—Poof! A dream appears and then it vanishes. If you shake a sleeping person: "Wake up, the house is on fire!" Poof! The smoke, heat, flames, and crackle of the fire appear as you run for safety.

All phenomena are preceded by the mind's substrate, the bhavanga, from whence they issue forth. In the terminology of the early Pali Canon, no distinction is drawn between the substrate and the substrate consciousness—it's a system, which makes good sense. When the conceptual mind goes dormant and the substrate consciousness is experienced, there is no explicit bifurcation of experience between the substrate over there and the consciousness of it over here. Coming out of this experience, we may speak retrospectively about appearances of vacuity that we designate as the substrate. Awareness of it is not a separate thing being posited. One term, "bhavanga," describes the system. The bhavanga consciousness emphasizes the awareness that occurs.

Shifting our perspective, the objective side of this unified experience of the substrate consciousness is the substrate. All appearances, including the brightness of lights, the blueness of the sky, and the forms in your personal environment actually represent configurations of the space of your mind. This substrate, which is formless, shapeless, colorless, and dimensionless, generates every aspect of form, shape, color, and dimension. It appears as visual, auditory, and tactile forms, such as those we see in a dream; it encompasses every possibility.

Can you imagine the smell of a ripe banana? If so, the space of your mind becomes configured as that smell. The sour taste of lemon juice on the tongue manifests in the substrate. All such appearances consist merely of configurations of the empty space of the mind. They arise from this space, consist of this space, and dissolve back into this space. This is what the Buddha meant in saying that all phenomena issue forth from the mind. Where else could they possibly come from? The notion that all phenomena emerge from neurons is absurd—even our perceptions of neurons emerge from the space of awareness.

Understanding that all phenomena consist of the mind places the horse before the cart. Phenomena are configurations or formations of the substrate perceived by consciousness, which is connate and interdependent. When the substrate is configured as a dreamscape, the substrate consciousness is configured as a dreaming consciousness. Out of this same substrate manifest all the appearances of the waking state, and the mind that apprehends them is called the psyche. Even though they are strongly configured by the visual cortex, auditory cortex, genetics, language, and culture, all such appearances consist solely of the mind. This is the Buddha's teaching in the *Dhammapada*.

In the *Ratnamegha Sutra* of the Mahayana canon, also attributed to the Buddha, is found a similar statement: "All phenomena are preceded by the mind." This is followed by the extraordinary statement: "When the mind is comprehended, all phenomena are comprehended." Since Buddhism starts with the world of experience, "all phenomena" refers to appearances to consciousness rather than to an independent, objective reality as perceived from a God's-eye view. Once we completely fathom the world of experience, we may see that there is nothing else. The Buddha's third assertion is truly astonishing: "By bringing the mind under control, all things are brought under control."[98] How can we understand this? Bear in mind that the Buddha said he was awake, while we're not.

Imagine that you are in the midst of a lucid dream. All appearances in the dream are simply configurations of your substrate. The dream state is like the waking state with no objective, physical constraints. If someone in your dream says, "All phenomena are preceded by the mind," being lucid, you respond, "Of course they are—I'm dreaming." When the mind is comprehended, all phenomena are comprehended. If you thoroughly fathom the nature of the substrate—from which all appearances emerge—this illuminates the nature of everything that appears.

In a lucid dream, you might experiment with transforming the contents of your dream by shifting, modifying, and reshaping them to reveal anything that is not malleable under the influence of your mind. Bringing your mind under control by truly fathoming the nature of the dream, you will find nothing impervious to your wishes. You can obliterate the whole dream or reshape it by changing anything you like, limited only by your imagination. You are completely free—the master of your lucid dream universe.

At this moment, you undoubtedly assume that you are actually awake, with no such ability to shift, modify, and master your universe. Relative to last night's sleep, you are awake, but relative to the Buddha's state, you might still be asleep. What would be the result of bringing your mind under control and thoroughly fathoming the nature of waking experience—as he did?

The idea that all phenomena are preceded by the mind, referring to the substrate, has an interesting parallel in twentieth-century physics. Quantum field theory includes very elegant theoretical systems and experimental methods to probe and characterize the nature of space. My undergraduate work in physics was focused on the energy that is implicit in the essence of space itself, called the "zero-point energy." When Paul Dirac (1902–1984) mathematically integrated special relativity and quantum mechanics into quantum field theory, the concept of space was altered radically. In classical physics, space is inert—simply a location in which things can happen. In general relativity, space becomes far more interesting because it can be warped by massive objects. In quantum field theory, the very nature of empty space is characterized by the zero-point energy.

Besides containing ordinary matter, space can contain energy in thermal, gravitational, electromagnetic, and other forms. When all such matter and energy is removed, what remains is the zero-point energy: the energy of empty space. The very nature of space can be thought of as an equilibrium, symmetry, or homogeneity—the same in every direction. But circumstances can break this symmetry, causing virtual particles to emerge spontaneously from "empty" space. A virtual electron or another elementary particle might be detected, but it will rapidly vanish with little effect.

Other more durable phenomena also emerge from empty space, and we call them particles and fields. According to quantum field theory, all particles of matter and fields of energy, virtual and real, are simply configurations of empty space. From galaxies to wristwatches to dark matter and energy, everything emerges from and consists exclusively of configured space. Everything eventually dissolves back into space. Whether phenomena are ephemeral or durable, quantum field theory describes their common ground as the nature of space.[99]

Likewise, observe the space of the mind, and you will see a luminous vacuity, saturated with creative energy and ready for anything. While you are passively witnessing this space, a thought may pop up and then dissolve with no further effect. If you are able to rest without grasping, an arising thought is simply noticed, like a virtual particle with no durability. Whether it is neutral, virtuous, or nonvirtuous, the thought triggers no intention and influences no behavior. There is no chain of associated thoughts and no disturbance to your mental equilibrium. On the other hand, if you identify with thoughts and images—seeking them or rejecting them—the mind's grasping tentacles fixate upon these objects as real, and your intentions may trigger behavior. All the while, the objects of grasping exist only as configurations of the substrate, reified by grasping.

We have discussed three primary modes of shamatha. The first is mindfulness of the breath, which you can continue practicing throughout the day and night. As long as you are breathing, there is something to attend to. But there will come a time when you breathe out for the last time, respiration ceases, and the senses dissolve.

According to the Buddhist understanding, even after the breath stops, there will be lingering appearances and mental activities for some time.

You cannot practice mindfulness of the breath, but settling the mind in its natural state is quite possible. Watch the space of the mind and its contents with great interest as you die. Rest in the luminous space of awareness, attending to the mind as it falls away.

Eventually, the mind completely settles in its natural state; all appearances dissolve into the substrate, and all mental activities dissolve into the substrate consciousness. What remains is the appearance of the substrate and the awareness of the substrate consciousness, so no more settling is possible, but you can still practice awareness of awareness. Resting there, you can know what it's like to be dead. You might also see something more, but that's the practice of Dzogchen, which we'll address in the next chapter.

GUIDED MEDITATION:
Awareness of Awareness II

---

*Attend to the cognizant luminosity of awareness—
sustaining it without subject or object*

Settle the body in its natural state and the respiration in its natural rhythm.

Rest with your eyes open and gaze vacant, not attending to anything. Sustain the clarity and luminosity of awareness without latching on to an object.

Maintaining only a peripheral awareness of the flow of the breath, with each inhalation arouse your attention and invert your awareness, drawing it in upon that which is aware. Each time you inhale, probe deeply the inner space of awareness—without ever finding a subject who observes.

With each exhalation, utterly relax and instantly release any thoughts or contents of the mind that may have arisen. Sustain the awareness of awareness throughout the whole course of the exhalation—without ever finding an object to observe.

Repeatedly invert your awareness without latching on to an inner subject and then release your awareness without latching on to an outer object. With familiarity, you may disengage from the breath and oscillate at any rhythm you find comfortable. Observe the referent of the term "awareness": that which is luminous and cognizant. Sustain an ongoing flow of awareness of awareness, giving no attention to anything else.

Attend very closely, especially with each inhalation. Remedy laxity by paying closer attention. With each exhalation, continue to attend but with a deep sense of relief, release, and relaxation. Remedy excitation by relaxing more deeply. ❧

On Lucidity

Degrees of lucidity characterize both waking and dreaming experience. The practice of settling the mind in its natural state entails a quality of heightened interest and discerning intelligence that is clear, luminous, present, engaged, and highly attentive. This is a practice of becoming lucid with respect to our own minds in the waking state. When we lack awareness of our mental processes, we instinctively fuse our identity with our mental impulses: I want, I think, and I feel. Furthermore, we frequently take everything that manifests to our mind as being quite real. When a thought appears, we simply assume it's real. The ordinary state of mind—nominally awake but profoundly asleep—is caught up in endless thoughts and identified with everything, much like in a nonlucid dream. Most people's dreams are unpleasant and fraught with anxiety for good reason: they are fundamentally deluded.

Psychologists study rumination and worry, the obsessions with negative thoughts of the past and the future respectively. Sufferers are entangled in a vicious cycle, paralyzed by repetitive thoughts of anger, resentment, craving, anxiety, and low self-esteem. Much like a nonlucid dream, this is a nonlucid waking state. Without awareness of mental processes, these images are taken to be real.

In a lucid dream, we recognize that a fearsome monster is only a harmless mental image, and joy comes from knowing things as they really are.

Some dreams include indications of marginal lucidity. For example, a friend described an unpleasant dream that became quite scary, but after a while he noticed a lingering, semiconscious awareness: "This is a dream, and I'm going to stop it." This went on for some time before he woke up.

It can be quite rewarding to enhance one's degree of lucidity—really grokking that this is a dream, not just entertaining the possibility. One of my favorite quasi-lucid dream reports came from a woman who found herself clinging to steel beams atop a skyscraper under construction. She was enjoying the company of Richard Gere, but he slipped and was plunging to his death. She was lucid enough to think: "I'm not losing Richard Gere," as she reversed the effects of gravity and pulled him back to safety.

A number of people have demonstrated remarkable gifts for lucid dreaming. One fellow was having frequent lucid dreams, so I suggested he enhance his lucidity with certain exercises developed by LaBerge. One example is to practice walking through walls because all dream bodies and walls are merely configurations of the substrate. In his next lucid dream, he attempted to walk through a wall and got stuck halfway through. He tried running through the wall but found it to be very viscous. Even though he knew it wasn't a real wall, the tactile sensations of solidity were vivid. LaBerge and his students discovered a way to walk through walls without resistance: walk through backward. If you don't see the wall, you won't know when it's supposed to get hard, and you will pass through easily.

A woman in another retreat was very adept at lucid dreaming, and I gave her the challenge to unscrew her own head and examine her headless body. She nearly got it off but found it too disconcerting to disconnect her head entirely. The inkling that "I don't have to tolerate this; it's not real" is an early indicator of lucidity. In Tibet, it has been known for centuries that the surest way to induce lucidity is via a very unpleasant dream. Even without any special aptitude or training, in the midst of your nightmare, a little glimmering may surface: "This isn't real—I'm out of here." You might be lucid for about two seconds before hitting the ejector button and waking up with a sense of relief. A broad continuum of lucidity exists in both dreaming and waking experience, and transitional experiences occur until one becomes thoroughly lucid.

Passing Signs

As you engage in meditative practices such as those described here, various mental and physical experiences can manifest vividly as signs of progress on the path. Such meditative experiences (Tib. *nyams*) are defined as anomalous, transient experiences resulting from authentic meditative practice; they can be psychic, somatic, or both. Calling these experiences anomalous and transient is purely descriptive rather than being dismissive. The overriding instruction concerning all such experiences, regardless of their content, is to simply be present with them while avoiding any form of grasping, attachment, or aversion.

Of course, it is crucial to differentiate transient meditative experiences from physical or mental conditions that may require medical attention—these can occur whether you meditate or not. If you follow my instructions, practice in short sessions, and remember the primacy of relaxation, I am very confident that you will not be harmed by these practices. The risk of harm occurs due to thinking, "I must achieve something faster, try harder, and do more." For many people, relaxation is often difficult, the process of meditation is goal driven, and the preliminary practices are skipped to reach a mythical pot of gold at the end of the rainbow. Such spiritual materialism generates physical and mental obstacles that prevent one from actualizing the key points of practice.

You must maintain mindfulness of your body and not press on doggedly with your session when you need to rest. If you are experiencing low blood sugar, you might need a glass of orange juice. If you have a heart condition and notice your heart beating rapidly, you should take a break from meditation and rest, or take a leisurely walk. If you are concerned that a physical condition is manifesting, you should use common sense and seek medical care immediately. The more deeply you dredge the psyche in intensive practice, the more stuff that will come up, including traumatic memories, deep-seated fears, and powerful emotions. There are trained professionals who can assist you in healing psychological wounds—secure their help if you need it.

Without mentioning the bizarre and truly dangerous potential results of improper meditation, an enormous variety of experiences can be catalyzed by authentic practices. Dredging the psyche in the practice of shamatha can catalyze transient experiences of paranoia or disturbing feelings in the body. Some people experience nausea and vertigo; strange mental states manifest and vanish without a trace. Other transient, anomalous experiences may seem like shafts of sunlight breaking through the cloud cover or bolts of lightning illuminating the darkness, if only briefly. Such transient experiences catalyzed by authentic meditation can indicate the radiance of something far deeper and not transient. This blazing luminosity is the referent of the Buddha's "brightly shining mind" and one defining aspect of the substrate consciousness.

If the immediate experience is accompanied by a sense of bliss, this is a second characteristic of the substrate consciousness. Even without the third aspect of nonconceptuality, and long before the actual achievement of shamatha, this represents a manifestation of the substrate consciousness in your immediate experience. Even though such experiences are transient and anomalous, they are indications of the substrate consciousness. Continuing on the path, you are likely to have more such experiences. As you approach the mother lode, resting in the substrate consciousness is utterly luminous, blissful, and nonconceptual. But the purpose of shamatha meditation is not merely to enjoy bliss, luminosity, and nonconceptuality; it also enables a profound sense of empathy, loving-kindness, and compassion to be invoked. This is a platform—not the end point.

The result of achieving shamatha is experienced in postmeditation as extraordinary clarity and luminosity, even while one is actively engaged with the world. Everyday experiences take on a bright, high-definition luster, like a three-dimensional holographic display. Commenting on this, Tsongkhapa says that having achieved shamatha, even between sessions your sense of temporal and qualitative vividness may be so acute that you feel you could count individual atoms in the walls of your house.

Shifting Gears

We have covered a broad range of practices, and careful discrimination is needed to determine the most suitable methods for your own needs. If you sit down to meditate and merely let your mind wander around, try-ing a bit of this and a bit of that, nothing is likely to work out very well; you might end up visiting the refrigerator instead. Such a lack of disci-pline represents one extreme. The other extreme is to ruthlessly press on with a practice, even though you are doing it rather poorly, generating increasing frustration. The middle road requires you to adapt your prac-tice to the conditions at hand.

Think of shamatha as an all-terrain vehicle with a five-speed transmis-sion to handle any situation. On a rough day, plagued by disagreeable encounters, stress, and exhaustion, the thought of meditating for half an hour might seem intolerable. Even if you tried to push yourself, it probably wouldn't go very well. But anesthetizing yourself with televi-sion, food, or entertainment won't help either. On such occasions, find a softly lit, quiet space, such as your own bedroom; lie supine on your bed with your head on the pillow, and breathe with full-body awareness. You will begin to feel better immediately by releasing all tension, untangling the body's knots, and resting the mind in full-body awareness. In as little as half an hour, releasing thoughts with every exhalation, you are likely to feel much better. Full-body awareness is like engaging your four-wheel drive to safely traverse the roughest conditions—this is first gear.

On other occasions you may feel mentally scattered and excited, even though you're not particularly stressed. Once again, the supine position is superbly relaxing, and you can simply attend to the rise and fall of the abdomen. Be grounded in the firm support of the earth element and melt in its embrace. For stability, you might introduce a subtle count at the end of each inhalation. Relax deeply and progressively with each exhalation. Focusing on the abdomen safely releases the energy behind your agitation, grounds you, and allows you to enter into the flow of awareness—second gear.

At times you may feel relatively balanced, without being particu-larly excited or stressed, and meditation may seem inviting. This is a good time for an upright posture and mindfulness of the breath at the apertures of the nostrils. Simultaneously and synergistically cultivating relaxation, stability, and vividness is an excellent practice for everyday conditions—third gear.

Occasionally you may feel quite refreshed, bright, and clear. Settling the mind in its natural state, which requires finesse and clarity, could be the perfect practice. When conditions are smooth, this practice allows you to travel to subtler realms—fourth gear.

Finally, at times when you feel optimally composed and very sharp, you can streamline your practice to awareness of awareness—fifth gear.

Everyone is different, and only you can tell which practice will best fit your physical and mental state at any particular time. Some people immediately gravitate to awareness of awareness. Others find settling the mind in its natural state to be a mainstay. Mindfulness of the breath can be as soothing and healing as a good massage.

Because of the diversity of conditions as well as personalities, inclinations, and aptitudes for meditation, it's best to become familiar with the strengths and limitations of a variety of techniques. If you attempt to settle the mind in its natural state but notice that you're wandering all over the place, you can downshift to awareness of the breath or full-body awareness, finding the practice that meshes with your current capability. The type of meditation you engage in should be appropriate to your quality of mind at the moment. You need not perform it perfectly, but it's very important to know that you are practicing correctly. With confidence in your trajectory, you will realize the benefits.

Upon finishing this book, you will understand a number of fundamental practices and will know how to perform them correctly and confidently. When you detect an imbalance, you should quickly recognize this and take corrective steps. Even within one session, you should monitor your performance and shift gears up or down if necessary, choosing a practice to suit actual conditions. You can always shift your posture; an upright position promotes vividness and counteracts laxity, while a supine position promotes relaxation and counteracts excitation.

Walking Mindfully

In the Buddha's discourse on the four close applications of mindfulness, he explicitly refers to walking, standing, sitting, and lying down. Walking practice is superb, but be mindful not to walk into things. Simply sustaining mindfulness can lead to profound results, even though mindfulness alone does not constitute vipashyana. You can practice vipashyana while walking by employing some of the specific methods the Buddha taught. Observe the arising of feelings with respect to the five physical senses and the mind while walking. Observe the arising of the earth, water, fire, and air elements with some of the sophistication the Buddha offered, rather than simply being mindful. Keep your eyes open, pay attention to your step, and choose a safe, quiet place.

It is often easiest to simply pace back and forth, focused on mindfulness of the mind and mental events as they arise. One can also explore the interplay between mind, body, and environment with closely applied mindfulness, observing the causal nexus of events arising. This can be done as a very simple practice of mindfulness of sensations, or as informed by the sophisticated theory taught by the Buddha. In the Theravadin tradition, it is generally suggested to walk rather slowly. One is less likely to trip, more likely to sustain mindfulness, and more able to generate crisp, vivid appearances while walking slowly, watching phenomena arise moment by moment. Slowing down your activity allows the pace of your mind to engage with the present moment, and you are able to detect increasingly subtle events arising in body and mind.

ALL PHENOMENA INCLUDED

Now we venture into the practice of open presence—the close application of mindfulness to all phenomena that appear to the mind. In the Tibetan term for the practice of open presence (*rig pa cog gzhag*), *rigpa* means pristine awareness and *chok shak* means letting it be. One simply lets awareness be—wide-open, nonpreferential, and not excluding anything. The eyes are not closed but open to reality. Having no preferences, no appearance to the mind constitutes a distraction.

The "enemy" in this practice is not the appearances to any of the six senses but the distraction of becoming caught up in them via grasping. For this practice, it is essential to be totally relaxed, as if you were simply taking a break from reading and enjoying a cup of tea. Without looking at anything, your eyes are open and completely relaxed, blinking naturally.

GUIDED MEDITATION:
Open Presence I

Attend to the space of the mind and all appearances—
hovering in the present moment, wide-open

Settle the body in its natural state and the respiration in its natural rhythm.

From the six experiential domains, select the tactile domain. Direct your awareness to the entire field of the body and whatever tactile events arise there; attend to them without distraction or grasping. Relax with each exhalation, releasing all thoughts. Arouse your attention during each inhalation.

Now let your eyes be naturally open along with all six senses. Observe all sensory appearances, mental events, images, and emotions that arise—excluding nothing. Hover with awareness wide-open in the immediacy of the present moment, where everything is fresh and unprecedented. Abide in a mode of bare attention, free from conceptual elaborations. Witness the space of the mind as the all-encompassing domain of sensory and mental appearances. Direct your awareness to this omnipresent space and whatever manifests within it, without distraction or grasping. Let your awareness rest in its own place, not chasing after objects, labeling them, or engaging with them. Let it stay home.

Maintain an unwavering flow of mindfulness. Monitor the process with introspection, noting as swiftly as possible when you are caught up and carried away by thoughts. Conceptualization is a poor substitute for reality! Release, relax, and rest your awareness in the present moment, remaining wide-open as appearances present themselves.

If you find yourself becoming spacey, without an object of mindfulness, or falling into laxity, refresh your awareness by rekindling a vivid interest in the immediacy of the present moment. Periodically check up on the body, posture, and breath. Let your awareness be motionless like space—unmoved, but illuminating all that appears within it. ↤

On the Eyes

Movement in one's visual field can be distracting, particularly in the peripheral field. Ideally, one will find a solitary, quiet place with soft lighting, no movement, and no visual distractions. Twilight is my favorite light; it's very soft but not dark.

Mindfulness of the breath can be practiced with the eyes in any comfortable position, open or closed. The shamatha practices of settling the mind in its natural state and awareness of awareness are generally practiced with the eyes at least a bit open. This instruction is not based on dogma but on the experiential results of deepening levels of practice. The eyes can be hooded, while letting in some light and enabling awareness to extend outward. The gaze should rest vacantly in the space in front of you.

The fourth close application of mindfulness to phenomena excludes nothing whatsoever, so the eyes should be open. This practice is also directly relevant in daily life, where we continuously encounter myriad phenomena in a tapestry of tastes, odors, sounds, and visual appearances, both natural and man-made. Rich, multisensory experience is a feast for the close application of mindfulness to all phenomena.

Grist for the Mill

Open presence can be a foundation for the cultivation of insight, or vipashyana. If you were to practice settling the mind in its natural state for ten hours a day over a six-month period, then you would likely find that your senses were gradually withdrawing. You would rest increasingly in your mind rather than your senses, which would begin to fade out. Even with the eyes open, the visual field might occasionally become monochromatic. Some people perceive a lavender sheen, while others report a blackout with their eyes wide-open. Photons are striking the retina, but no attention is being given to the visual field. We don't understand it neurophysiologically, but this is what happens experientially.

In settling the mind in its natural state, the trajectory is to gradually withdraw awareness from the five physical senses, attending exclusively to mental events. Thoughts and mental images gradually unravel and dissipate, and the space of the mind becomes more sparsely populated. Eventually, the psyche settles and dissolves into the silent, luminous, blissful substrate consciousness. The achievement of shamatha is like falling deep asleep while remaining wide awake—your only awareness is of a luminous vacuity called the space of the mind, or substrate.

The practice of awareness of awareness entails the observation of awareness itself, without directing awareness to any appearance. You are not interested in any of the five physical sense fields, the space of the mind, or anything arising in the space of the mind—only in awareness itself. When you achieve shamatha on this trajectory, your awareness is of the substrate consciousness, which is a mode of awareness. Your ordinary psyche has dissolved into the substrate consciousness, and all appearances have dissolved into the substrate.

In open presence, the fundamental instruction is to remain equally attentive to all visual, auditory, tactile, olfactory, and gustatory sensations, as well as to anything arising in the mind. All phenomena are equally objects of mindfulness. Rather than slipping into the vacuity of the substrate, the practice is simply to hover in the immediacy of the present, with all senses wide-open. As relaxation deepens and grasping is released, one's clarity of attention becomes enhanced and refined. Whatever arises is seen nakedly, without the habitual tendency to reify or superimpose a concrete substantiality upon objective phenomena. Everything is grist for the mill.

Looking at a massive object, we think we see its weight and substantiality. But visual perception cannot detect weight, heat, or cold—these are tactile sensations. In the seen, let there be just the seen. Use Ockham's razor to shave off everything except what is actually being presented and see it as nakedly as you can. Likewise, as much as possible, hear sounds without slipping into evaluations and preferences, all of which are projected. The Buddha said, "In the heard, let there be just the heard." Let tactile sensations appear naked of superimpositions. Simply be present with all sensations and mental events. Awareness is wide-open and fully present, and all appearances are seen with increasing clarity, unencumbered by veils and projections. This practice is very much in the spirit of empirical science, like calibrating a finely tuned instrument to collect clean data, free of artifacts.

Undirected Attention

We are developing the skill of being present without the deeply ingrained habit of directing the attention. In daily life, the ability to direct one's attention is essential because some things are much more important than others. Directed attention is crucial to survival while driving in traffic. In ordinary activities, we can arouse great vividness of attention simply by trying hard. Notice how the forehead and jaw muscles tighten when we exert ourselves determinedly. After expending such effort, we typically feel fatigued. In open presence, we are broadening our repertoire. We remain attentive to all sensory fields, which are not as static as they might seem, even when little is happening. The goal in this practice is to avoid anything catching our attention and constricting our vision—something we already know how to do.

In the contemplative practice of shamatha, we simultaneously enhance the stability and vividness of attention while relaxing increasingly deeply. This is a skill not taught in the ordinary world, where highly aroused attention is generally accompanied by a sharp focus, strong effort, and contraction. People who cultivate their attention in skillful shamatha meditation can sustain a state of very high arousal and vigilance, with extraordinary vividness and stability of attention, and still feel utterly fresh after many hours. This ability constitutes a highly advanced platform for vipashyana.

When open presence is practiced correctly, there is no narrowing of perception and no selectivity. It is imperative that awareness remains in its own place, illuminating all directions without moving toward any object. Everything appearing to visual, auditory, tactile, olfactory, gustatory, and mental perception is grist for the mill. The eyes should be open naturally, without selectivity or looking around, which constitutes grasping. If I look to my left, I've just excluded everything to my right. The gaze is not unfocused, which entails a retraction of discerning awareness. Instead, you are equally aware of everything in your field of vision. Imagine holding a lantern high to illuminate everything evenly in all directions. This is the quality of open awareness.

Present-Moment Awareness

In an interesting unpublished study, an experienced meditator practicing open presence was tested for the acoustic startle response—experimenters generated the sound of a gunshot about six feet away from a subject who was not expecting it. The startle response comprises reflexive reactions in the eyes, muscle contractions, and other physiological effects that are beyond voluntary control. Even if subjects are warned about the sound, they typically cannot help flinching. However, one meditator resting in open presence reacted so little that the scientists were surprised. They had never seen anyone respond so minimally. As a control, his startle response was tested when he was simply letting his mind wander, and he flinched like everyone else.

I asked this meditator what it was like. He said, "It's not such a big deal. When I'm resting in open presence, my attention is hovering right here in the present moment. At the instant of the gunshot, my attention is already vigilantly aware of the present moment, so the sound doesn't draw my awareness anywhere. There is no place to go. On the other hand, if my mind is caught up in ordinary thoughts and distractions, the gunshot yanks my chain and I react reflexively." This meditator was practicing open presence correctly, and his report gives us the flavor of the subjective result.

Fusing Stillness and Motion

This practice is not like falling asleep at the wheel. You're not spaced out: "I don't care about anything—I'm just sitting here." That would be an exercise in dullness. Neither is this a practice of active scanning, like a leashed dog that growls and lunges at all passersby up to the reach of the leash. Attending to phenomena does not entail the mind's darting out to grasp at whatever appears. Active, engaged reactions are overkill here. The instruction is to let your awareness rest in its own place, not chasing after objects, labeling them, or engaging with them. Let it stay home.

A nice metaphor from the Buddhist tradition is of an old man watching other people's children play. I'm getting to that stage myself. I enjoy watching Little League games, even without a kid of my own. The parents become very excited, but I can attend with a lot of interest and no concern over which side wins. The children are in good hands, they're not my responsibility, and no intervention is necessary. Similarly, in open presence you vigilantly attend to whatever comes up, while awareness remains motionless and unattached.

As your practice deepens, you will get the taste of what is called the fusion of stillness and motion (Tib. *gnas rgyu zung 'jug*). This means that awareness is still, loose, and relaxed, while attending with clear perception and discerning intelligence to myriad phenomena coming and going. Appearances arise and dissolve continuously, and you are aware of a great deal of motion in this fanfare of impermanence. Even though everything rises and falls in a fizzy display, you remain at rest and still. The quality of simultaneous stillness and motion is enabled by releasing grasping on to thoughts and sensory impressions. Awareness becomes spacious, and events arise within a space of stillness.

GUIDED MEDITATION:
Open Presence II

Attend to the space of the mind and all appearances—
interacting in causal patterns

Settle the body in its natural state and the respiration in its natural rhythm.

With eyes open and gaze vacant, settle the mind in its natural state. Attend to the space of the mind and its contents without distraction or grasping.

Now open this same quality of awareness to all six sense fields, attending to all appearances without distraction or grasping. Besides noting what arises from moment to moment, establish a higher-order view that notices larger patterns of causality over time. Look for relationships, such as one appearance—a mental process, sensory perception, emotion, or state of mind—giving rise to another. Notice how a thought leads to an emotion and a sensory impression generates a thought. Observe patterns of interdependence among the appearances in all six sense fields.

Appearances do not arise randomly but emerge from a causal nexus of dependent origination. Observe closely the patterns of causality, witnessing in a purely phenomenological mode. These are simply regular patterns of appearances giving rise to appearances, without underlying mechanisms. Do not look for mechanical explanations—none will be found.

Let your will be passive, while maintaining an intelligent, discerning mindfulness. Closely attend to phenomena arising from moment to moment, along with causal patterns stretching over time. Exert no influence or control over the mind or appearances to the mind. Simply allow all thoughts, images, sensations, and memories to arise without interference, regulation, or ownership.

Witness appearances just as they are. In the felt there is just the felt; in the seen, just the seen; in the heard, just the heard; in the cognized, just the cognized. Observe these phenomena and their causal interactions nakedly—bare of conceptualization. ❧

On Proper Preparation

The myriad practices in the Buddhist tradition can be classified as technologies with specific purposes. Shamatha is designed to produce exceptional mental health and balance—a potent equilibrium of attention with stability and vividness rooted in deep relaxation. Vipashyana is designed to free the mind from mental afflictions—severing the very root of delusional notions of reified self, reified mind, and reified phenomena. Finally, having accomplished these goals, one is prepared to effectively practice the theory, meditation, and way of life of Dzogchen. But such stepwise preparation is rarely followed nowadays, especially in the modern world. Many people try to practice Dzogchen prior to any accomplishment in shamatha and with little knowledge of vipashyana. The lack of profound benefit from such attempts should not surprise anyone.

When you enter into open presence with the proper preparation advocated by the great masters—with extraordinary mental balance, having shattered the reification of the mind and the bifurcation between the mind and its objects, and having had the nature of uncontrived, pristine awareness pointed out to you—resting in open presence ultimately means doing nothing. This sounds deceptively easy. The Dalai Lama commented that when you rest in nonconceptual meditation—putting the mind out of work—the vital energies naturally become refined, and the mind and vital energies slip into the clear light of pristine awareness. This requires settling in complete inactivity. And then he added, "But it's not so easy!" I can hear him laughing at the irony of this statement.

We are all pretty good at doing nothing, so why bother to practice shamatha, vipashyana, and the six perfections, when we can just do nothing instead? As the Dalai Lama said, it's not so easy doing nothing. Attempting to remain in open presence, the untrained mind is distracted within seconds. Now what? Letting the mind be distracted is merely daydreaming, which is doing something. Correcting a wandering mind is also doing something. Neither one is the practice of Dzogchen. This is why shamatha precedes vipashyana in the classic sequence. Furthermore, without having challenged, penetrated, and dissolved the reified notions of self, mind, subject, and object via vipashyana, one might merely be resting in a cozy nest of reification instead of resting in open presence, and dormant mental afflictions will inevitably be reactivated.

Highly accomplished beings, even nowadays, do sustain the practice of resting in open presence—sitting with the body still as a mountain and pristine awareness still as space, in classic Dzogchen imagery—doing nothing with body or mind. Furthermore, engaging in spontaneous activity with thoughts arising and speech emerging, these adepts sustain pristine awareness and continue to do nothing with body or mind. Their practice is to sustain pristine awareness at all times. Accomplishing activities while resting in pristine awareness is emulating the conduct of a buddha. In spontaneous arising there is no premeditation, no controlling ego, no exertion of will, and no expenditure of effort. Practicing inactivity in the midst of activity is taking the fruition as one's path.

Open Mindfulness

The fourth close application of mindfulness is the grand finale: all-inclusive mindfulness. In the first three applications of mindfulness, the emphasis was on observing clearly and nakedly in the present moment. What is your immediate experience of the body in terms of the elements, internally, externally, and both internally and externally? How do feelings arise, how are they present, and how do they disappear? Where does the vast range of mental phenomena originate, persist, and dissolve? With careful inspection and intelligent monitoring, we have examined all the constituents of reality in our world of experience.

The Buddhist understanding, which is empirically testable, is that the five modes of sensory experience have nonoverlapping domains: the five sense spheres. Disregarding the question of synesthesia, the tactile sense detects solidity but not colors, the eyes see colors and forms but not sounds, the ears hear sounds but not scents, and so forth. Mental perception is unique in having its own domain, inaccessible to the other five senses, along with access privileges to those five domains.

For example, if you imagine a banana, you don't physically see it, hear it, smell it, taste it, or feel it—you perceive it solely in the domain of the mental sense. When you are fast asleep and the five physical senses are dormant, the mental domain becomes the field of dreams in which the gamut of sensory phenomena appears. It has been shown that activity in the visual cortex during waking sensory experience is replicated during dreaming. There are not separate processes to generate dream images and waking visual appearances. The only difference is that waking appearances are constrained by objective physical input, such as photons and sound waves. In a dream, even though the visual cortex is operating, no photons arrive from the outside world—we don't see with our eyes.

In an old metaphor, the five physical modes of perception are like five princes with their own private princedoms. The mind is king, so the sixth kingdom of the mind includes access to the other five domains. When you detect something with visual perception, mental perception is simultaneous, allowing you to recognize an object you have previously seen. Mental perception roves among the six domains, following the attention. Using mental awareness, we can discern regular patterns and causal sequences. Something occurs, and some result follows, constituting a causal pattern of origination; something doesn't occur, and some result doesn't follow, in a causal pattern of nonorigination. We are bringing an entirely new dimension of insight to the practice. Instead of focusing on a particular domain and ignoring the rest, we take a step back to observe all domains of experience, moment by moment. Furthermore, we bring our intelligence to bear, drawing from experience and memory in order to recognize patterns. Although events arise continuously in staccato fashion, they are not merely random happenings.

One classic sequence occurs in sensory experience. Although this happens very rapidly, it can be observed. The first step is contact, or encounter between the sensory faculties and a stimulus—such as sound waves activating receptors. Contact ignites mental engagement, but the event has not yet been placed in a conceptual framework—there is just noise. Then recognition clicks, and a raw tactile sensation or sound becomes a familiar one—it's a lawnmower. In the midst of this process, a feeling is bound to arise as a concomitant mental factor, simultaneously engaged with the same object. This is not another object, but a pleasant, unpleasant, or neutral mode of awareness that flavors our apprehension of the object. Feelings are affected by attitudes, such as a belief that noise will interrupt one's meditation—it's a horribly loud lawnmower. Then a desire might arise: "I hope it stops." Anger could follow: "Why can't those gardeners be quiet!"

Ordinarily, the experiential sequence of contact, mental engagement, recognition, feeling, desire, and various conceptual elaborations might activate your intentions, which could precipitate actions. However, in the practice of close application of mindfulness to phenomena, you observe this process and think before acting: There are no impediments to open presence—only grist for the mill.

Wisdom and Skillful Means

Observing these sequences, we see that they are not random but cohere in patterns. In this practice, we do not seek to alter, adjust, or redirect our experience; however, this does not imply that such interventions are never required. If we find ourselves fixated on a negative memory, reliving it repeatedly and becoming resentful, an attitudinal adjustment is necessary.

There is a faddish quality to the current interest in mindfulness. Over-simplification rules as the popular media crowd onto the bandwagon. Sometimes the practice of mindfulness is presented as a panacea, but it is wrong to suggest that simply observing experiential phenomena will solve everything. Instead of curing all your ills, this could make things worse. Mindfulness is not all there is to Buddhist insight practice, not to mention the broad range of valuable contemplative practices in other traditions.

The purpose of the Buddhist practice of mindfulness is to cultivate wisdom by way of direct, experiential insight. Even though acts of intervention are not part of this practice, they are completely appropriate in many contexts. Wisdom must be balanced with practices of skillful means, including cultivation of the four immeasurables: loving-kindness, compassion, empathetic joy, and equanimity. Such practices are interventions designed to shift attitudes, enhance empathy, and so forth. Within this rich context of practice, mindfulness brings synergistic benefits.

One example of skillful means is the practice of mind training (Tib. *blo sbyong*), which focuses on attitudinal adjustments to train and purify the mind. When phenomena present themselves, our reflexive attitude is often one of disagreeability. By adjusting attitudes, shifting perspectives, and cultivating insights, we can experience the same phenomena in radically different ways. Those who maintain ordinary, habitual attitudes may experience a particular phenomenon as highly objectionable. However, for someone with a transformed perspective, appearances may be quite different: phenomena are not independent of experience.

Our inquiry has become an epistemic one: What can we know about the nature of reality that we experience? We are also facing an ontological challenge: What sorts of phenomena actually exist? What could be more fascinating than experiential insight into the very essence of being? Nevertheless, our pursuit of knowledge is not for the sake of knowledge itself. Our explicit purpose is to heal and liberate: Seek out those truths that will set you free.

STRATEGIC CATEGORIES

Hearing about the categories of four close applications of mindfulness, five aggregates, six sense spheres, and so forth, one could easily get the impression that the Buddha and the ancient scholars were obsessed with lists. In fact, the practical purpose of these classical systems for categorizing reality is to untangle our confusion by increasing clarity, resolution, and differentiation. The universe is not like a pot of homogenized cream-of-reality soup. If we examine things carefully, we can distinguish myriad aspects and elements of reality.

Confusion means fusing together. For example, if I'm practicing open presence and hear some music that I enjoy, there is contact, mental engagement, recognition, and a pleasant feeling along with the recognition. I may begin to anticipate the future: "What will they play next?" Perhaps a desire will arise: "I hope they continue, this is nicer than meditating . . . I wish I had been a musician. . . ." In the midst of experiencing this pleasant sensation with running mental commentary, we might very naturally think: "This music is really great." Now we have confused our subjective feelings with the object. Hearing this same music, someone else may say, "Isn't that music irritating?" We might question their hearing or their common sense because we clearly heard how great it was.

Similarly, an appearance to perception can be regarded as an attractive person, a horrible place to live, boring weather, or a fascinating book. Neglecting the merits of any of these judgments, in each case we act as if our superimposed feelings are intrinsic to the object—fused together. This confusion of our feelings with objects ultimately leads to fusion of the whole world into reified clumps. Descartes posited two reified clumps: things with spatial extension, or *res extensa*, and thinking things, or *res cogitans*. But fusing together appearances to perception and our subjective reactions to them—along with reification of this amalgam—is confusion.

Our approach to vipashyana entails observing phenomena nakedly, seeing them for what they are by peeling away all superimpositions. We don't mistake the impermanent for permanent. We don't mistake suffering for a true source of happiness. We don't mistake empty appearances for a truly existent "I" or "mine." Stripping away projection and superimposition, we see things as they actually are—impermanent and unsatisfactory, as long as the mind that experiences them is subject to afflictions. Phenomena are not intrinsically unsatisfying, but a mind enslaved by afflictions experiences everything as such.

Mental, Physical, and Other

Mindfulness of phenomena includes all things mental and physical, but we are not subscribing to the Cartesian split that reifies mind and matter—not everything is mental or physical. For example, time is not physical; it's not composed of atoms and has no spatial location. Time is not mental either because time passes whether or not anybody knows it. The first billion years of the universe transpired without any sentient organisms like us. The days and seasons are periods of time that are neither physical nor mental, yet time is as real as anything we know.

Physical phenomena occur in two varieties, the first being material things like elementary particles, atoms, molecules, and cells. The second category of physical phenomena includes energy fields, rainbows, mirages, and many things that can be photographed and affect the physical domain but are not composed of matter and have no real spatial location. One of my favorite examples is easy to demonstrate. Stand five feet away from a mirror and look into it. You'll see an image of yourself, ten feet away. You can photograph this image, but if you focus your camera on the surface of the mirror, the picture will be blurry. The image actually appears to be five feet behind the mirror, which could be in another room. In fact, this image does not exist anywhere in physical space.

Justice and beauty are other examples of things that are not physical or mental. One that is right in your face, perhaps too close to see, is your very own "self." As you read this, you are someone who exists right now in a certain place. It's true and meaningful to say that you have a body and a mind, both subject to your intentional control. You are not equivalent to your body or your mind, although you have both. Your very self is neither physical nor mental—it's something else. All the major philosophical schools in Buddhism would agree that you do exist and you are impermanent. Like all people, you are getting older and changing over the course of time, which means you are real. Your actions give rise to real effects. Nevertheless, you are not simply compounded of atoms, nor are you a mental process or state.

Five Hindrances to Liberation

An interesting aspect that now becomes explicit, even though it pervades all four applications of mindfulness, is that we do not attend to causal sequences to gain knowledge for its own sake. Furthermore, unlike in some versions of scientific materialism, there is no absolute dichotomy between facts and values; subjective and anthropocentric elements are not censored from our contemplative inquiry. On the contrary, the close application of mindfulness to phenomena and their causal interactions carries a clear agenda, which is the pursuit of genuine happiness and liberation. Since we already care so much about suffering and wish to avoid it, we attend very carefully to uncover the root of the matter. Is it possible to eradicate suffering by severing this taproot?

Countless yogis of the past have found that certain mental obscurations can do a lot of damage. These afflictions obscure the natural luminosity of awareness. They hinder the pursuit of genuine happiness and freedom from suffering. The ancient methods teach us to become aware of five types of hindrances—sensual craving, malice, laxity and lethargy, excitation and anxiety, and uncertainty—and to observe their effects when they arise.

Shantideva described two ways to pursue happiness and freedom from suffering, particularly while we are socially engaged. When life isn't going well, people are behaving selfishly, or the traffic is brutal, we can give rise to unpleasant feelings. In Shantideva's metaphor, the first approach is to identify all the world's thorny people, things, and situations and cover all their thorns with leather. We won't be pricked if we can make everybody and everything conform to our desires, like covering the world with leather. The second approach is to wear a pair of sandals, requiring a lot less leather. If we transform and heal our own mind, we can encounter the beautiful, the ugly, and the ridiculous, while always maintaining our composure. Only the second approach has a chance of success.

In our daily lives, we often become upset when our desires are thwarted, but we cannot control people's behavior, the weather, the economy, or even our own bodies. Any control over these things is only superficial and temporary. But what about the mind? Can we recognize the features, patterns, and impulses that make us so vulnerable to suffering when things go wrong? Our goal is to identify the mental impulses and tendencies that generate craving, hostility, and unrest, thus giving rise to suffering. As we attend to these phenomena arising, instead of merely noting appearances with bare attention, we make informed observations.

Become a private sleuth instead of a simple witness. Keep on top of things, checking out the effect of the obscurations and hindrances from moment to moment. Are they present? If they have not yet arisen, how do they arise? Once they have arisen, how do they persist? How do they dissipate? Can mental afflictions be prevented? Preventive medicine is the best kind for psychological health and well-being. If we can avoid the arising of malice, craving, and so forth, there will be no need for antidotes, and no risk of such afflictions taking control.

Causal Interactions of the Five Aggregates

The central theme of this practice is the examination of causal interactions. Theoretical knowledge gained by studying the accounts of past adepts informs our inquiry intelligently and nondogmatically. In the Buddha's teachings, he classified all the constituents of our worldly embodiment into form, feeling, recognition, compositional factors, and consciousness: the five aggregates subject to clinging.

In the first application of mindfulness we investigated form—our body. In the second, we developed mindfulness of feelings. The third aggregate is sometimes translated as perception, but this is the ability to distinguish one phenomenon from another, better called recognition. Compositional factors include the entire array of mental processes, wholesome and unwholesome, associated with mental consciousness.

The five aggregates are categories of phenomena that we hold very closely; upon them, we habitually superimpose the sense of "I and mine." Mindfulness of the aggregates is a process of careful observation of all the patterns of causal interactions and relationships among these constituents. Is there any evidence for "I and mine" within the aggregates or apart from them? Can we overcome our habitual attachment to these phenomena and see them for what they are?

Six Sense Spheres

Next, the Buddha's discourse examines the six sense spheres internally and externally, and he comments: "A monk knows the eye, he knows visible forms, and he knows the fetter that arises dependent on both." When we attend to the coupling of the visual faculty of the eye and the forms that appear to the eye, the fetter is a mental affliction, hindrance, or obscuration that may arise, such as craving or aversion.

The Buddha continues: "He also knows how an unarisen fetter can arise, how an arisen fetter can be removed, and how a future arising of the removed fetter can be prevented." It is quite clear that in the practice of mindfulness, we are trying to remove obscurations, not merely observe them. It is a misrepresentation of this practice to suggest that one must never intervene; simply watching whatever comes up and being present with it can be bad medicine. At times, we must actively eliminate a hindrance. Even better, we might see how a future arising of affliction can be prevented—the best medicine.

The Buddha repeats this formula for each of the physical sense spheres. In each case, the sensory faculty and its object arise interdependently, and we see how they are obscured by afflictions. The final case is the mind, the sixth sense sphere:

> He knows the mind, he knows mental objects, and he knows
> the fetter that arises in dependence on both; he also knows
> how an unarisen fetter can arise, how an arisen fetter can be
> removed, and how a future arising of the removed fetter can
> be prevented.[100]

The mind means mental awareness, and mental objects means the phenomena that are accessible exclusively to the mind. Thoughts, mental images, dreams, and so forth cannot be detected by any of the other five senses or by any instrument of technology. Even ordinary sensory appearances are accompanied by mental awareness—if awareness is so directed—making them mental objects.

Seven Factors of Enlightenment

In this therapeutic orientation toward awakening, a classical enumeration includes seven factors that are like seven pistons that can accelerate awakening. Mindfulness, investigation, effort, joy, tranquility, concentration, and equanimity are your engine's seven cylinders. It's always helpful to recognize and overcome fetters, hindrances, or obscurations; but even more beneficial is the generation of active forward propulsion. Are all cylinders firing?

These seven factors act synergistically, and mindfulness leads the process. The result of increasing mindfulness is that one is motivated to investigate phenomena more closely, which leads to persevering effort that generates insightful results: discovering the truth of one's existence is a joyous experience that catalyzes peaceful tranquility, the abode of concentration, wherein one develops unshakable equanimity. Just as the hindrances restrain your progress, these seven are your best friends, propelling your journey of awakening.

The Buddha's well-informed and discerning investigation uses categories as its instruments, but it is important not to become attached to them; relinquish these instruments once they have served their functions. Examine how an unarisen factor of awakening can arise. Once arisen, how can it be developed and perfected? What is the nature of its fulfillment? In the close application of mindfulness to reality with no exceptions, everything that arises is grist for the mill.

Four Noble Truths

Finally, we carefully investigate the Four Noble Truths. The reality of suffering becomes extremely poignant when the First Noble Truth is witnessed internally, externally, and both internally and externally. Clearly perceiving the manifestations of explicit suffering due to grasping and attachment is a refrain running through all four close applications of mindfulness.

Tragic suffering arises due to our implicit mistaking of the aggregates for "I and mine." It's a deathtrap! Even prior to any explicit manifestation of attachment and clinging, our instinctive grasping on to the aggregates of body and mind as "I, me, and mine" sets the trap of suffering. We are inherently vulnerable because we are fundamentally deluded. Transcending mere beliefs, we directly see the causes of suffering—the Second Noble Truth.

Now the most daunting of all Buddhist claims becomes a showstopper: this suffering does not end at death. There is no relief when we die because the story is not over. Samsara is a perpetual motion machine, spinning on and on. But the story never gets any better if we heedlessly put in our time, punching the clock from lifetime to lifetime. The Third Noble Truth asserts the existence of an alternate possibility—liberation.

In the Fourth Noble Truth, the Buddha described the path to liberation. He said to begin by knowing well the reality of suffering, confronting these symptoms of existence internally, externally, and internally and externally. We can intimately witness our own dissatisfaction in the spectrum from mental malaise to existential anguish and from physical discomfort to searing pain. Knowing well our internal suffering, we direct our awareness externally and find a lot of company. It is revolutionary to discover that everyone else is not merely a source of assistance or hindrance in our selfish pursuit of happiness. The childish, solipsistic view of the world—one subject surrounded by a universe of objects—crumbles when we recognize all sentient beings as our equals.

Spirit of Awakening

Our common predicament becomes obvious when we attend externally, particularly in daily interactions with our families, coworkers, and communities. Furthermore, thanks to the "clairvoyance" of telecommunications, high-definition images of suffering pervade our news of the world. Tragic stories are amplified, cloned, and spun into multimedia webs to capture the attention of legions of our fellows seeking entertainment or diversion. This unprecedented ability to witness the gory details of the whole world's suffering can also bring a profound benefit—others' suffering becomes real for us.

If we choose not to attend, we can revert to Buber's exploitative "I-It" relationships. But if we attend closely—internally and externally, supported by wisdom, in "I-You" relations—the arising of compassion is automatic and the heart's floodgates open. Suddenly the artificial distinction between my suffering and everyone else's suffering vanishes. This division exists conventionally, but it is no more real than the notion that my glasses belong to me. These are merely shared understandings subject to transient conditions. Separating my suffering from yours is simply a conventional way of thinking.

Shantideva was a gifted poet, and he describes this situation with unmatched poignancy. He grapples with the bodhisattva ideal of opening his heart to all sentient beings. He accepts the responsibility to strive for and eventually realize the highest state of enlightenment, however long that might take, in order to be of greatest possible benefit to all sentient beings. He aspires to lead each and every one to liberation. Shantideva's bodhisattva aspiration, actualizing the spirit of awakening, is mind-boggling in its scope. But in his soliloquy, there is a point where we sense his resolve weakening. This might take forever! So many beings are not even remotely interested in liberation; they only want mundane pleasure, money, and power. How could he possibly lead them all to liberation? Of course, we have to be patient and wait until people become interested. But how long before they will develop interest in purifying their own minds and finding the source of genuine happiness? Looking at the enormous challenge of achieving perfect awakening in order to be of greatest possible service to all sentient beings, we might get cold feet.

Bear in mind that the Buddhist worldview is at least as vast as that of modern cosmology, whose hundred billion galaxies have hundreds of billions of stars each. Moreover, the Buddhist description includes countless world systems with massive populations: our planet is not unique. The legions of sentient beings in the universe dwarf the seven billion humans on Earth.[101] Contemplating this incredibly vast vision, Shantideva says his heart quails when facing the enormity of this bodhisattva ideal. It occurs to him: Why should I attend to the suffering of others? Why should their problems be my problems, as if I don't have enough of my own? He considers the possibility of abandoning his bodhisattva vow. Every man for himself! Your mental afflictions are yours, and mine are mine. You don't even want to deal with your problems—you blame them on other people. I'm not going to wait for you because samsara is too painful. I just want to achieve nirvana for myself. Shantideva sympathizes with this natural sentiment, allowing it to float for a bit. Then his heart floods with compassion, and he recognizes that he must attend to others' suffering because it is suffering—which has no owner. In his own words:

> As there is no owner of miseries, there are no distinctions among them all. They are to be dispelled because they are suffering. What is the use of restrictions there? Why should suffering be prevented? Because everyone agrees. If it must be warded off, then all of it must be warded off; and if not, then this goes for oneself as it does for everyone else.[102]

In the practice of the four close applications of mindfulness, the barrier between internal and external ultimately vanishes. The imaginary distinction between your suffering and my suffering disappears—only the suffering is real. The insight that emerges from this profound sense of union is not dry, abstract, or detached. It is saturated with juicy, personal import. This is knowledge for the sake of genuine happiness and ultimate liberation.

GUIDED MEDITATION:
Open Presence III

Attend to the space of the mind and all appearances—
distinguishing hindrances from wholesome factors

Settle the body, speech, and mind in their natural states of equilibrium: relaxed, still, and vigilant.

Now open your awareness 360 degrees to illuminate all fields of experience—the five sensory fields and the mental domain. Attend to the continuous arising of momentary events and their causal patterns. Without positing any mechanisms, observe the relationships between these occurrences phenomenologically. Influence or cause simply means that when A occurs, B occurs, or that when A doesn't occur, B doesn't occur.

Explicitly invoke a pragmatic purpose for this pursuit of knowledge. Examining the appearances to all six senses, apply discerning intelligence to distinguish those mental phenomena that hinder the path to liberation with disturbance, unhappiness, and conflict from factors like effort, joy, and equanimity that support and enhance the purification and awakening of the mind.

Attend closely to these afflictions and wholesome mental factors. How do they arise? How are they present? What effect do they have on the body, mind, and other aspects of reality? Actively contemplate how unarisen factors might arise in the future. The common denominator of all these modes of contemplative inquiry is the close application of mindfulness. Remain face to face with reality, attentive, engaged, and vigilant, without slipping into distraction or excitation. Maintain an ongoing flow of luminous mindfulness. ❧

On Progress

It is essential to distinguish between practicing vipashyana correctly and simply letting the mind wander. This is precisely why shamatha is taught as the foundation for vipashyana. Shamatha develops the ability to ascertain whether your mind wanders or not. Achieving stability means that your mind does not wander. Introspection is refined and sharpened like a surgical scalpel to detect and excise even the subtlest attentional perturbations and imbalances.

When you bring a solid repertoire of shamatha techniques to the practice of vipashyana, you are well equipped to dissect and destroy your delusions, eliminating them for good. On the other hand, attempting to practice vipashyana without accomplishing relaxation, stability, and vividness is like attempting surgery with a headache, a shaky hand, and a dull blade—the results may not fulfill your expectations. What need is there to mention the futility and dangers in attempting advanced practices such as the Great Perfection without the necessary preparation?

On the other hand, it can be meaningful to explore advanced practices even before having achieved shamatha. One might attend a qualified teacher's Dzogchen retreat to become acquainted with these teachings and practices. Nevertheless, as my teacher Geshe Rabten often said, make sure that the primary focus of your daily practice is appropriate to your current quality of awareness and way of life. Ensure that the benefits are really being achieved. Then, you can profitably sow seeds for the future by spending some time studying the more advanced practices.

Manage your practice as you would a family farm. While you might plant an orchard that won't bear fruit for years, your immediate sustenance depends on seasonal crops. Similarly, the daily harvest of your practice should nourish your life with peace, meaning, and mindfulness. Interpersonal relationships should improve and negative circumstances diminish. Confidence that your practice is effective and certainty that you are on the right track are more powerful than blind faith in a teacher, text, or tradition. When you see that the medicine you are taking is working, you will be motivated to finish the prescription and achieve a clean bill of health.

Pattern Recognition

This is a practice of observing causal sequences rather than theorizing about mechanisms. We see a recurring pattern that A is followed by B—it is not random. Phenomena can be real even if we cannot imagine causal mechanisms to explain them. We simply observe various mental processes interacting among themselves. One traditional Buddhist metaphor for awareness is a mirror that reflects everything impartially. Modern metaphors include cameras and audio recorders that capture images and sounds with high fidelity and low distortion. Recall that a primary definition of mindfulness is the all-important faculty of memory. Just as a recording device captures images or sounds for later review, mindfulness captures experiences and recalls them later. Scottish philosopher David Hume (1711–1776) made the analogous point that were it not for memory, we would not be able to recognize causality. Without memories of past events, we would not notice recurring sequences and could never infer causal relationships.

Mindfulness also includes remembering the practice instructions, of which the Buddha gave quite a few, especially for the fourth close application of mindfulness. This is a very compact sutra, but the advice is deeply meaningful. Over time, mindfulness develops increasing awareness of patterns, such as contact, mental engagement, feeling, recognition, and desire arising, which generates thoughts, leading to other thoughts, which ultimately precipitate actions.

Studying complex patterns of causal sequences, it becomes perfectly obvious that certain thoughts will trigger specific emotions and desires and certain fears will generate characteristic thoughts and reactions. A vast array of causality operates strictly within the mental domain. A full understanding of mental phenomena as such is sufficient to liberate the mind; there is no need to know anything whatsoever about the brain or mechanisms.

Even before modern science appeared, it was perfectly obvious that mental states influence the body. Anyone can observe that his or her own intentions and thought processes lead to deliberate physical behavior. This can be replicated as often as needed to establish the reality of a causal sequence. Why do the capillaries open precisely where the attention is focused within the body? Why do sugar pills and sham surgeries sometimes generate results similar to active ingredients and invasive procedures? Our expectations and beliefs have powerful, measurable effects on the body and mind, whether the mechanisms are understood or not.

Mechanisms have become an antiquated notion, particularly in modern physics. Mechanical models describe only the big, chunky aspects of reality, like billiard balls colliding. In many other realms of reality, such as electromagnetism, quantum mechanics, and string theory, mechanistic explanations are not very useful. When it comes to interactions between the mind and body, mechanical notions are likely to be misleading.

Buddhism has successfully explored the phenomenal world for 2,500 years without quantitative behavioral science or neuroscience.

Enlightenment can be achieved without understanding statistical models, brain mechanisms, or neural correlates, as useful and relevant as these may be. Nevertheless, the Dalai Lama is one of many people, including me, who are eager to fill this gap in Buddhism. Brain science certainly provides valuable insights into the neural correlates of mental processes. Scientists may help meditators cultivate attentional stability and vividness with objective measures of psychosomatic states and brain correlates. Inexpensive biofeedback devices may promote relaxation.

Tania Singer at the Max Planck Institute in Leipzig is doing marvelous work studying the brain correlates of compassion and empathy.[103] She briefly described her research to the Dalai Lama, and her results were intriguing to me as a contemplative. I'm much more interested in meditative practice and experience than in the brain as such, but this research reveals phenomena hidden from first-person observation. Similarly, Ekman has cast a very revealing light on emotions by studying facial expressions quantitatively. Buddhism has no quantitative behavioral science, but why shouldn't we employ every tool in our investigations? Multiple instruments and modes of research illuminate each other.

GUIDED MEDITATION:
Open Presence IV

Attend to the space of the mind and all appearances—
inspecting the inherent identity of yourself and all objects

Settle the body, speech, and mind in their natural states of equilibrium. Settle the breath in its natural rhythm.

With eyes closed, turn the full force of awareness to the tactile field and all types of tactile events and sensations that arise. In the felt, let there be just the felt. Attend to naked tactile perception.

Direct the full force of awareness to the sound field and auditory phenomena. In the heard, let there be just the heard, with as little conceptual overlay as possible.

With eyes open, bring awareness to the visual field, attending very closely in your best approximation of bare attention. In the seen, let there be just the seen.

Direct awareness to the domain of the mind and all events arising there.

Now allow the attention to move quite deliberately among these four domains of experience, neglecting smell and taste for now. Is there any overlap in the immediate contents of these fields of experience? Can anything be directly perceived both visually and tactually? Is there any auditory appearance that is also perceived visually? Do mental events overlap with the sensory fields or are they mutually exclusive?

The four spheres whose appearances dominate our world are those of visual, auditory, tactile, and mental phenomena. In our daily lives, we engage not only with these appearances but with various entities as well. Among these entities, search for your very self—a specific person with a body, mind, memories, hopes, fears, sensations, and emotions.

Examining your immediate experience, is there any evidence that the entity called by your name is present within this matrix of appearances? Are you real and findable within the immediate contents of experience? Or are you something conceptually projected upon appearances, with a merely conventional, or nominal, existence defined by agreement? Search carefully for any entity within your-self—your mind, body, emotions, thoughts, and awareness—that is the referent of your name.

Direct your awareness externally to someone very familiar to you. Bring to mind this person's name, body, voice, touch, mannerisms, hopes, fears, and so on. Drawing from all the memories of your various encounters, have you ever perceived the actual referent of this person's name? Can you find any external entity that corresponds to his or her name?

Direct your awareness to the body with which you habitually identify so strongly: the solid mass composed of molecules that exhibits spatial dimension, color, and texture. Is the referent of the word "body" a real and substantial entity that occupies a region of physical space? Is it equivalent to the whole array of tactile sensations experienced when you attend to the body? Or are these sensations simply phenomena of solidity, fluidity, heat, and motion emerging within the tactile field?

Examine your reflection in a mirror. Does this massless visual image constitute your body? Do the tactile sensations that you perceive define the boundaries of your body? Do the sounds emerging from your body—speech, song, breath, heartbeat, popping joints, gurgling digestion—belong to you? Is your body something you can directly perceive? Or is it something you have conceived, conceptually imputed, and projected on appearances, none of which are actually your body?

When you investigate the diversity of physical objects in the world—each characterized by multidimensional attributes, such as shape, color, texture, chemical composition, mass, and location—have you ever perceived an actual entity that bears these physical attributes? Or are these entities conceptually projected upon appearances, none of which constitutes the object itself? Carefully examine the relationship between the objects in the world and the appearances they seem to manifest.

In the seen, there is just the seen; in the heard, just the heard; in the felt, just the felt; in the cognized, just the cognized. Do the myriad forms of visual, auditory, tactile, and mental appearances possess inherent identities or only relative ones? Could the interdependent appearances of form arise, persist, and dissolve if these objects had absolute, inherent identities?

Rest in the awareness that all appearances are completely devoid of substantiality and empty of inherent existence. ❧

On Heroic Endeavors

The trajectory of these practices is to gradually relieve the ego of employment by discontinuing grasping at progressively subtler levels. In the Dzogchen practice of open presence, one settles so deeply that even the sense "I have chosen to practice open presence" dissolves. At first there is an ongoing flow of intention, remembering to practice open presence, becoming familiar with it, and overcoming habitual focusing and grasping. Open presence only becomes a Dzogchen practice when it is embedded in a larger framework of the view, meditation, and way of life.

When beginning to practice sustaining this attention, we might become distracted and think, "I'm lost again," as we yank our attention back to open presence. Whenever we pull it back we are not practicing open presence—we have reasserted the sense of "I am." The bona fide practice of open presence in the Dzogchen context assumes that one no longer needs to retrieve the attention from distraction or arouse it from dullness. All such methods are contrary to Dzogchen meditation instructions because they are activations of "I am."

You do not have to fight this same old problem all your life. Continuing to be overcome by excitation and laxity is a bit like being stuck in kindergarten, still learning your A-B-Cs. It is essential to master the basics before advancing to higher practices like Dzogchen. The culmination of the path of shamatha is the effortless maintenance of stability and vividness. Even prior to achieving shamatha, in developmental stages eight and nine there is no need to introduce introspection to monitor the meditative practice; this itself is an interruption. An exertion of will is required to think, "I have to check up." You don't have to check up anymore. Mental balance is spontaneous and effortless, and the flow of awareness is stable and clear—uninterrupted even by subtle laxity or excitation—making monitoring and intervention unnecessary.

Having developed the superb mental balance of shamatha as a sound basis for vipashyana practice, you are poised to effectively challenge the behemoth: the sense of "I and mine." With shamatha, the overt, reified sense of self has largely become dormant. But like a hibernating bear, it will eventually reawaken, and you will revert to habitual patterns. This was why Gautama was not satisfied with samadhi itself; he wanted to defeat the bear, not simply put it to sleep.

This heroic endeavor is described metaphorically as a team effort with the fearless warrior of shamatha protecting the wise minister of vipashyana. You summon your adversary: "Come out, habitual sense of reified self! Let's have a look at you." The practice of vipashyana includes the close scrutiny of the body, feelings, and so forth until the reified sense of self dissolves under the bright light of inspection. There are also daytime and nighttime dream yoga practices of vipashyana that probe into the nature of the mind. Such inquiries always entail an expression of grasping. You must get the bear out of its den rather than letting it sleep. You must carefully investigate the reality of your sense of self. Does such a self actually exist? Is it separate from the body and mind and in charge of them?

In the increasingly subtle questions of vipashyana, we not only investigate whether the self exists independently of body and mind, but we examine all types of phenomena. Does your mind exist as a real entity with its own inherent nature, distinct from all other phenomena? Does your mind have its own intrinsic borders that demarcate it from your body, from other people's minds, and from everything else? Does your mind have its own character, qualities, and thoughts? Where is this agent that illuminates and knows?

Perhaps we don't exist at all, and the word "I" has no referent in reality. It's possible that our existence is completely illusory, no more real than a zebra's wings. But it seems absurd to think: "There's no such thing as mind." If the mind is not nonexistent, how does it exist? Does it generate thoughts, emotions, and experiences? Does it know? What is this agent that enacts the mind's many activities? Does the mind exist independently, with its own inherent nature? Direct your mind toward itself. Conventionally, we can speak of the mind in a meaningful way as something that does many useful things. But does it exist as the independent entity that Kant called the "thing-in-itself"?

The Buddhist practice of vipashyana probes repeatedly into the very nature of the mind, ultimately determining that which thinks, knows, illuminates, has emotions, and so forth to be completely empty of inherent existence. The mind is not found as a thing-in-itself. It is not found in any specific mental events, thoughts, emotions, or desires—these are simply experiences. The mind is found to be an interdependent phenomenon, just like oneself and all other phenomena. Backed by the power of shamatha, you overcome the habitual identification of your mind as a separate, reified entity and saturate your awareness in the sheer empty nature of your own mind.

Middle Way View

ABOUT THIRTY YEARS ago, I was a monk living in a beautiful monastery overlooking Lake Geneva in Switzerland. A highly accomplished master, Geshe Ugyen Tseten, visited us for a few months, and I translated for him. He offered us profound teachings concerning the Middle Way view and the relationship between emptiness and dependent origination. The central theme is the emptiness of inherent identity of all phenomena, internally and externally, including even the bifurcation of outer and inner. This same meaning is also conveyed in the corollary statement that all phenomena exist as dependently related events.

While I was receiving these teachings, I was developing an interest in modern physics because it seemed that physicists might be coming to a similar conclusion. I clearly remember my teacher's friendly admonishment: "Alan, be careful not to refute the existence of atoms; you should investigate how they exist, not whether they exist." I have found this to be valuable advice. We ask many leading questions in this practice, but they are not leading to philosophical idealism. The Middle Way view does not assert that only the mind and appearances to the mind exist; it does not refute the existence of the physical world.

OBJECTS AND APPEARANCES

Our goal is a fundamental reassessment of the very nature of all objects and entities that populate our world, including the entity referred to by your own name. Your name has a referent—it's not like the example of a zebra's wings. Just as we don't refute the existence of atoms, we don't refute the existence of people; this leads down a treacherous slide to nihilism.

Challenging the foundations of metaphysical realism that underlie virtually all of modern science can be quite startling. The powerful conviction dominating humanity for most of our history is that we are living in a world of real things, and we hold our own selves to be real entities. What is the actual relationship between appearances and objects? The referent of a name is an object with certain attributes. If the necessary attributes are present, we can truthfully say that the object exists, but what is it that bears these attributes? The attributes are clearly observable; but can you observe an entity that possesses them?

One of the Sautrantika criteria for what is real is that it can be a direct object of experience. This practical, robust school of metaphysical realism defines as real anything that is directly perceived or can be perceived with adequate technology. Just because we cannot currently detect life on other planets does not mean it's nonexistent. With a powerful enough telescope, alien life might be undeniably demonstrated to us—made real. This criterion of reality, the potential to become manifest, qualifies all our visual perceptions, auditory impressions, and tactile sensations as being real. Furthermore, from our inside perspective, we have privileged access to myriad mental phenomena, so they are real as well. All the interactions we observe between thoughts, sensory perceptions, and sequences of causal relationships are real. But where are the attribute-bearing entities?

No Thing Itself

A good place to start is at ground zero with "I am." Are you real? Looking internally, have you ever actually seen the entity that is the observer or agent in your inner life? You have been assuming all along that you must be a real entity, but where is the referent designated by your name? Look externally at someone whose appearance, voice, and behavior you know well and whose mental states you can reliably infer: is this person real or imaginary?

Consider the example of something as simple as an ordinary bottle of water. The Sautrantika view would classify it as real because it was created by causes and conditions. The bottle was manufactured and filled with water, which had its own causes, and so forth. In the metaphysical realist view, a bottle of water is real. At first glance, it seems as though we can directly perceive the entity that bears these attributes—until we begin to peel away the layers of conceptual designations.

As we approach bare attention, everything boils down to qualia, such as visual impressions of form and color and tactile impressions of temperature and texture. But where is the actual bottle of water that bears these attributes of coolness, smoothness, and color? If we strip away all conceptual imputations, visual perception cannot distinguish a "real" object from a holographic image. Similarly, a bottle of water could appear in a nonlucid dream just as distinctly as it does in waking experience. The dream bottle is indistinguishable from a "real" bottle.

The point is not that these objects don't exist, but that the realist view has a soft underbelly. It is impossible to directly perceive the bottle of water as it exists in itself. The only things we directly perceive are visual, auditory, and tactile impressions—we never directly perceive an inherently existent object that bears these attributes. There is no intrinsic entity in a bottle of water. Similarly, we can never directly perceive the fact that an object is ours. We might believe that a bottle of water is ours because we purchased it, but this is merely a convention. We might learn that it was stolen and never really ours. Ownership cannot be determined by examining an object—it's a conceptual superimposition.

Moving beyond the view of metaphysical realism, with its naive confidence in a material world, the Middle Way approach is to conduct an ontological probe into the actual nature of the objects, entities, people, and so forth that seem to exist and bear observable attributes. What is the nature of the objects we impute upon visual, auditory, and mental appearances? The appearances are manifest, but what about the objects themselves? We are explicitly searching for the attribute-bearing entities that possess the qualities we directly perceive. Are these entities real by virtue of being immediate contents of experience? Do they have their own intrinsic nature? Do they actually do anything? Do we ever perceive the attribute bearers, or can we observe only appearances leading to other appearances?

For example, looking at someone close to us, we can see her visual form, hear her voice, and observe her behavior. Looking from the inside, she can see additional things that others cannot, such as her emotions, thoughts, memories, fantasies, desires, and so forth—but these are simply mental events. Can either one of us actually see the person who possesses these external and internal forms? Can we directly perceive the true entity of any person or thing? Are the attribute bearers real or imaginary?

Deconstructing Phenomena

The close application of mindfulness to phenomena investigates the relationship between objects and appearances in a further way. Examine something very ordinary in your possession, such as a pair of eyeglasses (which is a single object, even though we call it a pair). It would be absurd to say that these eyeglasses don't exist, but what precisely is their mode of existence? Your visual impressions and tactile sensations are not the eyeglasses themselves.

If you drop the glasses on the table, they will make a noise, but what actually made the noise? Wasn't the table equally responsible? Saying that the falling glasses made a noise is like saying, "It's raining." Have you ever seen the entity that rains? We refer to things like the weather as "it" and everyone understands what we mean, but precisely what and where is "it"?

Examine a functional pair of glasses. How did they come into existence? They were obviously assembled, and we can mentally disassemble them into lenses, frame, temples, screws, and nose pads. None of these parts constitutes a functional pair of glasses, but they could be reassembled into one.

Imagine the process of reassembling these parts one at a time. When do they become a pair of glasses? If only a single screw were missing, would it qualify as a pair of glasses? What if there were a loose nose pad? If all the parts were present, with one lens badly scratched, would it still qualify if you only needed to see your cell phone's display? What if the tip of one temple were chewed off by the dog? Is there any unambiguous point at which this assembly of parts actually becomes a pair of glasses or ceases to be one? Is the identity of the pair inherent in its own nature, or is it dependent on human conventions, specific perceptions, and the purposes we have in mind?

A pair of glasses comes into existence when we designate it as such and it goes out of existence when we withdraw the designation. This is true for everything. The power of designation evokes all things into existence, including the entities we feel ourselves to be: the referents of the word "I." The referents of all the people and things that populate our world are designated, imputed, and projected upon appearances—they are never directly observed as things in themselves.

Measurement Matters

Can we at least be confident in the reality of matter, that chunky stuff that reigns supreme for materialists? Has anyone ever actually seen matter? It was taken for granted as the basic ingredient of the universe until the turn of the twentieth century. Then physicists began looking more closely at the fundamental constituents of the physical universe. They identified elementary particles, such as photons, electrons, and so forth, in order to characterize them with experimental and theoretical precision. These researchers were surprised to discover that all their characterizations were completely dependent on their systems of measurement—nothing could be said about the absolute nature of these particles. Observations arise in relation to the mode of inquiry.

For example, what is light? Is it a wave or a particle? The answer depends on the system of measurement you choose. If you're looking for waves and employ a wave detector, you'll find out that light behaves like ripples on water, with waves that cancel each other to form distinctive interference patterns. Employing a different apparatus, light appears as a discrete entity called a photon. Einstein received the 1921 Nobel Prize in Physics for his explanation, in 1905, that the photoelectric effect, an emission of electrons when light strikes a metal plate, was due to the particulate nature of light; this quantum theory was revolutionary.

How can one thing be both a wave that forms interference patterns and a particle that ricochets off other particles? Waves and particles seem like entirely different phenomena, as different as apples and giraffes. But depending on how you look at light, it behaves as a wave or a particle. You might say, "Enough already! What is light, really, independent of the experimental apparatus?" That question is fundamentally unanswerable. As Heisenberg said, we must not attribute existence to that which is unknowable in principle. It makes no sense to assert the existence of something that can never be known. Merely being unknown at present is different. We don't know if there is extraterrestrial intelligent life, but it's not unknowable.

If something is unknowable in principle, then what does it mean to say it exists? Pauli, who had a reputation for delivering scathing dismissals of theories he found lacking, reserved his most withering criticism for theories that were untestable and hence could never be proven wrong: "Not only is it not right, it's not even wrong." Wheeler said that the very notion of matter itself is simply something we have constructed out of a more fundamental element, information, which consists only of appearances. The same can be said for energy, space, time, and our own selves.

Appearances are congealed into solid objects by conceptual superimposition. We designate and impute entities in the external world to bear the attributes we perceive. We never observe these objects as real, objective entities existing in their own right. Nevertheless, we often take them to be more real than the attributes we do observe, which is exactly the contradiction that materialism has embraced. Intelligent, well-educated people actually assert that qualia do not exist—for them, only matter and its emergent properties exist.

Qualia, such as the sounds we hear and the colors we see, are not material phenomena. Even though sounds may be associated with waves in the atmosphere and colors may be related to photons reflected by surfaces, the phenomena we perceive are not composed of atoms, and they do not exist apart from us. Similarly, the odors we smell, the tastes we savor, and the tactile sensations we feel have no molecular structure, no mass, and no independent existence.

If matter is an entity that truly exists, independent of all systems of measurement, no physicist has ever seen it—it's unknowable in principle. Everything we know is by way of specific systems of measurement and sensory perceptions. There is no security camera with a God's-eye view. We have only humanly created instruments, augmenting human perception. Our concept of matter has been constructed by us, based on measurements and superimposed on our observations.

Has anybody ever directly seen space, time, mass, or energy? Can they be perceived as immediate contents of experience? What about our own selves? Do these things have absolute existence, as we habitually assume, or merely nominal existence based on consensual agreement? Can anyone have a God's-eye view of our physical world on planet Earth? Who has actually seen this massive object? We have all seen beautiful photographs, and a few lucky astronauts have directly seen large portions of the earth's surface, but our visual images are not the planet. We have walked on the earth, but our tactile sensations are not the planet. What do we really know about the earth itself?

Veil of Appearances

The motivation for much of the scientific inquiry that began four hundred years ago was the quest for a God's-eye perspective: absolute knowledge of the world, independent of appearances to the mind. Theists assume that God exists whether or not anybody is looking. Materialists make a similar assumption, except that matter replaces God as the ultimate reality underlying appearances. Neither God nor matter is directly seen as existing independently, but everything is said to derive from one or the other.

Can we go beyond the veil of appearances, to use a medieval metaphor? What can we know that doesn't depend on our perceptions and conceptual constructs? To me, the assertion that what truly exists from God's perspective, or as absolutely objective reality, might conform to a human notion like matter seems optimistic and anthropocentric. Human beings have defined terms like "matter." Nature has not defined these terms for us; in fact, our ever-changing definitions are diverse and pragmatic. Presuming that our concepts can define that which is absolutely real, independent of all human experience, is actually to make gods of ourselves. By creating these constructs, superimposing them on appearances, and reifying them as absolute entities separate from ourselves, we have created our own reality. In a way, we have spoken our world into existence.

We must not become trapped in solipsism, the egocentric hypothesis that nothing exists apart from appearances to *my* own perception. Myriad worlds exist relative to the perceptions of myriad beings, whether *I'm* looking or not. Furthermore, direct perception is not our only means of knowing. Reliance on indirect evidence as well as authoritative statements concerning things we cannot perceive directly, such as the mental phenomena of another being, aids our search for intersubjective truths, knowledge, and wisdom. The challenge of mindfulness is to ensure that the visual, auditory, tactile, and mental appearances to which we are attending closely are the immediate contents of experience.

Dependent Origination

The six perceptual faculties and their corresponding six domains of appearances, called the twelve sense bases (Skt. *ayatanas*), are not self-existent, independent entities that have newly come into contact. They exist only relative to each other. The qualia we perceive arise relative to our sensory faculties and the methods of investigation we bring to bear. Whether the body appears as tactile, visual, or mental depends on the mode of perception we employ. Seeking to understand the nature of the body, if we attend to the tactile sense, the impressions we perceive will be tactile ones. If we attend to the body visually, we will get visual impressions. Is there any overlap between tactile sensations and visual images? Does any tactile sensation exhibit color? Does any color manifest as solidity or warmth? According to Buddhist epistemology, the five *physical* sense fields are nonoverlapping, although *mental* perception has access to all of the physical sense fields.

The interdependency of perceptual faculties and their objects becomes particularly interesting if we consider fundamental mental constructs like mass, force, or acceleration. We can use these concepts to make meaningful statements like "Force equals mass times acceleration," or my favorite, "Energy equals mass times the speed of light squared." I believe these to be true statements. But what truly exists as the referents of the terms "energy," "mass," and "acceleration"? Does the mathematical notion "the speed of light squared" have any existence whatsoever independent of the mind that conceives it? Does the conceptual mind have any existence apart from its conceptions? In fact, the mind and its concepts are interdependent.

There is no question that subatomic particles and electromagnetic fields exist; the question is how they exist. In fact, all the entities we name to describe the world around us—ostensibly from an absolute perspective, but unseen by human perception—arise and exist only relative to our conceptual designations. Atoms, as we conceive them, arise relative to our mode of questioning. It is meaningless to speak of these entities independent of all systems of measurement and conceptual frameworks. Nobody has ever directly perceived conceptual objects such as justice, beauty, space, matter, time, energy, probability waves, and electromagnetic fields as they exist independently of our modes of observation. They do exist but only relative to the mind that conceives them, and that mind exists only relative to its conceptions.

Even without any mechanisms to be found, causality manifests. This understanding is difficult to achieve, requiring deep insight. We are not refuting the regular patterns of causal sequences. Observable causal relationships do exist, in both the physical and mental domains. These patterns may be regular, robust, or even universal in their manifestations.

Phenomena that arise in causal relationships can do so precisely because they are empty of inherent nature. If they had their own inherent nature and immutable existence, they could not interact interdependently with other phenomena. Because they are empty of that reified existence, they are able to manifest in the world of conceptual and sensory appearances, giving rise to regular patterns of causal interactions. Because phenomena are empty, they can enter into relationships of interdependence. Because they manifest interdependently, they must be empty.

This theme is summed up in two wonderful quotes from the Mahayana sutras. Although seeds of these ideas are clearly present in the early Pali Canon, their full expression occurred in the later *Perfection of Wisdom* sutras, systematized as the Middle Way view. In this paragraph from the *Lalitavistara Sutra*, the Buddha discusses the aggregates that constitute our bodies, minds, and the physical world:

> The aggregates are impermanent, unstable, naturally brittle like an unbaked pot, like a borrowed article, like a city built in the dust, lasting for a time only. By nature those conditions are subject to destruction, like plaster washed away by the rainy season, like sand on a river's bank, dependent on contributing conditions, naturally weak. They are like the flame of a lamp; their nature is to be destroyed as soon as they arise, unstable as the wind, sapless and weak like a clot of foam.[104]

All phenomena are characterized by this impermanent nature, which immediately implies the following realization from the *Lokanathavya-karana Sutra*:

> Nameless are all conditions, but illuminated by name; nevertheless, that which is of the nature of a name has been neither seen nor heard, is neither arisen nor disappeared. Of what do you ask the name? Name is a matter of habit, declarations are made by name. This man is Ratnachitra by name; that other man is Ratnottama.[105]

The words "all conditions" refer to all phenomena—outer, inner, and the very bifurcation of outer and inner—which do not possess names and definitions. Nevertheless, we engage in a world of objects that are illuminated by the act of mentally conceiving of them and identifying them using names. Who are you? I am Alan, and that name illuminates and separates me from all that is not Alan. That which is the inherently existent referent of a name does not appear to direct perception, has never arisen, and never disappears, because it does not really exist. If you closely examine the relationship between appearances and objects, you will find that names are established by human convention for purely practical purposes and do not correspond to objects that exist by their own inherent nature.

Atoms do exist and must be taken seriously. The energy described by Einstein's famous equation $E=MC^2$ was very real for those present when the first atomic bomb was dropped on Hiroshima. This energy was not simply an illusion. Energy exists relative to the mind that conceives it, and it does things as well, such as incinerating cities. Nevertheless, it is an empty entity.

Here are two quotes from the *Perfection of Wisdom Sutras* that sum things up:

> A bodhisattva views all phenomena as . . . similar to an apparition, a dream, a mirage, an echo, an image, a reflection of the moon in water, a magical creation, a village of celestial beings. . . . Even nirvana, I say, is like a dream, like an illusion. If I could apprehend any phenomenon more exalted than nirvana, of that also I should say that it is like a dream, like an illusion.[106]

Bad things happen in dreams as well. People suffer horribly and perish in dreams, and yet they are merely dreams. And the great Bodhisattva Subhuti says this:

> The Lord [Buddha] has said that dream and waking are indistinguishable . . . ultimately all phenomena are like a dream.[107]

Notice that he said, "are like a dream" and not "are a dream." In the midst of a nonlucid dream, we take everything that appears to be real. In the midst of a lucid dream, appearances still manifest, but we don't reify them. If we are truly lucid, we may take appearances seriously, but they will not trap us.

GUIDED MEDITATION:
Open Presence V

Attend to the space of the mind and all appearances—
observing relationships between objects and appearances

The Buddha declared that the mind settled in equilibrium comes to know reality as it is. Settle the body, speech, and mind in their natural states of equilibrium: relaxed, still, and vigilant.

To the best of your ability, rest your awareness in its own nature—a nonconceptual, nondesignative mode. Simply witness the appearances that arise from moment to moment via the six doors of perception. Observe carefully all six domains of experience and notice when objects arise from the midst of these appearances, such as airplanes, cars, birds, or people. Observe the relationships between appearances that constitute our world and the objects we take to be real.

On Golden Cages

Open presence seems very much like *shikantaza* or *zazen*—just sitting. Taking the practice of open presence far enough, might one actually duplicate Bahiya's enlightenment? I find the Buddha's short discourse to Bahiya tremendously seductive, and the Dzogchen teachings are very similar to Zen and Chan koans. These quintessential nuggets in a few lines or paragraphs evoke a strong intuitive sense: "Ah, that's it!" A great temptation is to abandon everything else and emulate Bahiya. "Am I done yet?"

Doing nothing but sitting like this for a long time, you must ensure that you are making real progress—one tragic possibility is that you are merely sitting in a nest of reification. Bahiya had very little "dust in his eyes," but some of us still have mud in our eyes. We can simply sit in our nice, cozy nests with mud in our eyes and never break out of our golden cages of reification. We wind up as happy hippies, and everything is cool, but our minds are still utterly ordinary.

We need to sit with the probing inquiries of vipashyana, such as investigating the nature of the body. Is there anything to a body other than emergences of solidity, fluidity, heat, and motility—like froth on a boiling pot of soup? Where is the stable, unchanging part? Is there more to this body than ephemeral events bubbling up and passing away? Is there any indication that this body is really mine as opposed to being mine by mere conventional agreement? Have I superimposed my ownership like owning my water bottle? Does my body by its own nature declare itself "mine," or is ownership simply a conventional designation? Does the fact that I can control my body, moving any part at will, prove that it's mine? For a person like Bahiya or the great Zen and Dzogchen masters, a pointed question can catalyze profoundly transformative insight.

Another example is the astonishing child prodigy Migyur Dorje (1645–1667), a young incarnate lama, or *tülku* (Tib. *sprul sku*), who spontaneously experienced profound realizations.[108] At the age of ten, he became a student of Karma Chagmé, a senior monk of tremendous erudition who was renowned as one of the greatest scholars and contemplatives of his era. Karma Chagmé was a lama with thousands of disciples. He gave extensive discourses and authored many works, displaying his vast knowledge and experience. Then he became Migyur Dorje's lama, charged with bringing the boy into the Kagyü lineage by giving him empowerments and teachings. But the boy also became the senior lama's lama, and Karma Chagmé sat at Migyur Dorje's feet to hear what was spontaneously arising in the boy's experience. It was a beautiful, bilateral relationship.

All of us would love to be gifted like Migyur Dorje or Bahiya. We'd like to say, "Sock it to me!" Or we would like to find the right rose apple tree on a hot spring day and say, "Now I'm withdrawing my awareness from sensory desires and avoiding all unwholesome things." Good luck with that— if you're not Gautama, you might have to wait a long time! If spontaneous realization doesn't occur, then you can't just sit there waiting for it to happen. You need to take a step back and rattle the cage of reification, really probing into matters. Investigate as the *Diamond Sutra*, the *Heart Sutra*, and other versions of the *Perfection of Wisdom* sutras teach. Nagarjuna's writings on the Middle Way merit a lifetime of study. Get in there and start shaking things up, probing into reality to see whether phenomena do have a substantial, self-existent nature.

If you're not developing insight through the practice of vipashyana, you might need to investigate the mind with which you're performing this inquiry. If you detect a bit of ADHD and an unstable mind that vacillates between laxity and excitation, it might be necessary to develop some robust shamatha before launching into vipashyana. You might spend weeks or months in shamatha and encounter nothing but obstacles, one after another. It might be necessary to take one step further back and examine the ethical aspects of your life. It is impossible to engage in successful meditation while simultaneously abusing, manipulating, and lying to others. Investigate the ethics of your own behavior and clean up your act.

It is essential to find the ground where the gears of practice really mesh. You will learn that it is better not to abuse and slander people. Your speech will become gentler and not abusive, which is a big step in the right direction. Then you will naturally progress toward greater mental balance and shamatha, followed by vipashyana and the development of insight. Ultimately, you will arrive at the simplest practice of all: just doing nothing. But, as the Dalai Lama warned, this is not nearly as easy as it sounds.

COGNITIVE RELATIVITY

It is a significant challenge to imagine that fundamental aspects of our world, such as atoms, matter, and time, are merely conceptual overlays or designations imposed by human beings. This issue has been addressed by some formidable theoretical physicists, such as Wheeler and Stephen Hawking, with support from experimentalists such as Zeilinger. In my book *Mind in the Balance,* I discuss a paper coauthored by Hawking and Thomas Hertog that concerns the relativity of time itself in the context of quantum cosmology.[109]

Who's Asking?

We ordinarily think of time as something that has flowed continuously for 13.7 billion years since the Big Bang, independent of occurrences within it. Homo sapiens appeared one to two hundred thousand years ago, so we are new to the world. Such notions of the evolution of the universe accord with metaphysical realism and classical physics. However, physicists Bryce DeWitt (1923–2004) and Wheeler envisioned a very different quantum universe that displays classical effects only under special circumstances. This was the origin of quantum cosmology.

Hawking and Hertog describe time from the perspective of quantum cosmology. As their paper mentions, no one was present to observe the genesis of the universe. In fact, all the information we have about the past 13.7 billion years has been gathered quite recently. The observations that led to the very notion of the Big Bang are less than a hundred years old. This is not God-given information, and Mother Nature did not write the story. We humans have developed this information in response to specific modes of inquiry.

The explanation given by Hawking and Hertog is actually quite intelligible to nonphysicists. They say that prior to the act of measuring the background radiation and other indirect evidence for the formation of galaxies billions of years ago, the entire past as well as the present existed in what quantum physicists call a superposition state—a mathematical abstraction describing an array of statistical possibilities. When measurements are made, a single possibility is determined. Interpreting this information allows us to construct theories, which can then be tested. The result is our concepts of strong and weak nuclear forces, elementary particles, fields, and the genesis of the universe.

In this view, our entire 13.7 billion-year story, with atoms that existed before Homo sapiens, is only true relative to the frame of reference of humans who have conducted measurements and made interpretations. There is no single, correct past that is absolutely objective and inherently existent. Concepts about the past arise in relation to the questions we pose in the present moment. The same is true for the immediate present and the future. Atoms, as we understand them, were not waiting for us to discover them: atoms were defined by us. Likewise, fields, forces, waves, space, time, matter, and the Big Bang are all human constructs based upon measurements made using instruments we developed. There are myriad potential pasts, depending on which measurements we make and how we interpret our data.

For example, explanations of the fundamental nature of light—particle or wave—have changed many times over the years as new experiments have led to revised theories. Today's quantum-mechanical explanations include the basic principle of complementarity, the notion that different experimental measurements can reveal apparently contradictory properties of an object, but not at the same time.

The principle of complementarity in quantum mechanics is famously demonstrated with light in what is known as the double-slit experiment. If you emit photons in the direction of a narrow slit in a metal plate with a screen on the far side, you will see a single bright spot on the screen. If you open a second slit, you might expect to see two spots. In fact, what appears on the screen is a broad pattern of fringes characteristic of waves interfering by addition and cancellation.

Strangely enough, this interference pattern emerges over time even when only one photon at a time passes through the slits—ensuring that each photon can only be interfering with itself. This has also been demonstrated with electrons,[110] neutrons, atoms, and even with a large molecule, the sphere of sixty carbon atoms known as the buckyball.[111] The brilliant physicist Richard Feynman (1918–1988) said that the double-slit experiment contains the only mystery of quantum mechanics.

It is very odd to think that photons, electrons, and even large molecules can display both particle and wave properties, but the principle of complementarity is uncontroversial in quantum mechanics. Furthermore, it is clear that observations can be made only in relationship to a cognitive frame of reference. Even information about the past arises relative to the system of measurement employed. If asked whether I believe that atoms existed before human beings, my answer is yes, but with an important caveat. Atoms existed in the past, but only relative to the cognitive frame of reference we share right now, in which atoms have been defined based upon our measurements in the recent past and our theories about these observations.

Einstein himself was troubled by the awkward interface between particles and fields. The mechanism for interaction between particles and fields is rather unclear. Einstein hoped that theoretical physicists would develop a pure field theory that explained all elementary particles such as photons, electrons, and neutrons. He tried for many years to develop an internally consistent theory to account for all the observed data without the awkward duality of fields and particles, but he failed. No one has yet achieved the integration of the general theory of relativity with quantum mechanics.

But let's imagine that twenty years from now, a brilliant physicist named Janice Strawberry develops a completely unified field theory that elegantly explains all the observed forces and elementary particles with compelling predictive power. Her theory revolutionizes our understanding of the world forever as "Strawberryfields," whose specific configurations account for the various appearances previously designated as a bewildering array of elementary particles. From this new perspective, electrons and photons don't exist—they are merely specific field configurations. Novel phenomena predicted by the new theory are rapidly proven, with benefits that everyone enjoys. The old concepts of fields and particles seem as antiquated as theories of the luminiferous ether, the geocentric universe, and witchcraft as the cause of plagues.

This scenario is not outlandish—human history records countless such revolutions. From our perspective today, atoms existed in the past. From the perspective of a future understanding, we might realize that atoms never existed in the past. Our notions of the past are dependent on our cognitive frames of reference.

A related issue in quantum mechanics is called the measurement problem. Wheeler conceived of the notion of the observer-participancy universe, but physicists have not made much progress in understanding the measurement problem in seventy years. Until you make a measurement, there is only a probability function—a mathematical abstraction. Heisenberg was insistent that the probability function described by the Schrödinger wave equation is not to be conceived as something truly existent. According to the Copenhagen Theory, which is the interpretation of quantum physics taught in most textbooks, when you conduct a measurement, the range of possibilities described by the wave function collapses. Only at that point do you observe a particle, such as an electron, with a specific location and momentum. What causes the shift from a state of potential to a state of actuality? Nobody knows.

We do know that the role of the observer has not been included in the quantum-mechanical equations. What is the effect of the participant who designs the experimental systems, makes the measurements, and analyzes the results? In order to solve the measurement problem and understand quantum mechanics, we can no longer ignore the observer. Classical physics, describing the world from God's perspective, cannot explain the world as we see it. It seems to me that you can account for the observer only by introducing consciousness itself.

Making Time

One of the most fascinating observations of quantum cosmology, eloquently described by theoretical physicist Paul Davies, is the problem of frozen time.[112] It turns out that when the equations of quantum mechanics are applied to the whole cosmos, one variable falls out: time. In the quantum cosmos devoid of an observer, there is no time, no evolution, and no change. The universe is frozen. To us, yesterday is not the same as today. We clearly experience time, so how does time enter the cosmic picture? The answer is that the perfect symmetry of the unchanging universe is broken by an observer, who does something quite profound by metaphorically saying: "Now." Establishing "now" immediately generates the perspectives of past and future relative to this "now," and we can talk about "yesterday" and "tomorrow." But without an observer to pick a specific "now," there is no relative framework to determine what is "future" and what is "past." Even the notion of causality requires the presence of an observer to make this conceptual designation.

This timelessness can be experienced in samadhi. From the perspective of one who enters the deep states of absorption in the form and formless realms, which had been thoroughly explored before the Buddha, time has vanished. It vanishes due to suppressing all conceptual processes along with the mental afflictions. The deeper the samadhi, the more timeless one's perspective, and ultimately, time is completely stopped. Nevertheless, coming out of samadhi, all the mental afflictions and conceptualizations return, and time manifests once more.

In contrast to that approach is an entirely different one. Releasing the psyche and all conceptualizations into the substrate, it is possible to break through this substrate and enter into primordial consciousness. Now, nothing is being suppressed—the whole conceptual apparatus has collapsed to the ground. This is open presence, which is the opposite of selective attention. Instead of zeroing in on very deep interior space, open presence means resting in pristine awareness, which is wide-open and timeless. Pristine awareness is not caught up in time; it is characterized by the "fourth time," which transcends and subsumes the three times of past, present, and future. In the deepest dimension of timeless, pristine awareness, there are no past moments, present moments, or future moments.

It sounds very poetic when the Buddha says that all phenomena are "similar to an apparition, a dream, a mirage, an echo, an image, a reflection of the moon in water, a magical creation, a village of celestial beings." What is he talking about? I might dream of you tonight, but all your appearances in my dream would arise from my individual substrate consciousness, not yours. If I were to die, my dreams would die with me. But you are not part of my dream, and if I fall dead, you will still exist.

In a nonlucid dream, we are completely identified with a particular persona in the dream; the notion of the substrate consciousness never arises because we take appearances to be real. When we are awake and look back on the dream, we realize that our persona and everything we encountered in the dream arose from a common ground: our individual substrate consciousness. Similarly, from the Buddha's vantage point, even the intersubjective "reality" we experience in our waking state is like a dream.

Emergent Features

The materialist's view is that consciousness emerges from increasingly complex configurations of atoms, molecules, cells, and ultimately, biological systems. The conceptual notion of the emergence of certain novel properties of a system that are not found in the underlying components is a valuable one that has inspired some to elevate this principle to lofty heights. Many examples of emergent properties in nature are given. For example, the property of surface tension does not exist in a single molecule of H_2O, but manifests when large numbers of water molecules cohere in a liquid state.

It is easy to accept the emergence of surface tension in water because we can measure the properties of H_2O molecules and groups of them, and we can measure surface tension. Similarly, we can measure the properties of neurons that are believed by materialists to be the basis for the emergence of consciousness; however, there the analogy breaks down— we cannot actually measure the consciousness that is said to emerge. A radical discontinuity exists between consciousness and the neural phenomena that are assumed to generate it. The notion that awareness will spontaneously emerge if you arrange electrons, atoms, and cells into a sufficiently complex configuration seems like magical thinking. Of all the known entities in the universe, nothing is more complex than the human brain. Nevertheless, repeatedly invoking the word "complexity" doesn't explain how consciousness might arise from inanimate matter.

The Buddha provided naturalistic explanations of human experience, including the nature and origin of consciousness, over 2,500 years ago. Based on his own direct experience, he rejected the belief, advocated by materialists of his time, that consciousness emerges from bodily functions. In stark contrast to scientific materialism, many Buddhist contemplatives have concluded that individual streams of consciousness ultimately emerge from a primordial consciousness that pervades the entire universe. All objective phenomena arise as dependently related events, and all are dependent on the consciousness that perceives and conceives them. This is an implication of what Wheeler meant by "Its from bits."

GUIDED MEDITATION:
Awareness of Awareness III

Attend to the cognizant luminosity of awareness—
maintaining an unbroken continuity of practice

Settle the body, speech, and mind in their natural states and the respiration in its natural rhythm.

Begin by grounding the awareness in the space of the body, attending in particular to sensations of firmness and solidity—the earth element. Attend to tactile sensations arising in the field of the body without distraction or grasping. Release and relax with each out-breath, letting go of all thoughts and mental images. Rest your awareness, quietly witnessing the field of the body.

Let your eyes be open and gazing evenly into the space in front. Maintain an ongoing flow of knowing as your attention alternates between focusing inwardly and releasing outwardly. You may conjoin this oscillation with the rhythm of the breath or allow it to flow naturally. Inverting your awareness upon that which is attending, focus inwardly upon awareness itself—without latching on to any subject. Then release this focus and any thoughts that may have arisen, opening your awareness into space—without latching on to any object. Arouse awareness while inverting it and relax more deeply as you release awareness into space.

Now rest your awareness where it always was, right in the middle, without inversion or release. Rest in utter simplicity, sustaining an unbroken flow of sheer luminosity and cognizance of awareness. Periodically check up on the body, ensuring against restricted breath and tension, especially around the eyes.

Following this session you will continue breathing, so you can practice mindfulness of the breath. Thoughts will arise, so you can settle the mind in its natural state. As long as you remain aware, you can also practice awareness of awareness. Maintain an unbroken continuity of practice. ☞

On Actual Accomplishment

Of the many revered figures in Buddhist history, some are highly distinguished scholars, while others seem to defy social conventions and shun formal institutions. The key factor is not erudition but sheer profundity of experiential insight. Some great contemplatives—people who have gained deep insight into the nature of pristine awareness—are also great scholars, and some are not. Padmasambhava was both an extraordinary scholar and a contemplative master, as were Tsongkhapa, Sakya Pandita (1182–1251), and the Soto Zen patriarch Dogen (1200–1253). Not all great contemplatives are scholars. For example, the beloved eleventh-century Tibetan yogi Jetsun Milarepa (c. 1052–1135) was not a learned scholar, but his realization was pristine. The Buddhist tradition does not posit diametric opposition between learning and profound experience. I find it quite unfortunate when scholarship is isolated from experience—these two must inform each other.

Actual experience matters most. One who dwells in a profound state of realization will exhibit spontaneously arisen behavior that is always appropriate to the situation at hand. On most occasions, such people will behave in completely mundane ways. Atisha Dipankara Shrijnana (982–1054),[113] another highly accomplished scholar and contemplative, teaches in his *Seven-Point Mind Training* that no matter how deep one's realization, one should behave normally, without calling attention to oneself.[114] Great lamas and yogis generally accommodate themselves to conventional expectations. Nevertheless, at the right time, something quite exceptional might manifest. Such people are not interested in drawing attention to themselves but to the Dharma—where the juice is.

THE DIRECT PATH

Overview of the Path

In the first phase of practice we ventured into mindfulness of the breath, starting with full-body awareness. On one hand, mindfulness of the breath is a method for developing attentional skills and shamatha since it is focused on the body and its rhythms. On the other hand, it can easily be oriented toward vipashyana practice and insight into the body. Mindfulness of the breath serves both functions, as the Buddha describes in his primary discourse. He begins with shamatha and progresses to vipashyana, using mindfulness of the breath as the vehicle for both practices. Mindfulness must always be conjoined with introspection. For example, when focusing on the tactile sensations at the apertures of the nostrils, we simultaneously employ introspection to monitor the meditative process. Introspection is bound to reveal insights into the nature of mind.

In settling the mind in its natural state, the primary focus of mindfulness is the space of the mind, along with all the mental activities that arise in this space. Once again, settling the mind in its natural state can perform double duty. From the most superficial introspective glance to the deepest probe that frees the psyche of suppressed impulses, memories, and emotions, the close application of mindfulness to the mind is a shamatha practice. At the same time, during the process of dissolving the psyche into the substrate consciousness, we glean insight into the nature of mind, which arises in dependence upon the body, genes, brain chemistry, language, acculturation, personal history, and more.

As we settle the mind in its natural state, the psyche dissolves into the luminous substrate consciousness, revealing a deeper dimension of mind that is free of gender, species, personal identity, and conceptualizations. This unconfigured state of consciousness is not conditioned by genes, biochemistry, or individual experience. The process of settling the mind in its natural state is like a guided tour of the psyche as it dissolves into the substrate consciousness.

On the other hand, for those who simply wish to reach the destination, without stopping along the way, the most direct vehicle is awareness of awareness. Here we take no interest in the mind at all, bypassing it to enter directly into the substrate. This practice is like an express elevator running directly from the surface level of the psyche to the depths of the substrate consciousness. The sign of the mind, with its defining qualities of cognizance and luminosity, is acquired by settling into the substrate consciousness. This is not some kind of a trance but a mode of sheer, nonconceptual knowing with three fundamental characteristics:

bliss, luminosity, and nonconceptuality. Here we have ascertained the nature of consciousness itself, though not its ultimate nature.

Having settled into the relative ground of the mind, we are well equipped for vipashyana practice. This is an ontological investigation into the ultimate nature of the mind and substrate consciousness. Scraping off the accretions of language, personal history, and social conditioning, we probe the essence of mind itself, investigating our individual continuum as an example of the substrate consciousness. How does this substrate consciousness emerge? How is it present? How does it dissolve? Does it have location, shape, or size? Is it ours? Is it us? This is a profound probe.

Vipashyana entails active inquiry, in a useful form of grasping that poses pointed questions rather than simply allowing our conceptualizations to go dormant. In order to observe and investigate the nature of the mind that grasps and reifies, we cannot simply relax in the hot-tub experience of the substrate consciousness. Düdjom Lingpa described resting in shamatha as bliss like the warmth of a fire because all reifications are temporarily dormant. Instead, with the goal of irreversibly liberating the mind, we deliberately arouse our sense of reification and examine the nature of this reifying mind.

It is crucial to note that, unlike the higher dhyanas, when we achieve access to the first dhyana, we retain our abilities of coarse investigation and subtle analysis. These two characteristics of the first dhyana were reported by the Buddha in his experience as a youth. Undistracted intelligence and comprehensive analytical skills are potentiated in the quiet domain of the substrate consciousness. A mind stripped down to the ground of the substrate consciousness is the ideal laboratory for probing directly into the very nature of mind because only the space of the mind appears—all distractions have vanished.

From within the substrate, vipashyana investigates the nature of mind. Does this substrate consciousness have an inherent nature and independent existence? If so, what are its qualities? By probing repeatedly, we ultimately realize the empty nature of our own substrate consciousness. Stripped down to the basics, the mind has no inherent nature: it's empty. The behemoth of reification and grasping on to inherent existence is slain by directly seeing that the mind is not inherently real and has no intrinsic identity. This is known as realization of the empty nature of mind. From this perspective, we are perfectly poised to enter into the practice of Dzogchen, which is closely similar to Mahamudra practice.

Having broken through the reification of the mind with vipashyana—seeing that the mind is not an inherently existing entity—there remains a conventional sense of the mind. Now the instruction is to release grasping on to even the conventional notion of mind in the Dzogchen practice of open presence. This subtle practice is critically predicated on the full context of the Dzogchen view, meditation, and way of life.

Resting without reification in the substrate consciousness, we experience bliss, luminosity, and nonconceptuality. Each of these has its own appeal, and some people are drawn to one aspect over another. The challenge is to release all preferences, maintaining detached nonchalance. Release all grasping on to bliss. Release all preference for luminosity. Release all clinging to nonconceptuality. Release even the preference for the quiet seclusion of the mind withdrawn from the five senses. Utterly release into open presence.

This is the practice called breaking through (Tib. *khregs chod*), which originated in the first century CE with Garab Dorje (Skt. Prahevajra), the first teacher of Dzogchen in our era. Just as we broke through the psyche to reach the substrate consciousness, we now break through the confines and limitations of our individual substrate consciousness to reach the infinite dimension of pristine awareness.

Pristine awareness is also known as primordial consciousness (Skt. *jñana*; Tib. *ye shes*). It is not individuated or localized but is omnipresent and atemporal. Pristine awareness defies all conceptual classifications, including the notions of existence and nonexistence. Because it does not arise in dependence upon causes and conditions, it is referred to as being originally or primordially pure. The Buddha referred to this ultimate dimension of awareness as "consciousness without characteristics," for it is undetectable by ordinary perception. It can be nondually known only by itself and not by any other means of observation. This is the dimension of awareness that persists even after an arhat has died, when the ordinary mind and body have been transcended and vanish without a trace.[115] The Buddha declared that the consciousness of an arhat who has died is "unsupported," for it has no physical basis, but this does not imply that it doesn't exist. Rather, he likens such awareness to a ray of sunlight that never contacts a physical object and so does not "alight" anywhere.[116] Such consciousness transcends all dualities, including that of good and evil.[117]

Although pristine awareness is inconceivable, it can be experienced by utterly releasing all grasping. The strategy to reach this experience is straightforward: Start with something feasible, such as mindfulness of the breath, and progress toward settling the mind in its natural state and awareness of awareness. Use vipashyana techniques to probe the very nature of the mind and realize its empty nature. Finally, engage in Dzogchen practice to realize pristine awareness.

Having ascertained this ultimate dimension of awareness, one's practice becomes profoundly simple: dwelling in pristine awareness at all times and sustaining it under all circumstances. Formal meditation consists solely of resting increasingly deeply in an unbroken flow of pristine awareness, with body, speech, and mind utterly inactive. Even the conventional self is fully unemployed. With increasing familiarity, one becomes so deeply attuned to this primordially pure way of knowing that it is sustained even between formal sessions. One rests in utter inactivity while engaging in ordinary daily activities. All action is spontaneous and every result is accomplished effortlessly with the energy of pristine awareness.

The final, most advanced stage of Dzogchen is the practice of direct crossing over (Tib. *thod rgal*), which is designed to actualize the infinite potential of pristine awareness. The practice is to fully manifest the virtues, creativity, and energy of spontaneously present awareness. Waking up entirely, one becomes a fully enlightened buddha.

The Result

The goal of these practices is not to terminate our individual consciousness, to adopt some other nature, or to merge with some cosmic mind. We have discussed three dimensions of consciousness, but speak of one pristine awareness. This is also called the dharmakaya, the mind of the Buddha, buddha nature, and primordial consciousness. It is unitary and not individuated. At the same time, it is who you already are. Fathoming the nature of your identity, you recognize it is who you have always been. Anything else was merely a dream.

Primordial consciousness is a mode of awareness that is said to be indivisible from the absolute space of phenomena (Skt. *dharmadatu*). This space is not ordinary Newtonian or even Einsteinian space, but the spacelike, transcendent dimension of ultimate reality. The term connotes that which is experienced by primordial consciousness, just as the substrate is experienced by substrate consciousness. Don't be misled by this analogy; primordial consciousness transcends subject-object duality.

In the Dzogchen view of emergence, primordial consciousness is that out of which everything else emerges. The materialistic notion that consciousness somehow emerges out of molecules, atoms, and ethereal elementary particles seems unbelievable, because these particles have no properties that suggest the power to give rise to consciousness. The alternate view is that from nonindividuated primordial consciousness emerges an individual substrate consciousness, from which emerges a psyche, which gives rise to all thoughts, emotions, memories, and other mental phenomena.

Primordial consciousness is nondual with the absolute space of phenomena, from which all relative configurations of matter, energy, space, and time emerge. Although primordial consciousness and the absolute space of phenomena are described separately, they are primordially nondual. The dharmadatu is not simply an empty vacuum—it is suffused by the infinite energy of primordial consciousness (Skt. *jñana vayu*; Tib. *ye shes kyi lung*). The union of primordial consciousness and the absolute space of phenomena abounds with energy that manifests in every way. The final stage of Great Perfection practice, the direct crossing over, is designed to tap into this unlimited energy source.

Primordial consciousness, the absolute space of phenomena, and the energy of primordial consciousness are inseparable. They constitute a unitary dimension of reality abiding in the fourth time, transcending the past, present, and future. Out of this eternal present emerge time, matter, energy, space, and consciousness, from which emerge myriad worlds moment by moment.

This is not a chronological account, as if long ago there were a sublime, transcendent unity that has been lost. On the contrary, from a buddha's perspective, the nature of the reality we experience in the world right now is a display of primordial consciousness. The space we experience is not other than the absolute space of phenomena. All forms of energy are simply expressions of the energy of primordial consciousness. This present reality emerges from moment to moment in a continuous flow; nevertheless, we sentient beings grasp on to whatever makes sense to us, label these phenomena with designations, and cling to our constructs as real.

GUIDED MEDITATION:
Open Presence VI

*Attend to the space of the mind and all appearances—
resting in the stillness of awareness*

Settle the body in its natural state and the respiration in its natural rhythm.

With eyes open and gaze vacant, settle the mind in its natural state. Attend to the space of the mind and whatever arises there, without distraction or grasping. If you wish, alternate between attending closely to thoughts and releasing thoroughly. Don't release the thoughts—only the grasping on to them. Conjoin this oscillating motion with the breath if that is helpful.

Now, instead of selecting the mental domain, open your awareness equally to all appearances in open presence. Maintain an unwavering flow of mindfulness, without distraction or grasping. Rest in the stillness of awareness, while myriad appearances arise and pass in all six sense fields. ☞

On Radical Healing

Complete healing of all afflictions, even in cases of extreme suffering, physical trauma, and psychological abuse, is possible. Such radical healing takes place only at the highest level of practice, for one who has achieved liberation. With an irreversibly clean bill of health, there is no possibility that reification, grasping on to "I am," craving, hostility, envy, arrogance, or delusion will ever arise again. No matter what happens to an arhat, the mental afflictions have been eradicated. Most importantly, these afflictions have been eliminated not only from the course of this lifetime but forever after. That there is continuity across lives is an amazing hypothesis, but that this can be transformed irreversibly is even more astonishing. While an arhat is completely free of mental afflictions, a buddha has transcended even this state. A buddha is perfectly awake and has fully manifested the potential of the deepest dimension of consciousness.

While the big picture is important to keep in mind, we all need to focus our practice closer to home. Is it possible to find genuine happiness in this lifetime without spending twenty years in a cave to become an arhat or a buddha? We have serious mental health concerns, including depression, anxiety, addiction, abusive relationships, and so forth. Will attentional training be effective if you are still blaming yourself for something traumatic that occurred in your childhood? Can any practice help your recovery if you are the victim of a natural disaster?

At the level of physical suffering, I know a number of Tibetans who endured horrific tortures in Chinese concentration camps. It is painful to hear the stories of atrocities told by the survivors. Having lived with Tibetans for fourteen years, I am convinced that people can indeed be healed from their traumas. Despite the Tibetan genocide at the hands of their occupiers, many have emerged as healthy, friendly, untroubled people who sleep well and remain at ease within themselves. They are compassionate and dynamic, not apathetic or despairing, and they continue to actively pursue their goals. Palden Gyatso is a glorious exemplar of the possibility of radical healing from the most extreme traumas.

Healing must occur on multiple levels. For example, one might draw from the wisdom of the psychotherapeutic tradition, while also engaging in an existential dialogue with a spiritual friend, teacher, lama, or priest. Tremendous sufferings have been reduced by drugs, which are sometimes necessary to ameliorate symptoms so that therapy can be effective. A person who engages at all levels participates fully in the healing process, rather than depending on external authorities and passive remedies, and is more likely to realize a full cure.

Powers That Be

Advanced practitioners are popularly credited with abilities that seem to violate the laws of physics. There are cases that I'm convinced are authentic demonstrations of the power of becoming lucid in the waking state, analogous to lucid dreaming. In a nonlucid dream, you are often an anxious, unhappy victim of circumstances, trying to escape your imaginary predicament. Acting primarily out of habit, you are vulnerable due to a fundamental delusion. In a lucid dream, because you know the nature of the reality you are experiencing, you can work miracles.

I've known yogis who have casually demonstrated seemingly miraculous feats before witnesses. Granite seems to be a favorite medium. By simply leaning into a granite boulder, they may leave a handprint. This is not very common, but it has happened recently. How could you make sense of such a demonstration if true? Such occurrences are not miracles. They are no more supernatural than a laser, but a laser would have been deemed supernatural a hundred years ago. Arthur C. Clarke's third law of prediction says that any sufficiently advanced technology is indistinguishable from magic for a person who does not understand it. The highly refined light of a laser can cut through steel. Consider that light is the most powerful metaphor for consciousness.

The natural display of an extraordinarily refined mind in samadhi could be called a paranormal refinement of consciousness, just as a laser is a paranormal refinement of light. Configured as a high-intensity beam of lucid insight into the illusory nature of reality, a yogi's consciousness may transcend ordinary limitations in pristine awareness. Tapping into the deepest dimension of consciousness might enable extraordinary, unimaginable powers.

Shamatha and access to the substrate consciousness will not enable you to leave your handprint in granite, but you could develop paranormal access to a lifetime's accumulated information in the substrate. The realm of possibility includes samadhi with laser-like focus of attention to illuminate memories from long ago. Once you have retrieved them, you may be able to determine whether these memories are veridical or not.

The ability to emboss your handprint on a boulder implies insight into the nature of phenomenal reality and may imply access to a nonlocal dimension of consciousness that is deeper than the substrate. In our contemplatively primitive culture, if someone demonstrates paranormal abilities, we either worship him or we kill him—sometimes both! We don't generally ask how we might do likewise. Jesus actually encouraged us to emulate his actions by saying, "He who believes in me, the works that I do he will do also; and greater works than these he will do."[118]

It is easier to worship than emulate someone. Many Buddhists worship the Buddha but don't meditate: "I'm not a yogi." The result is that faith overshadows wisdom. Making prayers and offerings due to faith in the Buddha is very worthwhile, but a disservice is being done if faith and devotion replace one's motivation to investigate intelligently for oneself. The Buddha said, "Come and see for yourself," and not "Come and worship me." Our teachers are here to help us awaken ourselves. Worship and devotion can be very useful on the path to awakening, but the notion of worshipping to get something in return is a lazy person's approach to religion. This occurs in Buddhism as well as Christianity—lazy people are found everywhere.

Paranormal Possibilities

Is it possible to directly know an occurrence in a distant place or time? As history has repeatedly demonstrated, new evidence may someday validate phenomena we currently believe to be impossible. In traditional cultures, there is often widespread acceptance of the existence of extrasensory perception. Many people in the modern world believe in some form of remote viewing, the ability to mentally perceive something beyond the range of the five senses. Obviously there are skeptics, and many people refuse to even look at the data.

If precognition and remote viewing do take place, they cannot rely on the psyche or the substrate consciousness, which have no knowledge of things we have not experienced. The substrate is simply a repository of memories. If some of these reports are valid, and the human mind does have extrasensory capabilities, how can we understand them? One possibility is a deeper dimension of nonlocal awareness that transcends and subsumes the three times of past, present, and future. The absolute space of phenomena pervades all space and is nondual from primordial consciousness. This space of omnipresent knowledge might reveal aspects of the future and appearances beyond the reach of the senses.

Remote viewing and precognition are universally accepted in most schools of Buddhism, especially those with a strong emphasis on samadhi. The practice of samadhi is crucial, but it may not be sufficient. Upon achieving shamatha, with some training one should be able to recall memories of past lives, perceiving them directly. This can be put to the test even without vipashyana. However, remote viewing and precognition require tapping into something deeper than the substrate. Resting in the luminous, boundless space of the substrate, it is possible that you might have fleeting access to primordial consciousness. By directing your attention, you might penetrate through the substrate consciousness to illuminate something far away in space or time, like slipping through a temporary wormhole into another domain. This is just an analogy, but from my perspective there is reason to believe that something like this happens.

I discussed this with His Holiness the Dalai Lama several years ago, and based on my understanding at that time, I commented that one would have to achieve shamatha in order to develop paranormal awareness. He immediately responded with great certainty, "That is not always the case." He said that there are highly accomplished meditators in the Dzogchen tradition who have not achieved shamatha, although their minds are very stable and clear. They have rested for thousands of hours in open presence and have gained a real taste of primordial consciousness. They are able to dwell in it and become quite accomplished—without having achieved shamatha. Adepts who have gained deep realization of primordial consciousness may display exceptional abilities, including remote viewing and precognition. This is not omniscience, but something like a flash of lightning illuminating distant regions of space, arising spontaneously and then receding. The achievement of shamatha makes such experiences more durable and intelligible.

The existence of a dimension of consciousness that is nonlocal and atemporal, beyond the psyche and the substrate consciousness, does not imply that the future is preordained. The Buddha took great care to say that it is not. We are agents cultivating and generating our futures right now, reaping what we have sown. We are not merely drifting in the flow of time, waiting for our fate to manifest. Nevertheless, there are cases where events in the future are ensured; if all the necessary causes and conditions have been accumulated, the result is unavoidable.

For example, in the finale of the movie *Thelma and Louise,* the protagonists are speeding suicidally toward a cliff. At first their fate is undetermined—anything could happen. But by the time they are fifty feet from the edge, you don't have to be psychic to see that they will plunge over the cliff to their deaths. All the necessary causes and conditions have been established. Precognition involves seeing future incidents for which the necessary causes and conditions are present, guaranteeing a result. Of course, even if one result is a sure bet, myriad aspects of the future are undetermined and unpredictable.

Starting Where You Are

As my primary Dzogchen teacher, Gyatrul Rinpoche, has commented many times, there is only one fundamental difference between buddhas, those who are awake, and sentient beings, those who wander in samsara: buddhas know who they are and sentient beings don't. The Dzogchen analysis of the Second Noble Truth of the origin of suffering is that we perpetuate our own suffering by grasping on to that which is not "I and mine," thinking it is "I and mine." In both waking and dream states, we fail to recognize who we really are, so we grasp on to that which we are not. The ultimate reality is that we have never been other than buddhas.

Such is the Dzogchen view, but we are not asked to simply believe it. It is most effectively absorbed as a series of provocative hypotheses that are tested experientially, step by step. It is good to envision the lofty pinnacles toward which this practice is headed. Nevertheless, right now our minds are still relatively unstable, alternating between excitation and laxity. Is this the intrinsic nature of the mind, with nothing to be done about it? Is human nature hard-wired for craving, jealousy, and aggression?

Freud saw the human capacity for virtue as quite limited. The deepest drives that motivate us—hunger, fear of death, and procreation—are not virtuous. We may sport a thin veneer of altruistic socialization, but it's inconsequential. With such powerful forces, it is crucial to determine which are inherent in human nature. Does meditation merely induce temporary shifts in consciousness, while biological imperatives to survive and procreate drive our behavior? The stakes are enormously high. Without being distracted by notions of advanced practices, we must start with our current situation.

By cultivating the mind, insight, and a wholesome way of life, can we decrease and even free ourselves from craving and hostility? Can we gradually calm the mind without collapsing into stupor? Can we pacify both agitation and dullness, bringing forth enhanced relaxation, stability, vividness, mindfulness, and metacognitive awareness? Can we achieve a higher degree of mental health and thrive in daily life? Is meaningful progress possible, or are we forever constrained by our genes and the evolutionary drive? These are simple questions of profound import.

One reason I admire Galileo so much is that he didn't pursue complicated theories—he put simple questions to the test of experience. He climbed the leaning tower of Pisa and dropped various balls to see whether the big ones hit the ground before the little ones. Then he rolled them down a ramp to see if they would accelerate or move at constant velocity. Galileo was able to answer his questions by observation. Newton built upon this work with a theory of gravitation and three laws of motion that explained Kepler's observations of the elliptical orbits of planets and a great deal more; his *Principia* is a grand vision of a universe ruled by mathematical laws.[119]

Galileo and Kepler asked basic questions that they could answer empirically, and some of these answers have held true ever since. They discovered intersubjective truths, not mere opinions. It is crucial to note that these truths arose in relation to their modes of investigation. Reality always arises in response to our questions, but this does not mean that reality can be fabricated as we wish. When we pose specific questions and find reproducible answers, we are learning truths about our world. The fact that rolling balls accelerate down a ramp is presumably true on any planet. This is a truth that holds across multiple cognitive frames of reference. Galileo launched the scientific revolution not by asking the most profound questions but by asking questions he could answer empirically. When others replicated his results, everyone could take them to be true.

In a similar fashion, we contemplative investigators must ask questions we can actually answer. A good place to start is the possibility of training our attention. Are we condemned to bounce between lethargy and agitation as we obsessively generate one thought after another and grasp on to everything? Or is it possible, through training, to achieve and sustain improved mental balance?

Is the Buddha's claim true? When mindfulness of the breath is developed and cultivated, does it lead to a peaceful, sublime, ambrosial dwelling in which unwholesome states vanish instantaneously? If true, this is highly significant; to conduct the experiment and confirm these results would be transformative. Can everyone's mental afflictions be subdued? Are some people innately more loving and others less so, regardless of how they train, or can anyone cultivate qualities of loving-kindness, compassion, and empathy? If this can be done, then how shall we identify the most effective means? What is the possibility of deliberate spiritual evolution as opposed to the slow process of biological evolution via natural selection?

Such juicy questions have been raised for a long time in contemplative practice. They are some of the most important questions we can ask about our own nature. We have witnessed an exponential growth in technological knowledge and power in the twentieth century—with little progress in ethics, compassion, or wisdom. Our voracious appetites for material consumption accelerate the degradation of our natural environment and threaten extinction for many species, including our own. What is the prospect for survival of our ancient heritages and the wisdoms of traditional cultures that struggle to adapt in modernity?

We must respond quickly to the unprecedented environmental changes we have precipitated. There is no time for natural selection to produce future generations that can flourish in ecosystems radically degraded by human activity. Unsustainable exploitation of the world's resources and negligent disposal of our waste now threaten the burgeoning human population with disease, famine, and destruction.[120] Genetic engineering will not restore the contaminated biosphere we leave to our descendants, and it may have unintended consequences. It is realistic to say that the only way we can possibly adapt to these changes is through spiritual evolution that is conscious and deliberate—not left to chance or technological innovation.

In the big picture, we can entertain many hypotheses and employ a variety of methods to verify them. If, like Galileo, we ask simple questions that can be put to the test, we will see from our own experience whether our practices generate good outcomes. Do they improve mental balance and lead to meaningful benefits? If they are effective, we will be emboldened in our practice. If they are not, we may test them again or search for something better.

My primary teacher in Switzerland in the seventies was Geshe Rabten, an accomplished scholar who had spent six years in meditative retreat. He was extremely articulate, and I attribute any clarity in the way I teach to having served as his interpreter. His teachings were so lucid that my English translations became effortless, and I remain eternally grateful for his practical instruction and advice.

Geshe Rabten would commonly give teachings for a week or so, and at the end he would say, "I was asked to teach on this topic and I've done so, offering you my very best. If you put these teachings into practice and find them beneficial, then I encourage you to continue practicing them to derive increasing benefit. On the other hand, if you put these teachings into practice and find no benefit, then don't worry. Leave them and find something else to practice because the goal is to derive benefit, not to blindly follow my teachings."

This pragmatic attitude is a hallmark of the teachings of the Buddha, who said, "Come and see." I can offer no better advice. Put this into practice and see if it is helpful. If so, continue practicing it. If not, then you should adapt, modify, or discard it. My aspiration is that you are now confident in your knowledge of how to practice correctly—and inspired to do so diligently.

GUIDED MEDITATION:
Loving-Kindness II

Radiate and reabsorb loving-kindness—
actualizing the highest aspirations

Settle the body, speech, and mind in their natural states.

Begin the meditative cultivation of loving-kindness by focusing on yourself. The essence of loving-kindness is the aspiration that all may find true happiness and the causes of happiness. Arouse this yearning for yourself: "May I find the fulfillment that I seek and cultivate the causes leading to fulfillment." What does your deepest fulfillment entail? Envision your own flourishing. Issue an open invitation to the happiness that is your heart's desire.

Consider that your imagination does not exceed your capacity. You do have the potential to realize such a result. Envision your own potential for well-being, awakening, and liberation as an orb of white light radiating at your heart. This represents the deepest dimension of your own awareness—a primordially pure fountainhead of virtue, well-being, and joy.

With each out-breath, radiate white light from the orb at your heart, while arousing the yearning: "May I realize the well-being that is my heart's desire." Imagine this light saturating your body and mind to actualize your deepest aspirations, here and now.

Consider what you would love to receive from the people around you and the natural world. What forms of friendship, guidance, and material assistance do you need to fulfill your highest aspirations? Allow the yearning to arise: "May I receive all that I need to realize the genuine happiness I seek." With each in-breath, imagine reality arising in the form of white light streaming in from all directions to provide you with everything you need.

The help we receive from the world includes necessities and cooperative conditions, but these are not sufficient causes for our realization of well-being and fulfillment. Inner transformation is essential. How would you love to transform and evolve as a human being? From which qualities would you love to be freed in order to realize your heart's desire? With which qualities would you love to be endowed? Picture your personal evolution and spiritual growth.

With each out-breath, imagine white light radiating from the inexhaustible source at your heart. Arouse the aspiration with each out-breath: "May I cultivate the causes of my own fulfillment." Imagine the white light of loving-kindness saturating your body and mind, as you actually become the person you would love to be, here and now.

Finally, for the sake of your own fulfillment and to make your own life as meaningful as possible, what would you truly love to offer to the world? Envision the best you can imagine, bringing maximum benefit to those near and far and profoundly enriching your life's meaning. With each out-breath, radiate the white light of loving-kindness in all directions, actualizing this offering to the entire world, here and now.

In conclusion, release all aspirations, imagery, desires, and mental objects. Rest your awareness in its primordially pure, nonconceptual nature. To derive the greatest possible value from your efforts, dedicate the benefit, merit, and virtue you have accumulated in the study and practice of mindfulness to the realization of your own and others' most meaningful aspirations.

⤔ Guided Meditation Practice Sequence ⟼

ABBREVIATED TITLE	PRIMARY INSTRUCTION	SECONDARY INSTRUCTION	PAGE
Settling the Body I	Attend to the tactile field	Balance relaxation, stillness, and vigilance	20
Mindfulness I	Attend to all mental and sensory appearances	Observe without distraction, grasping, or aversion	27
Mindfulness II	Sustain unwavering mindfulness of all appearances	Observe without distraction, grasping, or aversion	34
Mindfulness III	Sustain unwavering mindfulness of all appearances	Observe whatever arises in the present moment	54
Mindfulness IV	Sustain unwavering mindfulness of all appearances	Monitor with introspection	60
Mindfulness V	Sustain mindfulness of all appearances and projections	Consider everything grist for the mill	80
Breath I	Attend to the breath throughout the body	Relax and release with each breath	90
Breath II	Attend to the rise and fall of the abdomen	Balance stability with relaxation	92
Body I	Scan tactile sensations in three dimensions	Observe without mental projections	114

ABBREVIATED TITLE	PRIMARY INSTRUCTION	SECONDARY INSTRUCTION	PAGE
Body II	Attend closely to the field of the body	Observe solidity, moisture, heat, and motion	117
Sleep I	Attend to the breath throughout the body	Fall asleep in a smooth transition	131
Loving-Kindness I	Radiate and reabsorb loving-kindness	Actualize the highest aspirations	134
Feelings I	Attend closely to feelings	Observe pleasure, displeasure, and indifference	138
Feelings II	Scan feelings in three dimensions	Observe without grasping or identification	150
Feelings III	Attend to feelings in body and mind via all six senses	Observe emergence, persistence, and dissolution	153
Mind I	Attend to the space of the mind and its contents	Observe without distraction or grasping	157
Mind II	Attend to the space of the mind and feelings	Observe pleasure, pain, and indifference	161
Sleep II	Attend to the space of the mind and its contents	Fall asleep lucidly	172
Earth & Wind I	Attend to the domain of tactile sensations	Observe without distraction or grasping	176
	Attend to the space of the mind and its contents	Hover in the present moment	178
Mind III	Attend to the space of the mind and its contents	Observe arising, abiding, and dissolving	185
Earth & Wind II	Attend to the domain of tactile sensations	Rest awareness as still as space	191
	Attend to the space of the mind and its contents	Inspect for "I" and "mine"	191

Abbreviated Title	Primary Instruction	Secondary Instruction	Page
Earth & Sky I	Attend to the domain of tactile sensations	Monitor with introspection	206
	Attend to the space of the mind	Focus on intervals between thoughts	207
Substrate I	Attend to the space of the mind	Observe the domain of mental events	219
Awareness I	Attend to the cognizant luminosity of awareness	Invert on inhale and release on exhale	224
Awareness II	Attend to the cognizant luminosity of awareness	Sustain it without subject or object	239
Open Presence I	Attend to the space of the mind and all appearances	Hover in the present moment, wide-open	247
Open Presence II	Attend to the space of the mind and all appearances	Observe interactions in causal patterns	252
Open Presence III	Attend to the space of the mind and all appearances	Distinguish hindrances from wholesome factors	266
Open Presence IV	Attend to the space of the mind and all appearances	Inspect the inherent identity of yourself and all objects	270
Open Presence V	Attend to the space of the mind and all appearances	Observe relationships between objects and appearances	286
Awareness III	Attend to the cognizant luminosity of awareness	Maintain an unbroken continuity of practice	295
Open Presence VI	Attend to the space of the mind and all appearances	Rest in the stillness of awareness	302
Loving-Kindness II	Radiate and reabsorb loving-kindness	Actualize the highest aspirations	311

⇢ Citations of Texts from ⇠ the Pali Canon and Commentaries

THE PALI CANON (*Tripiṭaka*, the three baskets) consists of the *Vinaya Piṭaka* (basket of disciplinary rules), the *Sutta Piṭaka* (basket of discourses), and the *Abhidhamma Piṭaka* (basket of treatises). For a comprehensive outline of the Pali Canon see Russell Webb, "An Analysis of the Pali Canon" (Kandy, Sri Lanka: Buddhist Publication Society, 1991), available online as publication WH 217–20 from the Buddhist Publication Society, www.bps.lk/onlinelibrary_wheels.asp.

In the notes, my translations from the Pali Canon and commentaries are cited with the common name of the text followed by its volume and page number in the Pali Text Society's (PTS) roman-script Pali editions, in square brackets, using the abbreviations below. In some cases, chapter and verse are cited instead. Many translations of the Pali Canon include PTS page references, enabling comparisons between translations.

AN   Anguttara Nikāya
DN   Dīgha Nikāya
Miln Milindapañhā
MN   Majjhima Nikāya
SN   Saṃyutta Nikāya
Ud   Udāna
Vbh   Vibhanga
Vsm   Visuddhimagga

❧ Notes ❧

The epigraph to the preface is drawn from *The Debate of King Milinda: An Abridgement of the Milinda Pañha*, ed. Bhikkhu Pesala (Penang: Inward Path, 2001), 41. The original quote appears in the *Saṃyutta Nikāya* [SN V 115].

1   Several interpretations by fourth-century CE Indian Buddhist scholar Asaṅga are quoted in Artemus B. Engle, *The Inner Science of Buddhist Practice: Vasubandhu's "Summary of the Five Heaps" with Commentary by Sthiramati* (Ithaca, NY: Snow Lion Publications, 2009), 140.

2   *Saṃyutta Nikāya* [SN V 325]. See also *The Connected Discourses of the Buddha: A New Translation of the Saṃyutta Nikāya*, trans. Bhikkhu Bodhi, 2 vols. (Boston: Wisdom Publications, 2000), 2:1777. This translation of the *Saṃyutta Nikāya* comprises 2,904 sutras, arranged thematically in fifty-six groups; it is the third of five collections within the *Sutta Piṭaka*.

3   Nyanaponika Thera, *The Heart of Buddhist Meditation: Satipaṭṭhāna* (San Francisco: Red Wheel/Weiser, 1996). Nyanaponika Thera (b. Siegmund Feniger) cofounded the Buddhist Publication Society in 1958.

4   Sanskrit terms are rendered phonetically in the text; the endnotes include diacritics.

5   Kyabje Lati Rinpoche began his monastic career in Tibet at the age of ten, and he was eventually awarded the Gelug monastic system's highest degree, Geshe Lharampa. In 1959, he followed the Dalai Lama into exile. He continued to teach monks and laypeople worldwide, becoming the abbot of the Shartse Norling College of Gaden Monastery in India.

6   Geshe Rabten was one of the pioneering teachers of Tibetan Buddhism in the West. He founded the Rabten Choeling Center for Higher Tibetan Studies in Mont-Pèlerin, Switzerland, in 1977.

7   Kyabje Trijang Rinpoche was ordained by the Thirteenth Dalai Lama and was instrumental in spreading the Dharma to the West along with his disciples, including Lama Yeshe, Lama Zopa Rinpoche, and Geshe Rabten.

8 Balangoda Ananda Maitreya was revered in the Sri Lankan Theravadin community for his scholarship, meditative accomplishment, and humility.

9 Geshe Ngawang Dhargyey left Chinese-occupied Tibet for India in 1959. In 1971 His Holiness the Dalai Lama asked him to teach Westerners at the new Library of Tibetan Works and Archives in Dharamsala.

10 H.H. the Dalai Lama, Tenzin Gyatso, *Transcendent Wisdom: A Commentary on the Ninth Chapter of Shantideva's Guide to the Bodhisattva Way of Life*, trans. and ed. B. Alan Wallace (Ithaca, NY: Snow Lion Publications, 1988).

11 Ven. Jampel Tenzin, known to his Western students as Gen Lamrimpa, meditated in the hills above Dharamsala for over twenty years. In 1988 I assisted him in leading a one-year group retreat, which led to the Shamatha Project, a longitudinal study of intensive meditation practice.

12 Ven. Gyatrul Rinpoche is a senior lama of the Nyingma order. I served as his principal interpreter from 1992 to 1997.

13 Tibetan terms in parentheses use the Wylie system, which precisely transliterates the written script without indicating its divergence from pronunciation; for example, silent initial consonants are common.

14 *Dīgha Nikāya* [DN III 219]. See also Maurice Walshe, *The Long Discourses of the Buddha: A Translation of the Dīgha Nikāya* (Boston: Wisdom Publications, 1995), 486.

15 A brilliant scholar and accomplished master, Karma Chagmé is also known as the teacher of Migyur Dorje, who revealed the *Space Dharma* (Tib. *gnam chos*) cycle of hidden teachings.

16 Karma Chagmé, *A Spacious Path to Freedom: Practical Instructions on the Union of Mahamudra and Atiyoga*, commentary by Gyatrul Rinpoche, trans. B. Alan Wallace (Ithaca, NY: Snow Lion Publications, 1998), 85.

17 The practices of the Great Seal (Skt. *Mahāmudrā*) are most often associated with the Tibetan Kagyü lineages originating with the Indian *mahāsiddhas* of the eighth through twelfth centuries.

18 See discussion of this phrase, *"Ekāyano ayaṃ maggo,"* in Bhikkhu Bodhi, *The Connected Discourses of the Buddha*, 2:1915, n. 123.

19 Metaphysical realism refers to the belief in an independently existing reality, to which our conceptualizations merely correspond with variable accuracy. For a clear explanation of the Sautrantika view, see Anne Carolyn Klein, *Knowing, Naming and Negation: A Sourcebook on Tibetan Sautrāntika* (Ithaca, NY: Snow Lion Publications, 1991).

20 From the *Ghanavyuha Sūtra*, quoted in Alexander Berzin, *Relating to a Spiritual Teacher: Building A Healthy Relationship* (Ithaca, NY: Snow Lion Publications, 2000), 190.

21 Palden Gyatso was arrested in the Chinese invasion of Tibet, and he survived thirty-three years of imprisonment. The instruments of torture he smuggled out gave vivid evidence of the brutalities endured in Chinese gulags.

22 Pascal's wager suggests that even though the existence of God cannot be established, one should wager as though God exists because there is little to lose if you are mistaken (God does not exist) and everything to gain if you are right (God does exist).

23 The eightfold noble path consists of right speech, right action, right livelihood, right effort, right mindfulness, right concentration, right view, and right intention.

24 Cited in Kamalaśīla, "First Bhāvanākrama," in *Minor Buddhist Texts, Part II*, ed. Giuseppe Tucci (Rome: Istituto italiano per il Medio ed Estremo Oriente, 1958), 205.

25 Thomas Nagel, *The View from Nowhere* (New York: Oxford University Press, 1986).

26 B. Alan Wallace, *Contemplative Science: Where Buddhism and Neuroscience Converge* (New York: Columbia University Press, 2007).

27 Henry David Thoreau, *Walden* (New York: Thomas Y. Crowell and Co., 1910), 118.

28 See, for example, B. K. S. Iyengar, *Light on the Yoga Sūtras of Patañjali* (London: Thorsons, 2003).

29 See, for example, the *Sāleyyaka Sutta* [MN I 285] in *The Middle Length Discourses of the Buddha: A Translation of the Majjhima Nikāya*, trans. Bhikkhu Ñāṇamoli and Bhikkhu Bodhi (Boston: Wisdom Publications, 1995), 379. The *Majjhima Nikāya* comprises 154 medium-length discourses of the Buddha and is the second of five collections within the *Sutta Piṭaka*.

30 Upatissa, *The Path of Freedom: Vimuttimagga*, trans. N. R. M. Ehara, Soma Thera, and Kheminda Thera (Kandy, Sri Lanka: Buddhist Publication Society, 1995).

31 Buddhaghosa, *The Path of Purification: Visuddhimagga*, trans. Bhikkhu Ñāṇamoli (Onalaska, WA: BPE Pariyatti Editions, 1999). This commentary describes seven progressive stages of purification.

32 The seven points of Vairochana include detailed guidelines for the postures of the legs, eyes, spine, shoulders, head, mouth, and tongue; the hands and other aspects are often specified as well.

33 Like "the map is not the territory," this metaphor signifies that words are not the truth itself, or that the Buddhadharma teaches us to discover the truth in our own experience rather than becoming fixated on the teaching.

34 Edward J. Larson, *The Creation-Evolution Debate: Historical Perspectives* (Athens: University of Georgia Press, 2007), 58.

35 Albert Michelson (1852–1931) and Edward Morley (1838–1923) built an interferometer to detect expected differences in the speed of light due to the motion of its putative medium, the luminiferous ether; no differences were detected.

36 *Milindapañhā*, chap. 1, v. 12. See also R. M. L. Gethin, *The Buddhist Path to Awakening* (Oxford: Oneworld Publications, 2001), 37.

37 *Visuddhimagga* [Vsm 464]. From Gethin, *The Buddhist Path to Awakening*, 40. See also Buddhaghosa, *The Path of Purification*, 467.

38 *Bodhicaryāvatāra*, chap. 5, v. 108. From Śāntideva, *A Guide to the Bodhisattva Way of Life*, trans. Vesna A. Wallace and B. Alan Wallace (Ithaca, NY: Snow Lion Publications, 1997), 60.

39 *Mahāyānasūtrālaṃkāra*, chap. 18, v. 53. See also Maitreyantha/Āryāsaṅga and Vasubandhu, *The Universal Vehicle Discourse Literature*, ed. Robert A.F. Thurman, trans. L. Jamspal, R. Clark, J. Wilson, L. Zwilling, M. Sweet, and R. Thurman (New York: American Institute of Buddhist Studies, Columbia Univ., 2004), 265.

40 *Satipaṭṭhāna Sutta* [MN I 55]. From Anālayo, *Satipaṭṭhāna: The Direct Path to Real-*

ization (Birmingham: Windhorse Publications, 2007), 3, with modification of the original translation.

41 *Ādittapariyāya Sutta* [SN IV 19]. See also Bhikkhu Bodhi, *The Connected Discourses of the Buddha*, 2:1143.

42 Antoine Lutz, Heleen A. Slagter, Nancy B. Rawlings, Andrew D. Francis, Lawrence L. Greischar, and Richard J. Davidson, "Mental Training Enhances Attentional Stability: Neural and Behavioral Evidence," *The Journal of Neuroscience* 29, no. 42 (2009): 13418–27.

43 In two phases of three-month meditation retreats, researchers observed physiological, perceptual, emotional, and attentional changes in participants who engaged in the shamatha practices described here. See also note 74 (MacLean).

44 Mihaly Csikszentmihalyi, *Flow: The Psychology of Optimal Experience* (New York: Harper and Row, 1990).

45 *Bāhiya Sutta*, Ud chap. 1, v. 10. See also John D. Ireland, trans., *The Udāna and the Itivuttaka* (Kandy, Sri Lanka: Buddhist Publication Society, 1997), 19–21. The *Udāna* records eighty inspired utterances of the Buddha and is the third book of the *Khuddaka Nikāya* (Minor Collection), which is the fifth collection within the *Sutta Piṭaka*.

46 The Standard Model of elementary particles describes three of their four fundamental interactions but does not explain gravitation; hence, the search for a "theory of everything."

47 The Higgs boson, sensationalized as the "God particle," is central to the Standard Model and is the only fundamental particle in that theory not yet observed; scientists are attempting to do so utilizing the Large Hadron Collider at CERN.

48 Wilson Microwave Anisotropy Probe Five-Year Results, March 7, 2008, available at the Web site of NASA, http://map.gsfc.nasa.gov/news/5yr_release.html.

49 Lou Cannon, *President Reagan: The Role of a Lifetime* (New York: PublicAffairs, 2000), 38.

50 Paul Ekman, *Emotions Revealed: Recognizing Faces and Feelings to Improve Communication and Emotional Life* (New York: Owl Books, 2007), 57.

51 Laurence Freeman is director and spiritual guide of the World Community for Christian Meditation and founder of the John Main Center for Meditation and Religious Dialogue at Georgetown University.

52 *Mahā-Assapura Sutta* [MN I 274–75]. See also Bhikkhu Ñāṇamoli and Bhikkhu Bodhi, *The Middle Length Discourses of the Buddha*, 366.

53 See discussion of this simile from the *Sāratthappakāsini* commentary to the *Saṃyutta Nikāya* [SN IV 194–95] in Kheminda Thera, *The Way of Buddhist Meditation: Serenity and Insight according to the Pali Canon* (Colombo, Sri Lanka: Lake House, 1980), 9–10, and in Bhikkhu Bodhi, *The Connected Discourses of the Buddha*, 2:1428, n. 207.

54 *Mahāsaccaka Sutta* [MN I 246]. From Bhikkhu Ñāṇamoli and Bhikkhu Bodhi, *The Middle Length Discourses of the Buddha*, 340, with modification of the original translation.

55 *Ānāpānasaṃyutta Sutta* [SN V 321–22]. From Bhikkhu Bodhi, *The Connected Discourses of the Buddha*, 2:1774, with modification of the original translation.

56 Barbara Fredrickson, *Positivity: Groundbreaking Research Reveals How to Embrace*

the Hidden Strength of Positive Emotions, Overcome Negativity, and Thrive (New York: Crown Publishers, 2009).

57 *Ānāpānasati Sutta* [MN III 82]. From Bhikkhu Ñāṇamoli and Bhikkhu Bodhi, *The Middle Length Discourses of the Buddha*, 943–44, with modification of the original translation.

58 Ibid.

59 Ibid.

60 *Vishuddhimagga* [Vsm 126]. From Buddhaghosa, *The Path of Purification*, 125.

61 *Sāmaññaphala Sutta* [DN I 73]. From Kheminda Thera, *The Way of Buddhist Meditation*, 12, with modification of the original translation. See also Walshe, *The Long Discourses of the Buddha*, 102.

62 *Parāyana Sutta* [SN IV 373]. From Glenn Wallis, *Basic Teachings of the Buddha* (New York: Modern Library, 2007), 45, with modification of the original translation.

63 *Satipaṭṭhāna Sutta* [MN I 56]. See also Bhikkhu Ñāṇamoli and Bhikkhu Bodhi, *The Middle Length Discourses of the Buddha*, 146.

64 U Thiṭṭila, *The Book of Analysis: Vibhaṅga* (Oxford: Luzac/Pali Text Society, 1969). The *Vibhaṅga* analyzes phenomena in eighteen classes; it is the second book of seven constituting the *Abhidhamma Piṭaka*.

65 *Satipaṭṭhāna Sutta* [MN I 57]. From Anālayo, *Satipaṭṭhāna*, 6. See also Bhikkhu Ñāṇamoli and Bhikkhu Bodhi, *The Middle Length Discourses of the Buddha*, 148.

66 Ayurveda, the knowledge or science of life, is an ancient system of medicine from the Indian subcontinent.

67 *Rohitassa Sutta* [SN I 62]. See also Bhikkhu Bodhi, *The Connected Discourses of the Buddha*, 1:158.

68 The Big Bang refers to the theory that the universe expanded from an exceedingly dense, hot singularity, about 13.7 billion years ago, and that it continues to expand today.

69 Donald S. Lopez Jr., *Buddhism and Science: A Guide for the Perplexed* (Chicago: University of Chicago Press, 2008), 227. Lopez credits D. T. Suzuki with the first English version of this metaphor for the ground, path, and result, and he attributes the original passage to Chan master Qingyuan Weixin.

70 Neem Karoli Baba was a devotee of the Hindu deity Hanuman. His teachings have been propagated in the West by followers including Ram Dass, Bhagavan Das, Lama Surya Das, Krishna Das, and Jai Uttal.

71 *Kosalasaṃyutta Sutta* [SN I 75]. See also Bhikkhu Bodhi, *The Connected Discourses of the Buddha*, 1:171.

72 Antonio R. Damasio, B. J. Everitt, and D. Bishop, "The Somatic Marker Hypothesis and the Possible Functions of the Prefrontal Cortex (and Discussion)," *Phil. Trans.: Biological Sciences* 351, no. 1346 (1996): 1413–20.

73 B. Alan Wallace, *The Attention Revolution: Unlocking the Power of the Focused Mind* (Boston: Wisdom Publications, 2006), 118.

74 See, for example, Katherine A. MacLean et al., "Intensive Meditation Training Leads to Improvements in Perceptual Discrimination and Sustained Attention," *Psychological Science* 21, no. 6 (2010): 829–39. Further results from the Shamatha Project are forthcoming.

75 Düdjom Lingpa, *The Vajra Essence: From the Matrix of Pure Appearances and Primordial Consciousness, a Tantra on the Self-Originating Nature of Existence*, trans. B. Alan Wallace (Alameda, CA: Mirror of Wisdom, 2004).

76 V. S. Ramachandran and Sandra Blakeslee, *Phantoms in the Brain* (New York: HarperCollins, 1999).

77 Peter Harvey, *The Selfless Mind: Personality, Consciousness and Nirvana in Early Buddhism* (Abingdon, Oxfordshire: RoutledgeCurzon, 2004).

78 Sigmund Freud, James Strachey, and Louis Menand, *Civilization and Its Discontents* (New York: W.W. Norton and Company, 2005), 53.

79 B. Alan Wallace, *Genuine Happiness: Meditation as the Path to Fulfillment* (Hoboken, NJ: John Wiley, 2005), 4.

80 *Doṇa Sutta* [AN II 37]. See also Nyanaponika Thera and Bhikkhu Bodhi, trans. and eds., *Numerical Discourses of the Buddha: An Anthology of Suttas from the Aṅguttara Nikāya* (Walnut Creek, CA: AltaMira Press, 1999), 87–88. The *Aṅguttara Nikāya* includes eleven groups of discourses, numerically themed, and is the fourth of five collections within the *Sutta Piṭaka*.

81 Genesis 8:6 (New King James Version).

82 Buddhaghosa, *The Expositor (Atthasālinī)*, trans. Pe Maung Tin (London: Pali Text Society, 1920–21), vol. 2, 359–60. The simile of the falling mango appears in this commentary on the *Dhammasangani*, which is the first book of the *Abhidhamma Piṭaka*.

83 B. Alan Wallace, *Hidden Dimensions: The Unification of Physics and Consciousness* (New York: Columbia University Press, 2007), 54–57.

84 Daniel Wegner, *The Illusion of Conscious Will* (Cambridge: MIT Press, 2003).

85 Bertrand Russell, *A History of Western Philosophy* (New York: Simon and Schuster, 1945), 828.

86 Anton Zeilinger, "Why the Quantum? 'It' from 'Bit'? A Participatory Universe? Three Far-Reaching Challenges from John Archibald Wheeler and Their Relation to Experiment," in *Science and Ultimate Reality: Quantum Theory, Cosmology, and Complexity*, ed. John D. Barrow, Paul C. W. Davies, and Charles L. Harper (Cambridge: Cambridge University Press, 2004), 201–20.

87 Paul C. W. Davies, "An Overview of the Contributions of John Archibald Wheeler," in Barrow, Davies, and Harper, *Science and Ultimate Reality*, 3–26.

88 Andrei Linde, "Inflation, Quantum Cosmology, and the Anthropic Principle," in Barrow, Davies, and Harper, *Science and Ultimate Reality*, 426–58.

89 C. L. Hicks, C. L. von Baeyer, P. Spafford, I. van Korlaar, B. Goodenough, "Faces Pain Scale – Revised: Toward a Common Metric in Pediatric Pain Measurement," *PAIN* 93 (2001): 173–83. Available at www.painsourcebook.ca.

90 Stephen LaBerge, *Lucid Dreaming: A Concise Guide to Awakening in Your Dreams and in Your Life* (Boulder: Sounds True, 2004), 14.

91 *Aṅguttara Nikāya* [AN I 10]. From Harvey, *The Selfless Mind*, 166, with modification of the original translation.

92 The ten stages of attentional development described by Kamalaśīla in his classic text *Stages of Meditation* form the basis of my book *The Attention Revolution*.

93 The Indian Guru Padmasambhava (the Lotus-Born) founded the Early Translation

School of Buddhism, or *Nyingma* (Tib. *rnying ma*), in Tibet, where he is known as Guru Rinpoche.

94 Padmasambhava and Karma Lingpa, *Natural Liberation: Padmasambhava's Teachings on the Six Bardos*, commentary by Gyatrul Rinpoche, trans. B. Alan Wallace (Boston: Wisdom Publications, 1998), 105.

95 *Saṃyutta Nikāya* [SN V 152]. From Bhikkhu Bodhi, *The Connected Discourses of the Buddha*, 2:1636, with modification of the original translation.

96 William James, *The Principles of Psychology* (New York: Henry Holt, 1918), vol. 1, 488.

97 *Dhammapada* 1. See also Gil Fronsdal, *The Dhammapada: Teachings of the Buddha* (Boston: Shambhala Publications, 2008), 3. The *Dhammapada* is the second book of the *Khuddaka Nikāya*.

98 From the *Ratnamegha Sūtra* (Cloud of Jewels Sūtra), quoted in Nyanaponika Thera, *The Heart of Buddhist Meditation*, 198, with modification of the original translation.

99 Henning Genz, *Nothingness: The Science of Empty Space*, trans. Karin Heusch (Cambridge: Perseus, 1999).

100 *Satipaṭṭhāna Sutta* [MN I 61]. From Bhikkhu Ñāṇamoli and Bhikkhu Bodhi, *The Middle Length Discourses of the Buddha*, 152–53, with modification of the original translation.

101 U.S. Census Bureau's estimate from www.census.gov/ipc/www/popclockworld. html.

102 *Bodhicaryāvatāra*, chap. 8, vv. 102–3. From Śāntideva, *A Guide to the Bodhisattva Way of Life*, 102.

103 Tania Singer and Claus Lamm, "The Social Neuroscience of Empathy," *The Year in Cognitive Neuroscience 2009: Ann. N.Y. Acad. Sci.* 1156 (2009): 81–96.

104 Cited in Śāntideva, *Śikṣa-samuccaya: A Compendium of Buddhist Doctrine*, trans. Cecil Bendall and W. H. D. Rouse (1922; repr., Delhi: Motilal Banarsidass, 1971), 222, with modification of the original translation.

105 Ibid., 224, with modification of the original translation.

106 See also Edward Conze, *The Perfection of Wisdom in Eight Thousand Lines and Its Verse Summary* (San Francisco: Four Seasons Foundation, 1973), 98–99.

107 Ibid., 215.

108 Karma Chagme, *The All-Pervading Melodious Sound of Thunder: The Outer Liberation Story of Terton Migyur Dorje*, trans. Lopon Sonam Tsewang and Judith Amtzis (Pharping, Nepal: Palri Parkhang, 2008).

109 Stephen W. Hawking and Thomas Hertog, "Populating the Landscape: A Top-Down Approach," *Physical Review D* 3, no. 73 (2006): 123527.

110 See a movie of Akira Tonomura's results with electrons at www.hitachi.com/rd/re search/em/doubleslit.html.

111 Olaf Nairz, Markus Arndt, and Anton Zeilinger, "Quantum Interference Experiments with Large Molecules," *Am. J. Phys.* 71, no. 4 (April 2003): 319–25.

112 Paul Davies, *About Time: Einstein's Unfinished Revolution* (New York: Simon and Schuster, 1995).

113 Atisha was instrumental in the establishment of the New Translation School, or

Sarma (Tib. *gsar ma*), in Tibet following Buddhism's repression by King Lang-darma.

114 Atisha's orally transmitted mind-training aphorisms were written down a century after his death; they are the subject of my book *Buddhism with an Attitude: The Tibetan Seven-Point Mind-Training* (Ithaca, NY: Snow Lion Publications, 2001).

115 *Kevaddha Sutta* [DN I 223]. See also Walshe, *The Long Discourses of the Buddha*, 179–80. *Dutiyadabba Sutta*, Ud chap. 8, v. 10. See also Ireland, *The Udāna and the Itivuttaka*, 109–10.

116 *Mārasaṃyutta* [SN I 122]. See also Bhikkhu Bodhi, *The Connected Discourses of the Buddha*, 1:214–15. *Nidānasaṃyutta* [SN II 103]. See also Bhikkhu Bodhi, *The Connected Discourses of the Buddha*, 1:601. *Khandasaṃyutta* [SN III 53–54, 124]. See also Bhikkhu Bodhi, *The Connected Discourses of the Buddha*, 1:890–91, 1:941.

117 *Dhammapada* 39, 267, 412. See also Fronsdal, *The Dhammapada*, 12, 65, 97. *Sutta Nipāta* 547, 790, 900. The *Sutta Nipāta*, comprising seventy-one sutras, is the third book of the *Khuddaka Nikāya*. See also H. Saddhatissa, *The Sutta-Nipāta* (London: RoutledgeCurzon, 2003), 63, 93, 105.

118 John 14:12 (New King James Version).

119 Isaac Newton, *Mathematical Principles of Natural Philosophy* (London: Royal Society, 1687).

120 Millennium Ecosystem Assessment, *Ecosystems and Human Well-Being: Synthesis* (Washington: Island Press, 2005).

◈ Selected Bibliography ◈

Anālayo. *Satipaṭṭhāna: The Direct Path to Realization*. Birmingham: Windhorse Publications, 2007.

Barrow, John D., Paul C. W. Davies, and Charles L. Harper, eds. *Science and Ultimate Reality: Quantum Theory, Cosmology, and Complexity*. Cambridge: Cambridge University Press, 2004.

Bodhi, Bhikkhu, trans. *The Connected Discourses of the Buddha: A New Translation of the Saṃyutta Nikāya*. 2 vols. Boston: Wisdom Publications, 2000.

Buddhaghosa, Bhadantācariya. *The Path of Purification: Visuddhimagga*. Translated by Bhikkhu Ñāṇamoli. Onalaska, WA: BPE Pariyatti Editions, 1999.

Harvey, Peter. *The Selfless Mind: Personality, Consciousness and Nirvana in Early Buddhism*. Abingdon, Oxfordshire: RoutledgeCurzon, 2004.

Ireland, John D., trans. *The Udāna and the Itivuttaka*. Kandy, Sri Lanka: Buddhist Publication Society, 1997.

Karma Chagmé. *A Spacious Path to Freedom: Practical Instructions on the Union of Mahāmudrā and Atiyoga*. Commentary by Gyatrul Rinpoche. Translated by B. Alan Wallace. Ithaca, NY: Snow Lion Publications, 1998.

Kheminda Thera. *The Way of Buddhist Meditation: Serenity and Insight according to the Pali Canon*. Colombo, Sri Lanka: Lake House, 1980.

LaBerge, Stephen. *Lucid Dreaming: A Concise Guide to Awakening in Your Dreams and in Your Life*. Boulder: Sounds True, 2004.

Maitreyantha/Āryāsaṅga and Vasubandhu. *The Universal Vehicle Discourse Literature: Mahāyānasūtrālaṃkāra*. Edited by Robert A. F. Thurman. Translated by L. Jamspal, R. Clark, J. Wilson, L. Zwilling, M. Sweet, and R. Thurman. New York: American Institute of Buddhist Studies, Columbia University, 2004.

Ñāṇamoli, Bhikkhu, and Bhikkhu Bodhi, trans. *The Middle Length Discourses of the Buddha: A Translation of the Majjhima Nikāya.* Boston: Wisdom Publications, 1995.

Nyanaponika Thera. *The Heart of Buddhist Meditation: Satipaṭṭhāna.* San Francisco: Red Wheel/Weiser, 1996.

Nyanaponika Thera and Bhikkhu Bodhi, trans. and eds. *Numerical Discourses of the Buddha: An Anthology of Suttas from the Aṅguttara Nikāya.* Walnut Creek, CA: AltaMira Press, 1999.

Padmasambhava and Karma Lingpa. *Natural Liberation: Padmasambhava's Teachings on the Six Bardos.* Commentary by Gyatrul Rinpoche. Translated by B. Alan Wallace. Boston: Wisdom Publications, 1998.

Pesala, Bhikkhu, ed. *The Debate of King Milinda: An Abridgement of the Milinda Pañha.* Penang: Inward Path, 2001. Available from the Buddhist eLibrary, www.buddhist-elibrary.org.

Śāntideva. *A Guide to the Bodhisattva Way of Life: Bodhicaryāvatāra.* Translated by Vesna A. Wallace and B. Alan Wallace. Ithaca, NY: Snow Lion Publications, 1997.

Thiṭṭila, U. *The Book of Analysis: Vibhaṅga.* Oxford: Luzac/Pali Text Society, 1969.

Upatissa. *The Path of Freedom: Vimuttimagga.* Translated by N. R. M. Ehara, Soma Thera, and Kheminda Thera. Kandy, Sri Lanka: Buddhist Publication Society, 1995.

Walshe, Maurice, trans. *The Long Discourses of the Buddha: A Translation of the Dīgha Nikāya.* Boston: Wisdom Publications, 1995.

Wallace, B. Alan. *The Attention Revolution: Unlocking the Power of the Focused Mind.* Boston: Wisdom Publications, 2006.

———. *Buddhism with an Attitude: The Tibetan Seven-Point Mind-Training.* Ithaca, NY: Snow Lion Publications, 2001.

———. *Contemplative Science: Where Buddhism and Neuroscience Converge.* New York: Columbia University Press, 2007.

———. *Genuine Happiness: Meditation as the Path to Fulfillment.* Hoboken, NJ: John Wiley and Sons, 2005.

———. *Hidden Dimensions: The Unification of Physics and Consciousness.* New York: Columbia University Press, 2007.

———. *Mind in the Balance: Meditation in Science, Buddhism, and Christianity.* New York: Columbia University Press, 2009.

———. *The Taboo of Subjectivity: Toward a New Science of Consciousness.* New York: Oxford University Press, 2000.

◁ Index ▷

accomplishment. *See* result: of accomplishment
action, right, 14
Adittapariyaya Sutta, 64
afflictions, mental. *See* mental afflictions
aggregates (skandhas)
  causal interactions of, 261
  defined, 40, 261
  impermanence of, 284
  subject to clinging, 40, 261
alaya. *See* substrate
alayavijñana, 109, 166, 196, 208. *See also*
  substrate consciousness
Alexander the Great, 55
anapanasati, 102
Anapanasati Sutta, 102
Anguttara Nikaya, 221
apotheosis, 16
appearances
  actual, 76
  attachment to, 142
  aversion to, 38
  of blueness, 18
  clinging to, 39
  constrained in waking, 219, 255
  dependently arising, 41, 253
  dream, 62
  entities from, 277, 278, 280
  externalized, 142
  feelings vs., 44
  grasping on to, 39
  grouping into categories, 162

illuminated by awareness, 228, 234
information consists of, 280
mental, 46, 66, 154
mind and, 6
objects arise from, 286
patterns of, 47
pleasure and, 38, 149
projections fused with, 77, 258
relationship between objects and, 276,
  285
from substrate, 119, 211, 235–37
suffering and, 38
tactile, 44
unconstrained in dreams, 219
like unruly guests, 28
veil of, 281
visual, 44, 140
Aquinas, Thomas, 210
arhat, 55, 102, 106, 299, 300, 303
Aristotle, 16, 74, 99, 209, 210
asana. *See* postures
asceticism, 4, 96, 99
aspiration
  on beginning practice, 20, 33
  bodhisattva, 6, 265
  compassion and, 137
  on concluding practice, 22, 29, 33,
    34, 312
  defined, 137
  feelings vs., 137
  of freedom, 201
  immeasurables, four, 137

of insight and knowledge, 65
mundane, 265
association, free, 183, 193, 196
Atisha, 296
Atman, 40
atom, experiential, 18
attachment
  to aggregates, 262
  to enlightenment factors, 263
  from grasping, 144
  perception distorted by, 195
  suffering from, 39, 263
attention
  bare, 20, 57, 83, 121, 152, 159, 189, 277
  as common denominator, 137
  continuity of, 33
  creates reality, 137, 209
  defined, 138
  directed with effort, 250
  emotion and, 70
  focused, 32, 33, 100, 170, 188
  greatest gift of, 181
  inversion and release of, 226
  nonexclusionary, 249
  nonselective, 293
  undirected, 227, 250, 252
  undistracted, 273
  witnessing mode of, 20
Attention Revolution (Wallace), 156
attitudes, adjustment of, 257
attributes, primary and secondary, 125, 126, 127
Augustine of Hippo, 170
awakening (bodhi)
  to buddhahood, 300
  factors, seven, 263
  as lucid waking state, 171, 240, 241, 304
  perfect, 265, 303
  as self-knowledge, 307
  spirit of (bodhichitta), 5, 264–66
  See also enlightenment; realization
awareness
  at abdomen, 92, 131, 244
  centered, 226
  cognizant luminosity of, 34, 224, 226, 228–30, 240
  continuity of, 225
  defined, 228, 229
  of emotions, 156

full-body, 20, 44, 116, 117, 120, 131, 244, 296
fundamentality of, 211
mental, 24, 125, 130, 155, 223, 255, 262, 263
of mental processes, 240
like mirror, 268
like monkey, 148
motionless, 252
nature of, 2, 40, 62, 97, 101, 137, 229, 230
nonconceptual, 20, 29, 286, 297, 299
nondual, 299
nonlocal, 306
nonselective, 217
at nostrils, 114, 153, 231, 244, 297
obscured luminosity of, 110, 260
panoramic, 203
of patterns, 269
present-moment, 28, 80, 247, 249, 251
pristine, 7, 135, 246, 254, 293, 299, 300, 304 (*see also* consciousness: primordial)
process of, 226
proprioceptive, 44
pure, 14
reflexive, 120, 125
like rider, 104
sensory, 44
single moment of, 148, 225
like space, 254
spacious, 220, 252
spontaneously present, 300
of subjective impulses, 155
subtle continuum of, 208
timeless, 293
unbroken flow of, 300
underlies everything, 235
undirected, 189, 249
unified with object, 208
vividness and acuity of, 156, 208, 232, 243, 246
wide-open, 246, 249, 250, 251
ayatana. *See* sense bases, twelve

Bahiya, 75, 76, 103, 205, 286, 287
balance
  cognitive, 81, 82, 86, 87
  of practices, 133, 268

of relaxation and stability, 92
of relaxation, stability, and vividness,
    89, 244, 250
of relaxation, stillness, and vigilance,
    20, 21
of scholarship and contemplation, 296
of theory and practice, 1, 2
of wisdom and faith, 10, 69, 305
of wisdom and skillful means, 5, 256,
    257
Balangoda Ananda Maitreya, xvii
bashful maiden and playboy, 184
being, celestial, 171, 285, 293
beliefs
    affect mind and body, 269
    inadequacy of mere, 10, 264, 308
    ingrained, 217, 276
bhavanga (ground of becoming)
    access to, 166
    death and, 233
    defined, 166, 222
    free of mentation, 232
    javana and, 192, 222
    like pilot light, 235
    psyche from, 196
    pure mind of, 231, 232
    like sun, 234
    Theravadin, 166
Bodhgaya, 141
bodhi. See awakening
bodhi tree, 19, 96, 97
bodhichitta. See awakening: spirit of
bodhisattva, 58, 265, 285
body
    dream, 62, 241
    mind and, 105, 128, 146
    like mountain, 152, 254
    subtle energetic, 105, 223, 254
Brahman, 40
brahmavihara (sublime abode). See
    immeasurables, four
brain
    complexity of, 294
    correlates of compassion and empathy,
        270
    correlates of experience, 212
    mechanisms, 122, 269, 270
    mind and, 212, 213
    neuroplasticity, 218

research, 270
self not in, 8
breath. See mindfulness: of breath
brightly shining chitta (heart-mind), 221,
    222, 231
Buber, Martin, 181, 265
buckyball, 290
buddha nature
    as identity, ultimate, 301, 308
    mistaken for, 40
    obscured, 109
    as potential, highest, 135
    realization of, 7
Buddha Shakyamuni, xiii, xv, 4, 171
    career of, 102
    discourses of, 7, 35, 37, 55, 93, 100, 102,
        103, 104, 113, 141, 245, 286, 297
    innovation of, 4, 100
    path of, 7, 15, 19, 42, 74 (see also
        path)
    See also Gautama, Siddhartha
Buddhadharma
    aphorisms in, 10, 33, 37, 63, 64, 111, 127,
        145, 221, 222, 227, 234, 236, 305, 311
    decontextualized, 94
    eightfold path in, 14 (see also path)
    emergence in, 301, 302
    empiricism in, 10, 198, 305
    ethics, samadhi, and wisdom in, 4, 71,
        73, 74, 95, 100
    in fathom-long body, 127
    like finger pointing to the moon, 76,
        229
    Four Noble Truths in, 11, 12, 13, 14, 15,
        37, 63, 141, 263, 264
    good in beginning, middle, end, 33
    heroic endeavors in, 272
    naturalistic explanations in, 294
    from noble lineage, xvii
    pragmatism in, 11, 311
    shamatha and vipashyana in, 273
    summary of path in, 222
    view, meditation, and way of life in,
        273
    wheel of, 37
    See also Dharma
Buddhaghosa, 35, 56, 57, 102, 106, 192
Buddhism, 15, 16, 25, 97, 106, 141, 156,
    160, 163, 197, 305

prana and, 223
primordial, 293, 294, 299, 301, 302,
306, 307 (*see also* awareness: pristine)
primordial, and space of phenomena,
301, 306
reductionist theory of, 293
stem, 109
substrate (*see* substrate consciousness)
substrate connate with, 236
subtle, 208
unsupported, 62, 300
without characteristics, 299
contemplation vs. scholarship, 296
control, relinquishing, 179–84
Copernicus, Nicolaus, 16, 48, 73, 85, 228
cosmogony. *See* universe: genesis of
craving, sensual
attention counteracts, 90
avoidance of, 261
dormancy of, 107
eradication of, 14, 107, 303
grasping gives rise to, 144
obscuration of, 89, 260
pleasure gives rise to, 142, 143, 145
reality misapprehended gives rise to, 68
subjugation by, 201
suffering from, 12
walking to counteract, 35
world aflame with, 64
Csikszentmihalyi, Mihaly, 72, 104

Dalai Lama, xv, xvi, xvii, 2, 15, 64, 85,
86, 94, 122, 138, 202, 221, 254, 270,
288, 306
Damasio, Antonio, 147, 190
Davidson, Richard, 65
Davies, Paul, 292
death
bhavanga at, 233
certainty of, 39
consciousness at, 107, 200
fear of, 308
knowledge of, 108, 233
lucidity at, 233
mind at, 238
psyche at, 110
sleep as rehearsal for, 233
suffering continues after, 264
witnessing, 12

Dement, William, 218
Democritus, 210
Dennett, Daniel, 199
dependent origination (pratityasamutpada)
of concepts, 288
defined, 46
emptiness and, 6, 275, 283
human factors in, 279
of mind, 274, 297
nexus of, 205, 253
of phenomena, 275, 294
pristine awareness transcends, 299
of sense bases, 262
of sense of self, 130
twelve links of, 98
Descartes, René, 16, 83, 84, 185, 214, 258
DeWitt, Bryce, 289
Dhammapada, 234, 236
Dharamsala, xv, xvi, 51, 53
Dharma
framework of, 94
juice of, 296
misconception of, 105
path of, 15
revelation, 75
study of, 23
teaching of, 33
wheel of, 37
See also Buddhadharma
dharmadatu (space of phenomena, absolute), 301, 302, 306
dharmakaya (mind of Buddha), 301
dhyana (meditative stabilization)
access to first, 108, 197, 298
achievement of, 102, 105, 107, 108, 198
failure to achieve, 111
first, 96–99, 105–11, 197, 198, 298
fourth, 105, 197, 198
misconceptions of, 105
second, 97
Diamond Sutra, 287
Dirac, Paul, 237
DNA, 68
Dogen, 296
Dona the Brahmin, 171
dreams
cortical activity in, 255
delusional, 170

happiness
  authentic (positive psychology), 72
  due to ethical blamelessness, 169
  externalized, 73
  Freud's few causes of, 167
  genuine, xiii, 74, 168, 169, 170, 287, 303
  hedonic, 169
  due to insight into reality, 170
  loving-kindness basis in, 145
  due to mental balance, 71, 169, 260
  mundane, 14, 169
  power of, 101
  pursuit of, 12, 71, 73, 143, 260, 264
  science of, 85
  technology of, 71
  true sources of, 67, 68, 86, 107, 168,
    169, 258
  wealth and, 168
Harvey, Peter, 166
Hawking, Stephen, 288, 289
healing, radical, 303, 304
health
  care, therapeutic, 64, 101, 155, 165, 214
  clean bill of, 268, 303
  drug therapies and, 304
  mental, 76, 101, 303 (see also mental
    balance)
  via multilevel healing, 303
heart
  aspirations of the, 137
  chakra, 135, 223
  cultivation of, 5
  disease, 242
  following one's, 7
  heart-mind (chitta), 221
  of meditation, 171
  mind located in, 223
  openness of, 11, 265
  prana and, 223
  qualities of, 1, 133, 170
  somatic resonances in, 205
  substrate consciousness and, 223
Heart of Buddhist Meditation (Nyanaponika Thera), xv
Heart Sutra, 287
Heidegger, Martin, 18
Heisenberg, Werner, 162, 211, 280, 291
Hertog, Thomas, 288, 289
Hidden Dimensions (Wallace), 197

Higgs boson, 78
hindrances. See mental afflictions;
  obscurations
Hinduism, 16, 25
History of Western Philosophy (Russell),
  210
Homo sapiens, 13, 288, 289
homunculus, 212
Hume, David, 268
humors, three, 125
Husserl, Edmund, 18

ignorance
  domination by, 201
  innocent, 77
  of one's identity, 307
  suffering's taproot in, 69
I-It relationships (Buber), 181, 265
illness, mental. See mental disorders
Illusion of Conscious Will (Wegner),
  200
immeasurables (brahmaviharas, sublime
  abodes), four, 5, 7, 137, 138, 257
India, xv, xvi, 3, 10, 11, 55, 99, 100, 108,
  141, 165, 166, 184
information
  measurement gives rise to, 218, 289
  primacy of, 210, 217, 280, 294
insight (vipashyana)
  into causality, 283
  creativity and, 187
  cultivation of, 257
  disruptive, 187
  across domains, 256
  into equality of beings, 264
  experiential, 17, 32, 65, 98, 257, 296
  liberating, 228
  primacy of, 296
  into reality, 170, 296, 297, 304, 305
  spark of, 187
  transformative, 120, 189, 266, 287
  See also vipashyana
Institute of Buddhist Dialectics, xv, 51
intention
  of liberation, 260
  right, of eightfold path, 15
  therapeutic, 49, 263
interdependency. See dependent
  origination

internal, external, and both
  body, 120, 122, 124, 255
  defined, 123
  feelings, 145
  mental events, 189
  nature of reality, 138
  observation, 120
  phenomena, 205
  sense spheres, 262
  undivided, 206, 266
introspection
  defined, 43, 58, 59
  insight via, 17, 32, 65, 98, 257, 296, 297
  primacy of, 84
  refinement of, 267
  scientific movement of, 84, 85
  unneeded, 273
investigation
  categories employed in, 263
  close scrutiny in, 140
  coarse and precise, 96, 97
  contemplative, 5, 20, 23, 26, 31, 63, 65,
    70, 83, 84, 125, 162, 167, 228, 309
  empirical, 67, 108, 122, 148, 161, 163,
    167, 189, 194, 234, 255, 309
  epistemic, 11, 257 (see also knowledge)
  essential, 19
  experiential, xvi, 4, 308
  extrospective, 16, 17
  factor of enlightenment, 263
  hypothesis-testing in, 26, 85, 149, 216,
    234, 308
  imagination in, 8, 121, 145
  introspective, 17–19, 25, 26, 83
  multimodal, 270
  ontological, 6, 10, 159, 168, 189, 257,
    275, 277, 298
  phenomenological, 87, 201, 209
  purpose of, 70
  radical empiricism in (James), 27, 49,
    77
  of reality, 3, 6, 15, 17–19, 23–27, 41, 46,
    65–69, 98, 228, 257, 258
  scientific, 17, 73, 228, 281
  sleuthlike, 261
  of subjective impulses, 156
  uncensored, 260
  vipashyana, 85, 120
Islam, 25

its from bits (Wheeler), 210, 294

James, William, 23, 27, 49, 53, 84, 123,
  155, 156, 209, 210, 214, 228, 229
javana. See consciousness: bhavanga and
  javana
Jesus, 200, 305
jñana vayu (energy of primordial consciousness), 301
joy
  empathetic, immeasurable (sublime
    abode) of, 5, 137, 257
  factor of enlightenment, 263
  of freedom, 168
  innate, 135
  truth-given, 170, 171, 240
Judaism, 16, 25, 63, 74, 87, 99, 181
Jung, Carl, 196, 198
Junipero Serra, xiv

Kabat-Zinn, Jon, 64
Kagyü, 287
Kamalashila, 33
Kant, Immanuel, 108, 210, 274
karma
  accumulation of, 192, 194, 307
  defined, 98, 193
Karma Chagmé, 6, 287
Kelvin, Lord, 48
Kepler, Johannes, 16, 48, 308, 309
king and five princes (sense bases), 255
Kitti Subho, xvi
klesha. See mental afflictions; obscurations
knowledge
  absolute, 281
  certain, 224
  consensual, 25
  contemplative, 3
  of death, 233, 239
  direct, 68–70, 98
  dogma vs., 10
  for its own sake, 5, 11, 73, 257
  implicit, 187
  intuitive, 189
  measurement dependence of, 210
  omnipresent, 306
  omniscient, 15
  precognitive, 306, 307

pursuit of, 257, 267
of reality, 228
scientific, 15, 72
of technology without ethics, 310
traditions of, 74
of unknowables, 280

LaBerge, Stephen, 7, 170, 218, 235, 241
Lalitavistara Sutra, 284
Lamott, Anne, xv
Laplace, Pierre-Simon, 47, 48
Lati Rinpoche, xvi
Lebenswelt. *See* experience: world of
Leitch, Donovan, 129
liberation. *See* awakening; enlighten-
    ment; realization
Linde, Andrei, 211
livelihood, right, of eightfold path, 14
Locke, John, 210
lojong (mind training), 6, 257, 296
loka. *See* experience: world of
Lokanathavyakarana Sutra, 284
loving-kindness (metta)
    as antidote, 204
    cultivation of, 133, 257, 309
    defined, 137, 311
    immeasurable (sublime abode) of, 1
    for oneself first, 138, 145
    samadhi of, 170
Luther, Martin, 16
Lutz, Antoine, 65

Madhyamaka. *See* Middle Way
magnetic resonance imaging (MRI), 121,
    217, 228
Mahamudra (Great Seal), 6, 299
Mahayana (Great Vehicle), xvii, 5, 6, 58,
    59, 86, 219, 222, 236, 284
maitri. *See* loving-kindness
marga. *See* path
marks
    of existence, three, 65–68, 102
    of impermanence, 65, 284
    of selflessness, 67, 103
    of suffering or dissatisfaction, 66, 263,
    264
mathematics
    abstraction of, 210
    God's language of, 17, 126

Greek legacy of, 99
Plato's inspiration of, 210
Pythagorean ideal of, 16
reality of, 197, 209
space in, 209
technology and, 126
matter
    classical notion of, 79, 210, 217
    dark, 78, 79, 238
    from information, 210, 211, 218
    nature of, 198, 209
    quantum theory of, 238
    reality of, 52, 279
    reduction of all to, 200
    from space of phenomena, 200
    unknowable in principle, 280
    from unus mundus, 197
Max Planck Institute, 270
Maxwell, James Clerk, 53
medicine
    acupuncture, 223
    Ayurvedic, 125, 223
    preventive, 261
    Tibetan, 121, 125, 223
meditation
    aspiration at start of, 33
    awareness of awareness, 223–27, 239,
        245, 248, 249, 295, 300
    bird watching vs., 188
    blinking and, 152
    as brainwashing, 10
    comfort in, 32
    continuity of, 124, 295
    creativity and, 186
    dedicated times for, 32
    dedicating merit of, 33
    deepening of, 31, 252
    diagnostic and therapeutic, 196
    diligence in, 113, 244
    duration in, 33
    engaging in, 31–34
    ethical grounding of, 20
    experiences, 71, 203, 242
    failure to practice, 305
    incorrect, 242, 253, 254, 257, 268
    insight (*see* insight; vipashyana)
    long-term, 29
    manual of, xv
    matrix of practices, 2, 7

mental afflictions
  as defilement, 221
  as disease, 66
  dormant, 4, 69, 232
  in dreams, 170
  equilibrium disrupted by, 195, 230
  eradication of, 303
  like fire, 64
  freedom from, 63, 64, 108, 202
  habitual, 164, 167, 168
  like hair in one's eye, 95
  hardwired, 13
  insight as antidote for, 69
  perception distorted by, 194, 262
  phenomena tainted by, 68
  like pile of dirt in crossroads, xiv
  as poison, 145, 195
  prevention of, 261
  quelled on the spot, 101
  severed root of, 5, 93
  strong, 195, 230
  subjugation by, 201, 259
  subtle, 95
  from views, distorted, xiii
  like visitors, 193, 204, 222
  See also obscurations
mental balance
  of dhyana, 99
  ethical dependency of, 74
  for genuine happiness, 71, 169
  Olympic-class, 15
  as platform, 93
  as prerequisite, 254
  spontaneous and effortless, 273
  as technology, 71
mental disorders
  addiction, 201, 202, 303
  ADHD, 288
  beyond mere freedom from, 15, 72
  depression, 13, 64, 65, 86, 303
  obsessive-compulsive delusional, 61,
    97, 111, 231
  psychosis, 42, 77, 164, 202
  rumination and worry, 240
  tolerated unnecessarily, 111
mental factors
  concomitant, 56, 256
  introspection, 43, 58, 59, 60, 180, 183
    (see also introspection)

mindfulness, 43, 54 (see also mindful-
    ness)
merit, dedicating, 22, 33
methods
  attitudinal adjustment, 256
  counting breaths, 92
  enhancing lucidity, 241
  oscillating attention, 226
  visualization, 230, 231
  See also meditation
metta. See loving-kindness
Michelson-Morley experiment, 53
Middle Way (Madhyamaka), 6, 10, 53, 87,
    275, 277, 284, 287
Migyur Dorje, 287
Milarepa, 296
Milindapañha, xiii, 55
mind
  body and, 52, 269
  from brain, 108, 110, 199, 201, 211, 212,
    215
  brightly shining, 222, 231, 243
  of Buddha (dharmakaya), 301
  comprehended, 236, 237
  concept dependency of, 283
  controlled, 236
  conventional notion of, 274
  defilements of, 222
  defined, 222
  discontinuity of, 234
  empty nature of, 274
  energetic nature of, 223
  enhancement of, 221
  as epiphenomenon, 78
  falling away, 233, 234, 239
  heals itself, 195
  heart as, 223
  intrinsic nature of, 274
  like king and five princes, 255
  neural correlates of, 23, 270
  nonphysicality of, 222
  objects of, 160, 262
  observation of, 214
  pliability of, 221
  as primary instrument, 228
  pristine awareness and, 254
  purification of, 265
  in samadhi, 304
  sign of, 227

training (*see* meditation: mind
    training)
untrained, 254
Mind in the Balance (Wallace), 288
mindfulness (sati)
    of aggregates, 261
    as antidote to misunderstanding, xiii
    benefits of, 64, 81, 245, 257, 268
    of body, 8, 43, 113, 114, 120, 242
    of breath, 87, 89, 90–93, 100–105, 131,
        156, 179–82, 186, 187, 231, 238, 244,
        245, 248, 295, 296, 300
    like chariots dispersing pile of
        dirt, xiv
    close applications of, xiv, xv, 5, 8,
        43–49, 55, 63, 65, 71, 78, 102, 120,
        171, 208
    decontextualized, 94
    defined, 55–57, 59, 268
    direct path to nirvana, 64
    external, 120
    factor of enlightenment, 263
    of feelings, 9, 44, 133
    foundation for meditation of, 1, 8
    as gatekeeper, 231
    of instructions, 269
    internal, 120
    as memory, 56, 268
    mental vs. physical, 190
    of mind, 9, 46, 175, 189, 297
    of phenomena, 9, 46, 205, 246, 248,
        255, 256
    pillar of, 171
    present-centered, 22, 56, 156, 246
    prospective, 22, 57
    real-time, 154
    retrospective, 22
    right, of eightfold path, 15
    strategic, 56
    tying rope of, 230
    vipashyana foundation of, 5
    visualization in, 231
    wisdom purpose of, 257
Mindfulness-Based Stress Reduction
    (Kabat-Zinn), 64
moksha (liberation), 62
monastery, xiv, xv, xvi, 30, 165, 275
mudra, 5, 134
mysteries, perennial, 108

Nagarjuna, 6, 287
Nagasena, 55, 56, 234
Napoleon, 42, 47, 48, 52, 69, 103, 128,
    129
Natural Liberation (Padmasambhava),
    227
nature
    human, 308
    inherent, 10, 13, 222, 274, 283, 285, 298
    of mind, 2, 6, 19, 26, 47, 108, 159, 167,
        222, 232
    nonconceptual, 22, 34, 312
    of objects and entities, 275
    of space, 237, 238
    true, xiv
    universal, 86
    of words, 281
navigator and raven, 184
Neanderthals, 13
Neem Karoli Baba, 134
Newton, Sir Isaac, 16, 48, 53, 160, 308
nimitta. *See* sign
nirodha (cessation), 14
nirvana
    direct path to, 93
    dreamlike, illusory, 285
    via knowledge, 70
    for oneself, 266
    realization of, 55, 63–65, 74, 76, 93,
        95, 103
Noah, 184
Noble Truths
    First, 11, 37–42, 263
    Second, 12–13, 37, 264, 307
    Third, 14, 37, 93, 264
    Fourth, 14, 37, 93, 264
Nyanaponika Thera, xv, 171

obscurations
    enslavement by, 111, 273
    of excitation and anxiety, 89, 90, 107,
        260
    five, 89, 93, 106–11, 260–61
    of laxity and lethargy, 89, 107, 260
    of malice, 89, 90, 101, 107, 110, 145,
        260, 261
    prevention of, 261, 262
    samadhi counteracts, 89
    sense spheres and, 262

deconstruction of, 278–79
designation dependency of, 40, 279
as display of primordial consciousness, 279
as emergent features, 19, 77, 78, 110, 199, 211, 214, 233, 280, 293
experience dependency of, 257
magical, 110, 216, 285, 293, 294, 304
material, 259
mathematical, 209
mental, 23–26, 49, 79, 175, 190, 201, 208–19, 261, 268, 269, 276, 301
mind dependency of, 234–37
namelessness of, 284
nonmaterial, 259
nonmental, nonphysical, 259, 260
paranormal, 304–7
perceiver dependency of, 280
phantom limb, 159
physical, xiii, 26, 52, 78, 259
real, 51, 76, 210
subtle, 208, 222, 246
types of, three, 259
universal aspects of, 141
waking, 154, 218, 219, 236, 237, 255, 293
phenomenology, 18, 78, 160, 201, 228
photoelectric effect, 279
photons, 18, 53, 140, 216, 219, 228, 248, 255, 279, 290
physics
classical, 48, 51, 52, 53, 237, 289
Copenhagen Theory, 291
measurement problem, 291, 292
observer role, 292
quantum cosmology, 288–89, 292
quantum field theory, 237
quantum mechanics, 53, 279, 290
quantum superposition state, 289
Schrödinger wave equation, 291
Standard Model, 78
symmetry breaking by observation, 292
unified field theory, 291
Plato, 74, 97, 99, 197, 209, 210
Platonists, 214
pleasure
appearances and, 38, 149
attachment to, 145
brain correlates of, 212
clinging to, 39, 144

craving of, 142
feelings of, 44, 142, 208
grasping on to, 39
mental and physical, 45, 148
seeking, 142
worldly, hedonic, 13, 37, 71, 72, 169, 265
poisons, three, 145
postures (asanas)
corpse, 131, 172, 175
excitation vs. laxity and, 175, 245
four, 32
hatha yoga, 29
lotus, 35
personality type and, 35
seated, 29–30, 32, 35, 175, 245
supine, 32, 34, 35–36, 175, 191
vigilant, 21, 28, 34, 90, 93, 176
vipashyana, 35
walking, 245
powers, mundane psychic, 63
Prahevajra (Garab Dorje), 299
prajña, 6, 58. See also insight; wisdom
Prajñaparamita, 6
prana
channels and, 77
consciousness and, 223
pratityasamutpada. See dependent origination
Principia (Newton), 309
principles
closure, 78
complementarity, 290
conservation of consciousness, 108, 233
correlation is not causation, 218
prediction, third law of (Clarke), 304
therapeutic, 63, 141
uncertainty (Heisenberg), 162
unknowability, 280
Principles of Psychology (James), 214
Protestant Reformation, 16
psyche
afflicted, 167
configured, 109, 233
defined, 196
dredging of, 196, 242, 243
falling away, 233
ground of, 19
melting of, 109
origin of, 110, 301

Titchener, Edward, 84
tranquility. *See* shamatha
  factor of enlightenment, 263
Trijang Rinpoche, xvii
truth
  frame dependency of, 289
  intersubjective, 282, 309
  joy of, 170, 171
  liberating, 257
  mathematical, 197
  scientific, 25, 215
  ultimate, 16
Tsongkhapa, 59, 224, 243, 296
tülku, 287

union
  of horse and rider, 104
  of primordial consciousness and space
    of phenomena, 301, 302, 306
  of shamatha and vipashyana, 5, 69, 70,
    100, 179, 189
  of stillness and motion, 157, 251, 252
  of substrate and consciousness, 208, 235
  of wisdom and compassion, 5, 134
universe
  body as microcosm of, 127
  closed, 78
  composition of, 79, 279
  expansion of, 78, 79
  genesis of (cosmogony), 119, 197, 289
  heterogeneity of, 258
  holographic, 197
  mastery of, 237
  observer-participancy, 291
  population of, 265
  primordial consciousness pervades, 294
University of Massachusetts, 64
unus mundus (Jung, Pauli), 196, 198
Upatissa, 35

Vairochana, seven points of, 35
Vajra Essence (Düdjom Lingpa), 156
Vajrayana, 3, 5, 108, 219
vedana. *See* feelings
Vedanta, 3
Vibhanga, 123
view
  Buddhism, 265
  Dzogchen, 157, 299, 301, 308

empiricism, 15, 27, 49, 210
God's-eye, 16, 17, 18, 49, 125, 126, 159,
  217, 160, 236, 281, 292
idealism, 210, 275
materialism, scientific, 13, 110, 127, 210,
  213, 215, 281, 293, 294, 301
materialism, spiritual, 202, 242
mechanomorphism, 16
Middle Way (Madhyamaka), 6, 10, 53,
  87, 275, 284
nihilism, 276
one taste, 183
realism, metaphysical, 7, 16, 49–53,
  276, 277, 289
reductionism, 199, 215
right, of eightfold path, 15
solipsism, 211, 264, 282
theism, 281
vijñana kasina, 223
Vimuttimagga (Upatissa), 35
vipashyana (insight)
  Buddha's experience in, 47, 97–99
  correct practice of, 267
  creativity and, 186
  defined, 4
  exposition of, 4, 6
  goal of, 10, 68, 95, 103, 253, 298, 300
  inquiry in, 188, 274, 286, 298
  as instrument, 93
  mindfulness of the breath and, 297
  mundane, 98
  observation in, 258
  result of, 273
  shamatha prerequisite for, 250
  supermundane, 98
  like surgery, 267
  like wise minister, 93, 94, 103, 273
  See also insight
Vishuddhimagga (Buddhaghosa), 35
vow, bodhisattva, 266
vows, monastic, 94, 95

wager, Pascal's, 14
way of life
  a buddha's, 254
  Dzogchen, 253, 273, 299
  ethical, 19, 70, 71, 80, 288
  flourishing, 138
  insight grounded in, 20

Index   *349*